IF TROUBLE
DON'T KILL ME

IF TROUBLE DON'T KILL ME

A Family's Story of
Brotherhood, War, and Bluegrass

RALPH BERRIER, JR.

CROWN PUBLISHERS
NEW YORK

Copyright © 2010 by Ralph Berrier

Published in the United States by Crown Publishers, an imprint of the Crown Publishing Group,
a division of Random House, Inc., New York.
www.crownpublishing.com
CROWN and the Crown colophon are registered trademarks of Random House, Inc.

Grateful acknowledgment is made to the estate of Paul Edgar Johnson for permission
to reprint lyrics from "Don't Let Your Sweet Love Die" by Clarke Van Ness
and Zeke Manners.

Library of Congress Cataloging-in-Publication Data
Berrier, Ralph.
If trouble don't kill me / Ralph Berrier.—1st ed.
p. cm.
1. Hall, Clayton, 1919–2003.   2. Hall, Saford, 1919–1999.
3. Country musicians—United States—Biography.   I. Title.
ML395.B47 2010
782.421642092'2—dc22
[B]   2010002827

ISBN 978-0-307-46306-7

Printed in the United States of America

Design by Diane Hobbing of Snap-Haus Graphics

1   3   5   7   9   10   8   6   4   2

First Edition

For Lucy

Contents

Introduction

The old-timers are all gone. This is a little of what I know about them. They were our people, rising as untamed and beautiful as June's rhododendrons from hard soil. They worked tirelessly, played old-timey music, and told lies. They lived back in the good old days, which you and I will know only through the stories we inherit, like eye color and hairlines.

When they left, the old-timers took with them all the old ways: honor, faith, and work ethic; self-sufficiency and decency. Not to mention drunkenness and fornication; fighting and killing. Folks don't talk about those latter traits as much. Sentimental stories about the innocent soft-hair days spent swimming in the creek and helping Grandma string beans on summer Sundays are deemed more appropriate by us. Yet the mean old ways were undeniably as much a part of our proud mountain legacy as mules and country doctors. I wouldn't want it any other way.

Those are the good old days I want you to know about. Lord, lord, an old man once told me, the good old days were anything but. The unholy communion of desperation, poverty, hunger, and violence wrought abounding unpleasantness upon the hills of old Virginia, those Blue Ridge hills where I am from. The old-timers were complex, much deeper and harder to peg than the dog-eared picture of the illiterate hillbilly sittin' on a locust stump, whittlin'.

True, they were from a time as unknowable to us as craters of the moon. In the old days, people drank homemade potions to kill worms and washed newborn babies in dishpans. Old-timers made liquor, shot their own kin in blind-drunk rage, and fathered and mothered generations of children who knew the face of only one parent. That our people could claim any upstanding qualities in such a time is a testament to their true character and perseverance. They were good folks, mostly, trying to survive in a world they didn't create but wanted desperately to change.

I never knew captains of industry or passed time in the company of political leaders, yet I lived my whole life in the presence of greatness. I knew the last of the old-timers. In their honor, I offer this meager tribute.

Do not expect a tale of sorry old men reminiscing about the good old days. This is the adventure of young men, two brothers born pitiful and raised hard, who made beautiful things out of raw God-given talents. I think of them today not as I knew them: aged, crippled, silly, weak. I think of them as they appeared in their own stories: vibrant, happy, strong. Theirs is a story of brotherly love, war, and country music. What else do you need?

This is how I heard it.

THE
HOLLOW

Clayton and Saford, circa 1922

Saford was born first. That much I know. Clayton followed either ten or fifteen minutes later, depending on who was telling the story and when they told it. The twins fell from Mamo's loins into the bony, waiting hands of Granny Hall on May 4, 1919, just as the dogwoods bloomed and peaches sprouted fuzz and young men came home from the War to End All Wars. They were the last of Judie Hall's bastards born in The Hollow, a rough section of red dirt wedged hard between the Virginia mountains and the North Carolina line.

Clayton died last. I saw him the day he died. He had trouble staying awake—because of sickness or maybe the company—but when he was alert he talked about the birthday party Uncle Asey was going to throw in two weeks. He told me to bring my fiddle and we'd play music like we used to. Of course, he wasn't strong enough to hold a guitar, but I told him I'd bring the fiddle, the one Saford left me, and we'd play all day and night. I'd show him how I'd learned "Florida Blues" and "Natural Bridge Blues" just the way Saford had played them. But it didn't happen. Instead, Papa Clayton dropped dead in the living room that night after asking my grandmother to make him a tomato sandwich.

I returned to the house after I got the news to find family and neighbors standing glumly around the small, cramped kitchen, telling me how sorry they were about Papa Clayton. He was a good man, can't believe he's gone, he'll be missed. I wasn't that sad, to be honest. I was certainly going to miss Papa Clayton, but how could I be sad? The man helped MacArthur return to the Philippines and he sang with Roy Rogers, for heaven's sake. He lived enough adventure to fill two lives, so it's a good thing he had a twin.

I would have known my great-uncle Saford better had he not run off to North Carolina when I was a kid, but you can't do much with a rambler except let him go and hope he finds his way back. Clayton figured that out a long time ago.

Just a few hours before Papa Clayton died, he sent Grandma to Tilley's store to get some tomatoes. He also asked Grandma, since she was going that way anyway, if she would stop by the Mount Bethel Moravian Church cemetery to see who was being buried there. He'd heard it was a Smith. Clayton had a keen interest in Smiths, especially the ones he was related to. Grandma reported back that, yes, a Smith had been buried and, yes, she got the tomatoes.

Papa Clayton died of some kind of pulmonary fibrosis, scar tissue in the lungs, just like Saford and Mamo. The twins had smoked and worked in the bad air of furniture factories most of their lives, but the fibrosis was probably genetic. The twins died the same way, but they didn't always live the same way. Clayton was more laid-back and dependable than the wandering Saford, although he, too, had a short fuse. I saw his temper in action only one time, when I was seven, and it was a doozy. My younger brother Ricky and I were staying at Papa and Grandma's house one afternoon while my mom was working at the beauty shop. I was in the living room when Ricky, about four, charged like a loose beagle from the kitchen and fell smack-dab in front of the fireplace hearth. Papa Clayton raced in right on his tail and grabbed Ricky by the arm and commenced whipping him with a rolled-up magazine. Papa had told Ricky not to run so close to the hearth, because he could fall and hit his head. Ricky sassed Papa, which was not the thing to do to a former army sergeant who had fought the Japanese; then came the whipping. The story lived forever after Ricky cried to our mother later, "Papa whipped me with a paper switch!"

We laughed and told stories about Clayton the night he died. After everybody left, I helped Grandma stack up the plastic plates and cups. That's when I saw it on the table: the tomato-sandwich-in-progress, open-faced with a smear of mayonnaise. It looked lonely. Papa Clayton never got to eat it. He really liked those tomatoes from Tilley's store. Or maybe this time they were just an excuse to get Grandma to run by Mount Bethel and see if it was a Smith who was being buried. I picked up the bread and threw it away.

. . .

A year earlier, I had pushed Papa Clayton around the VA in a wheelchair, which hardly seemed fair. He had won the war just so he could live long enough to require the likes of me to push him past the carcasses of old soldiers? Other old guys at the VA glanced his way as I wheeled him down the hall, looking for some insignia on a cap or jacket that identified his military outfit. But Papa Clayton never wore anything like that. He wore a Braves cap.

I knew many of his war stories, like the one about how he got busted for eating the navy's apples on a troop ship after a crate busted on the deck and the one about getting shot in the head, and, of course, the one about falling into the tank trap. They were great tales, but they weren't everything. When his health failed him for the last time, I knew I didn't have much time to ask for more information.

I decided to interview him, really interview him, about the war. I went to Papa and Grandma's house and set up a tape recorder in the cozy living room decorated with photo albums and *National Enquirers*. Grandma brought us instant coffee and sandwiches. Papa Clayton sat in the recliner and repeated the same well-rehearsed anecdotes I'd heard since I was a boy. But I had the goods on him. I had discovered a brief history of his army outfit that one of his buddies, long since dead, had written, so I read him some of the accounts to see if they sparked a memory.

"And on October 26, it says you were at Tay-bon-tay-bon," I said, attempting to pronounce the name of the village where Company F of the 382nd Regiment of the Ninety-sixth Infantry Division, the fearless Deadeyes, had been baptized in combat.

Clayton's eyes widened and he grinned, like he had been waiting years for somebody to mention that place.

"Tah-bon-tah-bon," he corrected.

We had a couple of good interviews. He told me about Tabontabon and Mecham Ridge, about the escarpments of Okinawa and the final battle at Aragachi. The old guy from the hollows of the Blue Ridge couldn't pronounce "Michigan" correctly but sixty years later he could still say "Aragachi." I have the tapes. You can hear his oxygen machine in the background. A month after our last interview, he got up from the recliner, walked toward the bedroom, and died, just a few feet from where we had sipped instant coffee and talked about the war, where we had played music all those afternoons and where he had whipped Ricky with a paper switch.

Saford and Clayton were born May 4, 1919, in Patrick County, Virginia,
to Judie Elizabeth Hall.

—INTRO TO A BIOGRAPHY WRITTEN BY MY MOTHER
FOR A BIRTHDAY PARTY INVITATION, 1994

In 1994, the Hall twins, Saford and Clayton, celebrated their "150th
birthday"—their way of describing turning seventy-five. They liked to tell
other jokes about birthdays and ages. When they turned seventy, they were
playing lots of show dates with their band, the impeccably named Hall
Twins and the Westerners, and Saford would take the mike and announce
to the crowd, "I turned seventy years old this year." Right on cue, his twin
brother would reply, "And I'm seventy, too!" This gag surely dated back
to 1939, the year the twins turned twenty (except for Clayton, who was
"twenty, too!") and probably resurfaced every ten years from then on. Seventy was the last birthday they got to use it. Their big brother Asey—who
actually *was* seventy-two at the time—never got the joke. He heard them
do it on radio station WPAQ out of Mount Airy, North Carolina, when the
band played the Autumn Leaves Festival in '89 and he cried for days, "Oh,
poor little Clayton! He doesn't know his own age anymore!"

Mom made a big deal of that seventy-fifth birthday. She rented out the
Cana Rescue Squad building for a huge bash and printed tri-folded invitations on beige paper with pictures and a mini-biography that she wrote
herself. The old photographs showed the twins as young musicians (there's
Clayton with Roy Rogers!) and as old men in their satin shirts and cowboy

hats. She included a family photo of Clayton's descendents (there's Clayton with me!) but nothing from Saford's family. Saford had strained most of his family relations beyond all recognition, so there was no family to have a picture of. Mom even found sheet music from a song the twins wrote when they played with Roy Hall ("no relation," Mom noted in the bio). The song was called "Little Sweetheart, Come and Kiss Me" and was included in one of Roy Hall's songbooks from the 1940s.

The rescue squad building was packed. Family was there, grandsons, great-granddaughters, nieces, nephews, cousins, in-laws, neighbors, friends, and Asey, the last of their older brothers. The twins and the rest of the Westerners performed their trademark Western songs, such as "Cool Water" and "Tumbling Tumbleweeds." Saford fiddled "Orange Blossom Special" at a hundred miles an hour. The boys told stories, laughed, drank coffee by the potful, and ate sugary stuff that wasn't good for them. Everybody had a great time. Everybody except me. I wasn't there.

That very week, I had started a new job as a sports copy editor at the venerable *Roanoke Times & World-News*. I was scheduled to work the night of the party and was too timid to ask off, so I missed the fun. Ruth, my wife, went without me and shot dozens of photographs.

I saw them all a month later at a cookout, June 5, 1994, two days before my twenty-eighth birthday. Ruth and I went to my parents' house for a late-afternoon cookout. The first apples in the family orchard—the "June apples," sour Lodis and Yellow Transparents—would be ready for picking in a week, so this was one of the last lazy weekends my dad would know until winter. It wasn't as big a bash as the twins' sesquicentennial, but it was a day I'll never forget. That's the day we videotaped Saford talking about the war, and I got a fiddle.

Ruth bought the fiddle for $150, case and all, from our friend Karen Ziegler, who showed Ruth how to play a simple version of "Happy Birthday." Ruth practiced for several weeks unbeknownst to me, since I worked five nights a week on the sports desk, and on the day of the cookout, she stood on the front porch of my parents' log home in her long hippie-chick dress and sleeveless top and scratched her way through "Happy Birthday" on my present. We still have the videotape.

"Now play 'Orange Blossom Special'!" Ricky requested.

When they passed the fiddle to me, I held it in both hands as awkwardly as a new father cradling his baby the first time. What do I do with this thing? How do I hold it? Will it break if I drop it? Does it need changing? I set the fiddle under my jaw and dragged the bow across the strings, extracting a scratchy, shrill noise that sounded like a family of sick cats trapped inside a wall. "I sound like Jack Benny," I said. No, not that good.

I handed off the fiddle to Uncle Saford for testing. He pulled the bow across the G string and remarked what a terrific bass tone it had. He could be enthusiastic over the littlest things, sometimes sincerely. He fiddled a simple version of "Happy Birthday," complete with a bluegrassy sounding slide or two, and just as he played the last note Ruth chirped in his ear, "Show off!"

Saford, wearing a blue cap and short-sleeved checked shirt, held the instrument in front of me and plucked the strings with his fingers. That's your G string...D, A, E, he said, plucking each one for effect. He bowed two strings at once and told me it was a G chord. That was my first fiddle lesson. Like I said, we still have the videotape.

I like to believe that I inherited a love of music, if not necessarily the talent for it. We hillbillies do love that mountain music. You can't swing a banjo in Carroll County without hitting someone my family has played music with—and you can't swing a ukulele without hitting someone I'm related to. The phrase "tight as kin" takes on a whole new meaning where I'm from. That's why I married a Maryland girl. Clean up the gene pool a little bit.

Carroll and Patrick counties lie side by side like sleeping babies, with the Berriers from Carroll and the Halls from just across the line in Patrick. Papa Clayton and Uncle Saford—the Hall side, naturally—were raised in The Hollow by two remarkable women, their mama and their grandmother Susan, whom everybody called Granny Hall whether she was their granny or not. The boys grew up in Granny Hall's cabin, where they knew no father and where they heard their first music.

Mamo taught the boys those old mountain songs, ballads with so many verses you could hoe a row of corn before the song was over. Mamo knew them all—"Barbara Allen," "Down Among the Budded Roses," "Poor Ellen Smith" to name very few—and she sang as she worked in the fields or washed other people's clothes. Those unaccompanied melodies were the first music the twins heard. In the hills and hollers of Virginia, love of music isn't taught so much as bequeathed, like a precious brooch. You absorb it like vitamin D from the sun. It gets in your bones and becomes a part of your Blue Ridge DNA.

Just as Mamo passed on her love of music to her children, my own mother inherited her musical talents from her daddy, then passed those musical genes to her own three sons. All three of us—me, the oldest, and Ricky and Billy—can carry a tune for a fur piece. Ricky and I pick a little, but not like Papa Clayton and Saford.

I had wanted to get into traditional music for a couple of years, but then again, in my youth I had wanted to be a baseball player, a rock star, or a movie director. I never lost the dream, I simply never possessed the initiative to go out and become any of those things. I kept waiting for greatness to fall upon me, but, strangely, it never did. I wanted to learn my grandfather's music, but I was too busy or lazy to buy a fiddle, mandolin, or banjo. I played guitar, poorly. But that fiddle changed everything.

I grew up with my grandfather's music and even knew the words to "Cool Water" and some of his other favorite cowboy tunes, but I didn't fully appreciate or even understand his and Saford's musical legacy until I was older. I made the long, strange trip through the young hipster musical odyssey that every college-radio-loving loser went through: You start with the Top 40 phase in your early teens, writing down every song that Casey Kasem counts down, then discover the Beatles in high school and realize that all contemporary pop music is swill, so you enroll in the Classic Rock Immersion Program for two years, even staying home on Saturday nights to catch an oldies show from Charlotte while cool teenagers are out on dates, then you hear U2 for the first time and you descend into the rabbit hole of the American underground. Paul Westerberg caterwauling "Hold my life until I'm ready to use it" is far more relevant to you than "La la, how the life goes on," and just when you think you've got it all figured out, the '80s crumble spectacularly like the Berlin Wall, and you've used up your college eligibility and you become instantly nostalgic, not only for your own youth, which is ridiculous since you're only twenty-three, but for your roots, too, probably because you feel guilty about not knowing more about your family than you do, so you tumble back generations way before your own birth and go completely native. That's what happened to me, anyway.

I am embarrassed by how little I knew about mountain music, in general, and my grandfather's music, specifically, when I was in my early twenties. I knew just enough to prove I was an idiot when I tried to speak intelligently on the topic. I knew that Saford and Clayton had almost made it big with Roy "No Relation" Hall and His Blue Ridge Entertainers in the '40s. I knew they loved songs by the Sons of the Pioneers. I knew Bill Monroe was the undisputed "father of bluegrass," although I couldn't have sung you a verse of "Blue Moon of Kentucky." So, when I distilled all that information, it came spilling out of my mouth as "In the '40s when the war hit, the three biggest bluegrass bands were Bill Monroe, the Sons of the Pioneers, and Roy Hall and His Blue Ridge Entertainers." I don't remember who I told that to, but I am pretty sure I bragged about it to multiple people multiple times. I was very proud—of my grandfather, sure, but mostly of myself for knowing so much about my roots.

Without slogging through the nuances of bluegrass and "pre-bluegrass" or pointing out that the Sons of the Pioneers were a Western cowboy band from California, let's just say that since I now consider myself somewhat of a regional music historian, if I ever heard anybody say anything as foolish as "In the '40s when the war hit, the three biggest bluegrass bands were Bill Monroe, the Sons of the Pioneers, and Roy Hall and His Blue Ridge Entertainers," I would call the police and have that person arrested.

I would have definitely made a citizen's arrest on myself that June day Ruth gave me the fiddle for my birthday. How little I knew about old-timey music or fiddles. When Saford and Clayton inspected the fiddle and saw a Stradivarius label inside, I thought it was the real thing. "A Stradivarius!" I exclaimed like a goofball, thinking I held one of the five hundred or so violins made by the master instrument maker, Antonio Stradivari. I did not. (It's all on the videotape.)

* * *

That was the day Saford talked about the war. The next day was the fiftieth anniversary of D-Day. He knew all about it.

I had heard some of the twins' war stories before. Papa Clayton and Uncle Saford were never shy about sharing their experiences. That's what they did, told tales. Neither was the stereotypical Stoic WWII Veteran Who Never Talked About THE WAR. To them, falling into a Jap tank trap or getting shot in the helmet were merely the parts of their lives between the time they recorded with Roy Hall in Atlanta and the night Tommy Magness showed up drunk at the American Theater in Roanoke. It's part of the story.

Saford's stories were amazing, even though I didn't know the difference between a C ration and a Sherman tank. In fact, I couldn't have told you then whether any of it was true. I'm not even sure I can now.

Papa Clayton didn't say a word the whole time. He took a backseat to his gregarious, cackling older doppelganger. Clayton was a natural-born comedian, as good a musician and singer as Saford, but he was always the fop, the rhythm player, and the tenor harmonizer. Saford was the master of ceremonies, the lead singer, the star. Most country-music brother duos seem to possess these same characteristics. In the Monroe Brothers, Charlie was the gregarious one, and Bill hardly spoke to anybody, even as an old man. Carter Stanley shot the bull, talked to the crowd, and liked to have a good time, while little brother Ralph shunned the spotlight. But Bill Monroe and Ralph Stanley made the more lasting musical contributions long after their brothers had flamed out.

The Hall twins were two halves of the same whole, opposite sides of the same coin. They were small, Saford standing about five-foot-seven, an inch taller than Papa Clayton. The Hall Twins and the Westerners kept them busy in the 1990s. They played for our wedding party in 1992, as they had for Ricky's the year before. When we married, Ruth thought it incredibly odd that her fella's grandpa played in a band. Two years later, she bought me a fiddle.

Something about that fiftieth anniversary of D-Day turned the light on for a bunch of us in our twenties. Up until then, World War II veterans were salty old men who marched in their blue blazers and hats every Veterans Day. They were the crusty guys who ran the Boys State program every summer, when young men deemed the best and brightest that the mighty Commonwealth of Virginia had to offer gathered to spend a week learning the minutiae of state government. I attended Boys State in the summer of 1983, and I believe it still ranks among the longest, most boring weeks of my life. We had to wear the Boys State uniform of white T-shirts and white tennis shorts the whole week, and each morning, we were summoned for inspection, lined up in formation, and marched off to breakfast. We were all assigned to "communities" with names like MacArthur and Patton and instructed to vote for delegates and make our own laws and codes.

The communities were chaperoned by men in their fifties and sixties, real American Legion types, who'd holler at us to shut up, get back in line, and march in step. My fellow MacArthurians imitated our white-haired platoon leader's Olde Virginia accent: "MAC-Ar-thuh! No tawkin' in thuh RANKS!" We'd start every sentence with "Mac-ar-thuh" this and "Mac-ar-thuh" that. We were cool.

I know now that every damn one of those old guys probably fought in either World War II, Korea, or both. They had sailed on overcrowded troop ships, survived the jungles of the Philippines, fought Nazis in France, killed other men, and nearly been killed themselves, only to live long enough to waste their time babysitting a bunch of thankless brats who made fun of them behind their backs.

When the roll call of fiftieth anniversaries began in the 1990s, starting with Pearl Harbor in '91, then on through D-Day and Hiroshima, a lot of us Gen X boys quit horsing around and finally started paying attention. Those doddering elderly men at Memorial Day ceremonies and Veterans Day flag raisings were no longer just cute, stooped old guys in blue hats. That guy over there, the short guy with liver spots and Coke-bottle glasses, might've slit a German's throat in Belgium. The dude with the shock of white hair and leathery jowls who trembles a lot might have cut the ears off a dead Jap and now keeps them with his Purple Heart. The mayor, the high school janitor, the bus driver—they all could have committed acts so violent and murderous all those years ago on continents a world away, it's no wonder they never told you about them. It was none of our damn business what they did.

The day Saford talked about North Africa, Patton, Mount Etna, Normandy, and hedgerows was a day when the boy in the white T-shirt and short-shorts stopped cuttin' up in the ranks and started to listen.

They lived with their mother, their sisters . . . their brothers . . . in a small cabin in The Hollow community of Ararat.

—MOM'S PARTY INVITATION, 1994

The Hollow is the perfect place to grow up a bastard, because Virginia doesn't claim you and North Carolina doesn't want you. The Hollow is actually in Virginia, tucked deep into Patrick County's foothills like a penny in a pocket, but the Blue Ridge Mountains wall it off from the rest of the commonwealth. All the news, TV, and radio come from the flatlands of Piedmont North Carolina, which explains why there are so many Tar Heel basketball fans below the mountain today. That's what they call it—"below the mountain." You're looked down upon both literally and figuratively.

The Hollow was a rough patch of weeds with a reputation so bad that the Moravians sent missionaries from Winston-Salem in the 1850s like it was a subtropical island of godless savages in desperate need of civilizing. The task proved so monumental the Moravians had to build three churches within five miles of one another. To this day, those churches—Mount Bethel, Willow Hill, and Crooked Oak—are still the only three Moravian congregations in the Commonwealth of Virginia. My family has longstanding ties with the Mount Bethel and Crooked Oak churches.

Clayton and Saford were the babies of the family, and they called their mother "Mamo." I call her that, too, even though she died when I was two and I have no memories of her. She was small and sparrowlike, and was good at making things with her hands. She made a little ball for me out of wadded-up Christmas wrapping paper and string. Mom kept it for years. That ball and the intricate baskets she weaved from oak splits were the only vestiges of her that I ever knew. I learned a whole lot more about her as I got older. Like, for example, she had ten babies without availing herself of a husband, which apparently was not as scandalous back then as it sounds. Several women in The Hollow became mothers before wives, including a couple of Mamo's sisters.

Back when the twins were little in the 1920s, the government either couldn't or wouldn't help poor families, unless they wanted to pack up and move to the county farm. Unmarried women like Mamo were on their own to feed, clothe, and house their growing broods. The poverty and illegitimacy that wracked the Hall household in the early twentieth century sounds a lot like the problems we associate with urban areas in the early twenty-first century, which is why I have always believed that poor whites and poor blacks have much more in common with one another than they do with higher economic classes of their own shades. We have been divided and conquered.

Things were so tough for the Hall family that Saford and Clayton never wore a pair of britches until they were six years old, and only then because the teacher sent them home from school when they showed up in dresses. But, like unmarried mothers, boys in hand-sewn gowns were not an uncommon sight in The Hollow. Gowns were cheaper to make and patch than britches; they lasted longer and they provided easy access for little fellers to do their business without fumbling over buttons, zippers, and buckles and soiling themselves. For poor folks, gowns were a cheap, functional clothing alternative.

Even in The Hollow, however, most boys graduated to britches by the time they went to school. Saford and Clayton, though, marched bowlegged straight up the hill to Chestnut Grove School still draped in the little gowns a preacher's wife had made for them, all flimsy and practically see-through from years of wear. The hemlines that had hung to the boys' ankles when first made had risen about knee-high as the twins inched ever so slowly taller. When their teacher saw them, she scolded them for dressing like wild savages and told them they could not come to school without britches.

"But we ain't got no britches," Clayton shot back, defiant, proud, and, above all, honest.

Well then, the teacher said, you just go right back to Granny Hall's and you tell her and your mama to make you some britches.

. . .

Expelled on their first day of school, the twins whined to Granny Hall about their problem. That night, she and Mamo made britches from the worn-out denims of older boys who had moved on to overalls. The next day, all trousered up, the twins began their public education in Patrick County, Virginia.

Papa Clayton loved telling that story. Times were hard in The Hollow in those years just before the Depression hit (and a few more before anybody in The Hollow knew it had). But it does make you wonder: What kind of a mother sends her sons to school without any pants? The same kind of woman who has ten children but no husband, I reckon. These questions were never asked when I was growing up, possibly because we didn't want to know the answers, possibly because we didn't think fatherless sons and pantsless boys were all that odd. You just accepted the situation for what it was. The sky is blue, country ham is salty and delicious, and your Papa Clayton grew up without a daddy and without pants.

Once Clayton and Saford learned to put their britches on like every-body else, they did very well at Chestnut Grove School. The schoolhouse was cuddled by cornfields and apple orchards on a hill just a few hundred yards above Granny Hall's cabin, which was shoved down in the draw near a creek-fed pond. The white-frame school building boasted four rooms and seven grades, which meant young children learned alongside older class-mates. Most years, the school was open until May or June, except for the year the county ran out of money and closed it in February. The building burned to the ground in the 1930s, set ablaze by a poor country boy who didn't like school. The county never rebuilt it.

The twins enjoyed their time at Chestnut Grove. They were handsome boys, with high foreheads and dark hair. Even by twins' minuscule stan-dards, they were little. They were a bit bowlegged, probably from lack of proper nutrition, and their step pigeon-toed. They got by on their natural smarts and wits, especially Saford, who was quick to pick up on new sub-jects. They learned their ABC's and many new words, like the one Clay-ton heard when he and another boy emptied coal ashes from the school's woodstove.

"You a bastard," the boy said to Clayton.

"I'll kill you for saying that," Clayton snapped, even though he didn't know a bastard from a barn door. It sounded like a bad word, though, and it fired the hair trigger of Clayton's temper. He socked the boy in the snoot and knocked him into the ash pile. The boy got up, spitting and literally ashen-faced. Clayton said, "Don't call me that again," and clocked the kid a second time.

That boy probably learned his lesson, but it didn't matter. Plenty of other people knew the word, and there wasn't an ash pile big enough for Clayton to knock 'em all into.

. . .

The bigger boys posed more of a threat. Saford couldn't figure out why those beastly older fellows were in the same classroom as him and Clayton, marooned somewhere between third and seventh grades of the county educational system. A couple needed a shave, Clayton thought. They were mean, nasty boys, young men, really, who growled at the underprivileged and formerly dress-wearing twins and wagged their fingers as if to say, "Just you wait. You're gonna get yours and I'm the man to give it to you."

So the twins steered clear of the bullies. They aligned themselves with other boys, some of them cousins, some closer kin even than that. They were country boys running wild like Jersey cows that had broken down their fences. During recess, they roughhoused their way through baseball games and tag. They rolled down the hill behind Chestnut Grove School in old rubber tires and skidded down hillsides of dead leaves on tin signs as if sledding on packed snow.

But whenever Clayton and Saford strayed from the safety of the pack, the bullies were ready to pounce.

. . .

"Look, it's Dan and Fitzhugh," one of the fuzzy-faced beasts growled at the twins.

"Who you calling Dan and...Fiz-choo?" Saford demanded to know, running up to the hulking beast, his little fists balled up.

"Simmer down there, Dan," the mean boy said. Two more circled Saford like a pack of orchard mongrels.

"Why you calling us names?" Saford demanded to know.

"Them's your daddies."

Now, what the twins knew about having a daddy could have fit into a shot glass. No man ever pitched a ball to them, took them fishing, or brought them pieces of hard candy. Plenty of women were available to whip them for various offenses—which included, but were not limited to, sassing, cussing, spitting, smoking, fighting, and dipping Granny Hall's snuff—and their older brothers struck the fear of God into their hearts with basic orneriness and meanness, but otherwise the twins never had much to do with grown men. Despite the dearth of proper adult male supervision, Saford and Clayton knew this much: If they had a daddy, surely they had the same daddy. Right? After all, they were twins. So what's this "Dan and Fitzhugh" business all about?

"We ain't got no daddy!" Clayton shouted, defiant, proud, and honest as always.

The mean boys laughed. Well, somebody's bound to be your daddy.

The twins' brother Asey, two years older and a scrapper himself, ran up to the crowd and asked what the trouble was. Just then, the teacher rang the bell at the top of the hill and ordered the boys back inside. Confrontation avoided for now.

"See ya 'round, Dan," one of the mean boys said. "See ya 'round Fitzhugh."

The encounter so unnerved little Clayton that he told Granny Hall about it. The boys at school call us Dan and Fitzhugh, he told her. They call us bastards. Clayton asked if that was a name they called a boy who didn't have a daddy.

"Some of them other boys would be better off if they never had no daddies neither," Granny Hall said.

．．．

When I was a kid, maybe five years old, I saw what was left of the log cabin where Clayton and Saford were "partly raised" (as Saford liked to say, which suited him perfectly since he never grew up). I remember being there with my mom and grandma and some other women, tramping around the woods like we had discovered Mayan ruins. All that was left of the cabin was the foundation, maybe some logs and a fallen roof, situated at the bottom of a hill in a copse of scrubby trees. I don't remember much, except for a child's leather shoe lying in the rubble, looking as lonely as an orphaned child. I wondered if the shoe had been my Papa's. He and Saford wore shoes only in the cold of winter, hand-me-downs stuffed with brown paper in the toes so they'd fit. Maybe this had been one of those. Or maybe they had only one shoe and had to share it! No, they would've told me that.

I also recall how dark it was at the ruins. Honestly, fallen in like it was and with evening's light retreating, the old home place was pretty scary to a kid. It looked like it had been haunted, maybe was still haunted.

Turns out that it was! Young'uns thought Granny Hall was a witch. She wore black from bonnet to boots even on the hottest July days, when you could boil a frog in Booger Branch. Her long black dress hid her tiny feet, making it look like she floated as she carried a basket of magic potions on her arm. She was old, her toothless face resembling an apple-head doll left in the sun. Her hair was black and always pulled back into a tight bun, and her eyes and skin were dark. She might have been part Cherokee, a heritage people claimed in order to explain their swarthiness to neighbors who boasted of Scots-Irish ancestry. Her black attire spooked the local kids, but Granny Hall was actually a respected medicine woman and midwife who brought five hundred babies into The Hollow despite her better judgment. When the call came that a woman had gone into labor, Granny Hall mounted the sidesaddle of her old broken-down bay horse with "U.S." branded on its hindquarters and rode to the expectant mother's house. If it was a particularly difficult delivery, like a breech baby, she might stay gone two or three days. Sometimes she'd return late at night and fall asleep right in the sidesaddle and trust the old horse to find his way back to the cabin.

Susan Montgomery Hall was Mamo's mama, and she delivered the twins and all their siblings at her home. Granny Hall's one-room log house was home to her, Judie, Judie's young'uns, a great-grandbaby or three, and exactly zero daddies and grandpappies. The cabin's main feature was a large stone fireplace and hearth that served as a heating source and oven for making ashcake, a delicacy baked right in the red embers of a dying fire. Young'uns peeled away the layer of ashes and devoured ashcake to fill their empty stomachs while they dreamed of suitable dinners. Most of the children slept in a loft reached by a wooden ladder. They huddled against the wind and snow flurries that squeezed through the chinks in the logs back when it used to snow a lot more.

Granny Hall was the mortar that held the household together. She cooked, cleaned, and sewed and took odd jobs to put meat on the table. The twins never thought to ask if she had a husband. Clayton and Saford just assumed that she didn't, since men were as absent as food (and britches), but not nearly as necessary. The only menfolk the twins ever saw in those days were their tough older brothers, and they steered clear of them most of the time.

Granny Hall's standing in The Hollow exceeded her physical stature. In addition to delivering babies, she treated The Hollow's ill and infirm with cocktails of herbal remedies. She swore by peach bark tea for swimmy-headedness, mullen leaves for rheumatism, slippery elm for worms, and whiskey for everything. That last treatment made her quite popular in The Hollow.

Sometimes, it made her a little too popular with the no-good drunks, so she learned her way around a muzzle-loading shotgun. She could not control what her daughters did—a cabin full of fatherless children testified to that fact—but she was bound to chase off drunks the way you'd scare off a stray mutt, by filling their hindquarters full of birdshot if they didn't hightail it out of there.

"If I had killed every man I wanted to kill," she once said, "I could have laid them end to end and walked on them from here to Mount Airy."

That would've made nine miles of dead men.

. . .

Those who truly suffered, she doctored. The sheriff showed up one night with a blinding toothache. His cheek was so swollen it appeared to be stuffed with a chaw of tobacco the size of an apple. He begged Granny Hall for some relief. She sat him down in a cane-bottom chair and poked her finger in his mouth and stretched his lips open. He had an abscess on his gum and a rotten tooth that needed to be pulled. Granny Hall brought out her "gum knife," a slender, sharp blade that she used to slice boils on the grandbabies' gums. The sheriff eyed that knife warily, but before he could quarrel with her, Granny Hall slipped it in his mouth and slit the poisonous abscess open. Blood, pus, and spit flew and the sheriff erupted from the chair like it was on fire, breaking the arms off with his bare hands."

"If you wasn't a woman I'd knock the hell out you!" he shouted. To which Granny Hall replied, "Well, I am a woman so maybe you'd best sit back down and let me pull that tooth or find another dentist in The Hollow."

The sheriff cooled off and asked Granny Hall if she had any whiskey. Granny Hall stuttered and stammered that, well, maybe she did, but you's the sheriff so I ain't gonna tell you if I got any or not. The sheriff said he wanted the whiskey for himself to numb the pain. He'd bring her a replacement batch tomorrow. So Granny Hall poured him a dram and he guzzled it down. Fully medicated, the patient sat back down as Granny Hall rooted in his mouth with a pair of black pliers. With one ferocious tug, she liberated the rotten tooth and the sheriff again flew from the chair in dizzying pain. She showed him the tooth and offered him a second swallow of whiskey. After the sheriff went on his way, Granny Hall cleaned the blood from her gum knife and called the children to her. Might as well check them all for gum boils, so she commenced running her finger along the babies' gums.

The next day, the sheriff showed up with a jar of corn squeezings as payment for Granny Hall's dentistry. He handed it to her on the porch, right in front of the grandbabies. The sheriff rode off and Granny Hall turned to see all the babies staring at her as she held that jar of illegal liquor.

"Well, the Lord sent it even if the devil brung it," she told them.

. . .

Mamo wasn't the only Hall girl to have children without partaking of a husband, but nobody had more illegitimate babies than she did. Mamo's brood began with two girls, Roxie and Lee, then came the boys, Thamon, Mack, Romie, Sam, Simon (who died of an accidental gunshot when he was only seven years old); Asey, and finally the twins, Saford and Clayton, all delivered by Granny Hall. A couple of them might have had the same daddy (Saford and Clayton did, obviously, though they still had to figure out this "Dan and Fitzhugh" business), but Mamo never said so. She never said anything about any of their daddies or why she never got married.

My own mother always believed that Mamo was taken advantage of by the rowdy, often drunk, men of The Hollow, most of whom busied themselves ignoring their own families. Mom's theory was that Mamo would take a job doing laundry or working on a farm for a household where the woman was sickly or overworked. After a few weeks on the job, Mamo would come home with a sack of meal, some middling hog meat, and a baby in her belly.

Despite the dalliances that left her with ten fatherless babies, Mamo never seemed to care for men. Then again, if dalliances with men kept leaving you with illegitimate babies, you might not like men very much, either. One time she carried a load of laundry into a neighbor's house and was staggered to see the numerous pairs of men's britches the poor wife had to iron. The living room was festooned with trousers hanging from curtain rods, light fixtures, and rusty nails. Mamo practically skipped out of the house, crowing, "I sure am glad I'll never have to iron no man's long-legged britches!"

Mamo was pushing forty and showing it when she had the twins. Her dark hair was threaded with gray, and she wore it in a tight bun, like Granny Hall. She wore long dresses that buttoned up the front, which made her look even older. She never shirked her responsibilities to her family, even if it meant working past sundown only to have to fry up hog jowl at midnight for a passel of hungry children.

She was also a true artist. She weaved exquisite baskets from oak splits and sold them to the orchard men in Patrick and Carroll counties for a few pennies a piece. Her baskets were the number one vessel for apples until modern picking buckets arrived with their cloth flaps that made it easy to dump apples into crates. Baskets were rendered obsolete, yet their value increased. Years later, long after she died in the Catawba Sanatorium, one of her baskets sold at an auction for fifty dollars. If only she had gotten that kind of money when she was raising all those babies.

As she worked, she sang those mountain ballads, the ones as old as eternity and about as long. Her version of "Barbara Allen" could last for days:

> As she was walkin' through the fields
> She heard the death bells tolling
> And every toll they seemed to say
> "Hard-hearted Barbara Allen"
>
> She looked east, she looked west
> She saw his corpse a-comin'
> "Lay down, lay down the corpse," she said
> "And let me gaze upon him"
>
> "O mother, mother make my bed
> O make it long and narrow
> Sweet William died for me today
> I'll die for him tomorrow"

Many mountain ballads are about women in a mess of trouble, so it's fitting that Mamo preferred them. "Knoxville Girl," "Down in the Willow Garden," "Pretty Polly," and a slew of other songs all end badly for the female protagonist. "Poor Ellen Smith" was a true story about a gal from Mount Airy:

> *Poor Ellen Smith, how was she found*
> *Shot through the heart lying cold on the ground*
>
> *Her clothes were all scattered and thrown on the ground*
> *The blood marks the spot where poor Ellen was found*

Most of these morbid "murder ballads" were based on kernels of fact from real events. Some folk-music experts believe that many of the victims in these songs were killed because they were pregnant and refused either to marry or to have an abortion. Mamo could have been one of those girls. I wonder if she ever saw herself as such a character—a Polly begging for her life, an Ellen shot through the heart, or a Knoxville girl beaten to death and thrown into a river. Her own life was a murder ballad, minus the murder.

Born of a woman who had never married and delivered by a witch, the twins set out on their path to greatness.

．．．

"Clayton was the best," Asey said. "He had a better heart."

Asey is the last of Mamo's children still living. His full name is Silas Asa Hall. Some people actually call him Silas, but the family always called him Asey. He still drives every day even though he's ninety-two and doesn't see very well. So if you see a boat-sized Buick coming your way on Wards Gap Road, you might want to give it a wide berth.

Asey grew up the same way the twins did—the same way they all did—poor, hungry, and fatherless. But even he knew that the twins were special, and he was eager to talk about them. They had God-given talents and abilities that separated them from others in The Hollow, even their own brothers. Asey learned to pick a little "Wildwood Flower," the old song made famous by the great Carter Family of southwest Virginia, whose songs influenced Clayton and Saford immensely when they were boys, but he wasn't in the twins' league. He fought in the war, too, serving as a medic, and was grievously wounded and earned a Purple Heart. As a boy, he saw his seven-year-old brother Simon shot dead accidentally by a cousin who fired a loaded pistol discovered lying in a dresser drawer. The twins were only two when that happened, and they never had any memory of Simon, but eighty-five years later, Asey still dreamed about that boy and that tragic day.

Maybe that's why he felt like he had to take care of the brothers he still called "The Babies," even after they were both gone.

"Me, Saford, and Clayton were the youngest," he reminded me. "We lived in a world of our own."

Saford was the one always starting something. One spring afternoon when he and Clayton were boys, he swiped Granny Hall's spring chicks from her coop and carried them down to the pond past the springhouse.

"Let's make 'em swim," Saford said. He pulled out a chick in each hand. They looked like yellow cotton balls, fluffy and soft as rabbit fur, with stubby useless wings and bright orange feet. They cheep-cheep-cheeped when Saford set them in the water.

Clayton warned him that the birds couldn't swim.

"Yes, they can," Saford huffed. "Just watch 'em. I'll learn 'em to swim."

Clayton watched the first two chicks kick and flail in the shallow water. Their precious peeps sounded like panicked shrieks. Saford grabbed two more chicks and set them in the roiling water, then tossed the last two in with a splash.

The cheeping, doomed chicks sank one by one. The water bubbled a few seconds, then calmed, save for the circular ripples that radiated outward like the soul leaving a body. One by one, the chicks floated to the surface, still and quiet.

"See, they can swim," Saford hollered.

Asey ran down to the pond to see what was causing the commotion and got there in time to see a half-dozen dead chicks floating in the water.

"Saford, what did you do?" he said with alarm. "Granny Hall's gonna kill you for drowning her chicks."

Saford's self-preservation instincts kicked in, and he panicked and ran off. Asey and Clayton watched the chicks for a minute or two, looking for signs of life. Asey didn't stick around, though.

Left by himself, Clayton picked up a stick and held it out over the water and raked in a dead chick. He fished them out one by one and set their soggy, lifeless bodies on the red bank.

As he reached way out for the last one, a strong bony hand grabbed him by his shirt collar and jerked him to his feet. He looked up and saw the withered, reddened face of Granny Hall.

"You've drownded them chicks!"

She held him with her left hand and whipped him with her right, hard and swift.

She was as old as a Confederate veteran and no bigger than a bobwhite, but she was stout from a life of honest work. She whipped him good. Clayton did the best he could not to cry, but his eyes overflowed. Granny Hall demanded an explanation—"Why'd you do it? Why's the devil in you like it is?"—but he never offered one. This was the kind of thing Saford would and was expected to do, but not good little Clayton.

Clayton never broke. He never told her that Saford drowned the chicks and that he was just cleaning up Saford's mess. He accepted the beating as if it were a penance for the chicks, to be paid regardless of who did the deed.

Clayton sulked and sniffled as he sat on the edge of the pond where the last chick still floated lifelessly. He didn't know if he felt bad for the chicks or if it was from the whipping. Saford shuffled up and sat beside him. He offered the best apology he knew.

"I thought they was ducks."

. . .

People often got tongue-tied trying to say the twins' names together. "Saford and Clayton" would come out "Clayford and Satan." A preacher at Saford's funeral even slipped up and called him Satan. Sometimes, though, people said "Clayton and Satan" and they meant it. Granny Hall was known to say Saford had the devil in him.

One summer day when he was about ten years old, Saford convinced Clayton and a gang of cousins that it would be a real hoot if they all rolled down a hill of tall grass on Uncle Alfred Dawson's land. What's the harm, he said. It'll be fun. They rolled and rolled like runaway oxcarts, mashing the grass flat. Saford popped up like a prairie dog, looking for the others, then lay down and rolled away. Within minutes, they had flattened that field like it was biscuit dough.

When Uncle Alfred came along and saw his field of rye ruined, the stalks flattened, the buds squished, and a season's wages vanished, he nearly lost his religion, and he was a Moravian preacher. He banished Saford from his property even though he was the son of his wife Emma's sister.

When Granny Hall heard what the twins had done, she whipped them with a leather strop, Saford first.

"Why me?" Saford begged to know.

"You an old instigator!" Granny Hall hollered.

Clayton and Satan. Even their cousins called them that.

. . .

Despite Saford's penchant for landing him in trouble, Clayton usually stuck by his older twin.

Saford and Asey were fighting one day at Booger Branch, a spooky, rippling creek spilling from the mountain. Old folks said it got its name because some poor fellow wandered up into the mountain near the head-waters and was never heard from again—except for the moans that wafted down from the dark hollows. Saford started the fight, probably by spit-ting on Asey, cussing him, or throwing a rock at him—it could have been anything, really; Granny Hall didn't call Saford "the old instigator" for nothing—but Asey had him down and was really working him over when, from out of the blue, something cracked upside his head like a thunder-bolt and sent him sprawling. Asey saw stars. He looked for the rock slide that had waylaid him. Clayton was standing over him holding a tree limb as thick as a baseball bat. Clayton! Good little Clayton with the good heart, why on earth did you cold-cock me like that, Asey begged to know.

"You were hurtin' my brother!" Clayton said.

"But I'm your brother, too," Asey said.

He wasn't Clayton's twin brother, though, and that made all the difference.

. . .

Fighting was nothing. They all did it. Saford fought Asey, Asey fought Clay-ton, and the twins fought each other. They even scrapped with older broth-ers who punished them not for playing hooky but for going to school. Their brothers Mack, Romie, Sam, and Thamon all quit school as boys and went to work as soon as they were old enough to labor in the fields and apple orchards. They had no choice. The ever-expanding family had to eat. As a consequence, some of the older Hall children never learned to read or write. As bad as the twins had it, their older siblings had it much worse. They were on the front line for all the name-calling and meanness The Hollow had to offer.

Mack was the fightingest of them all. In a few years, he'd grow up to beat a sheriff's deputy to a bloody pulp after the deputy busted up his liquor still and smashed every jar, except for the ones he kept for himself. For now, though, Mack was just your normal, everyday whiskey-making illiterate teenager with a bad temper. He was ten years older than the twins, and everything about him, from his demeanor to his well-muscled limbs, was as hard as black walnut. He worked so the babies could eat and play. And he wasn't the least bit happy about it.

Asey and the twins were spoiled, Mack believed. Granny Hall made treats for the babies by spooning sugar into handkerchiefs, twisting them into cones, and dipping the tips in water for the twins to suck on. Doesn't sound like much of a treat, but it was the Depression, after all. The fact that the treats were called "sugar tits" should be reason alone to enshrine them in the confectioners' hall of fame. The twins sucked on sugar tits for days, even weeks, until they were dirty, rock-hard, and nasty. But they still tasted sweet.

Except to Mack. After spending ten hours climbing Henry Woods's apple trees picking Magnum Bonums, Mack couldn't stand the sight of a pair of look-alike urchins gallivanting carefree and sucking on sugar tits.

"All y'all babies do is play," Mack said scornfully, smacking the sugar tit out of Saford's hand and making him cry. Mack was right. The twins had advantages the older kids never had. They learned to read and write, to make friends and allies, and basically how to fit in socially. They also had ample time to goof off, play, and make music.

Ah, yes. Music.

* * *

The fiddle just showed up in Granny Hall's cabin like it was a mess of trouble. Of course, Saford found it. They don't call it "the devil's box" for nothing. Nobody ever said where it came from. One of Granny Hall's uncles might have left it. Maybe it was payment for an herbal cure. Fiddles and banjos were common in many cabins in The Hollow, where self-reliance was practiced in all arts, from cooking to liquor making to entertainment. The fiddle was there, and the craziest thing of all was that Mamo could play it a little. She pulled the bow down across the low G and pushed it back up, drawing a mournful tune from the instrument like water from a well.

That sound shook something in Saford's soul. Saford begged Mamo to show him how to play. She set him on her lap and propped the fiddle beneath his jaw. She clasped her right hand over Saford's little fist that held the bow. She fingered the notes with her left hand and together they pulled the bow across the low droning G. Mother and son played a sad nameless melody that sounded like the theme song of her life. That was the first fiddle tune Saford Hall ever played, and he never stopped. He played even in those last days when he situated the fiddle around the oxygen tubes that kept him breathing.

"That sound did something for me when I was real young," Saford told the local newspaper, years after war, marriages, and fame had passed.

Mamo played banjo, too. She could do it all! Except find a suitable husband, perhaps. Banjos were better than husbands. True, both laid around a cabin all day, but a banjo never wore long-legged britches that needed ironing. Plus, if you never liked what you heard from a banjo, a twist of a peg here, a tweak there, and you could make it say whatever you wanted.

Like the fiddle, the banjo just showed up from somewhere—musical instruments materialized in that cabin like babies—and Mamo gave it to Clayton. It was strung with gut strings that got sticky and kind of smelly when you played it a lot. Mamo twisted its wooden pegs until a plinka-plinka-plink resonated from the low strings. Clayton eventually played a banjo so well that he made enough money in one week to afford a brand-new Chevrolet. That was a ways off, though. He'd never even ridden in a car yet.

* * *

Saford got a fiddle to call his own by selling salve. The instrument was smaller than a regular fiddle, the right size for a boy, and was made completely from tin, save for the tuning pegs. A tin fiddle played by a beginner probably sounded worse than a fake Stradivarius played by me, but it didn't matter. Saford had a fever for the fiddle. Clayton was batty for the banjo. Life was about as good as it could be for two bastard boys from The Hollow.

The front porch of Granny Hall's cabin was the twins' first stage. Neighbors and cousins flipped pennies onto the porch in exchange for a verse of

"Going Down the Road Feeling Bad" or "Sitting on Top of the World" or some other song Mamo had taught them. Sometimes, the penny slipped between the boards and the boys scrambled over each other to retrieve it. Then they'd resume the song or dance a flatfoot until Granny Hall told them to come in and eat their beans and ashcake.

Saford could play any melody he could hear. Clayton beat a plinka-plinka-plink rhythm out of the banjo for accompaniment. The two made music that the Lord must have sent, even if it sounded like the devil brought it. The music grated on Mack's nerves, he smacked the fiddle out of Saford's hands like it was a rock-hard sugar tit.

"All y'all babies do is play," he said.

. . .

The twins lapped up music like it was plates of hog jowl and pintos. They played and sang every day. They worked a little here and there, picking apples for three cents an hour, but work only distracted them from their true calling.

In The Hollow, very few musicians have formal training. A choir leader or organist at a church might know a little music theory, but most folks learned to play by listening to other musicians (or "musicianers," as they called themselves). One reason why traditional music has remained prevalent in the rural Southeast is because people learn to play from the source—they learn from a daddy or a mama and try to play it just the way they heard it. But the twins had no daddy, and their mama just knew a little bit.

Bessie Boyd knew a lot about music. She was a trained musician who played piano in church and loved all kinds of refined music. Miss Bessie and her husband Dewey lived near Granny Hall, and she heard the twins playing their rough-hewn fiddle and banjo tunes on the cabin's front porch. The boys had raw talent, she could tell that, but they needed a little fine-tuning—or any kind of tuning. She invited them over to her house for a music lesson and some good grub. She fed them enormous hunks of warm cornbread slathered with melting country butter, which tasted sweeter than chocolate cake to a hungry boy who would still remember it seventy-five years later.

The twins had never seen or heard a piece of furniture like Miss Bessie's old Victrola. The wooden cabinet was as big as a washstand and had a crank on its side like the kind you saw on Model A's. Miss Bessie opened the cabinet's door and pulled out a large black platter the size of a dinner plate from a brown-paper wrapping. The platter had a label fixed to it, and she placed the disc atop the cabinet and turned the crank. The platter spun rapidly and made the boys swimmy-headed when they tried to read the words on the label. Miss Bessie pulled a short wooden arm with a sharp needle over the spinning black disc and dropped it onto the edge.

The cabinet began to sing a mournful song.

> Bring back my wandering boy
> For there is no other who's so apt to give me joy
> Tell him that his mother with faded cheeks and hair
> Is at the old home place awaiting him there

The cabinet sounded like Mamo. It sang with the melancholy voice of a woman who sounded strong and weary in equal parts, as if she bore all of the joys and sorrows the world could summon. Accompanied by an unseen guitar, the singing cabinet continued with a chorus of multiple voices, like a mountain church choir singing untrained and untamed. The twins had never heard any piece of furniture sound so beautiful.

Miss Bessie asked how they liked the new phonograph record by the Carter Family of far southwest Virginia. Just fine, the twins replied. Here is another, she said, by Mr. Grayson and Mr. Whitter. When she played a Charlie Poole record, the cabinet sang like a man who had worn out three lives and was on his last one.

Saford and Clayton listened transfixed. They turned the crank and played records repeatedly. Miss Bessie brought more cornbread and butter. She asked them to play their instruments and try to make the sounds they heard. They listened to the records again and again, Saford finding notes on his tin fiddle and Clayton playing plinka-plinka-plink on the tuneless banjo.

Miss Bessie sat at the piano where she practiced hymns. A bell seemed to chime when she pushed an ivory key. That is E, she said. She pressed another key. This is C. Here is G. She played several keys at once. That is called a C chord, she told them. Those same notes lived in their fiddle and banjo, she said.

Clayton and Saford went to Miss Bessie's house every afternoon after school, playing and singing with their new friend, the singing cabinet. With Saford on fiddle and Clayton on banjo, the twins accompanied the Carters, Charlie Poole, Jimmie Rodgers, and other disembodied voices as Miss Bessie listened and critiqued their performance.

"Now boys," she admonished them when they sped ahead of the voices. "You're getting off the song here. Aren't you listening to the song?"

No, they weren't. They played like their britches were on fire. Timing and tone didn't matter as much as volume and velocity.

Each was immersed in his own instrument, absorbed by his own playing. They had to play together, Miss Bessie told them, at the same speed and in the same tune as the record. "Can't you hear the music?" she'd ask. They listened. Clayton had natural rhythm. His steady playing provided the foundation that kept Saford's fiddling in check when he wanted to race ahead on his own. Even as a seven-year-old boy, Clayton had to be the steady one, the dependable one.

Eventually, Clayton picked up a beat-up Montgomery Ward guitar. Miss Bessie loaned him a pamphlet of chords and songs, and Clayton practiced shaping his skinny fingers across the neck, pushing down three strings at once to make a G chord, then a D, then a C. He practiced those patterns until he could switch from one to another without putting the brakes on a song. He figured out which chords sounded better underneath Saford's fiddling. For his part, Saford tried not to play too fast for Clayton's rapidly improving skills. He restrained himself and played right along with his twin.

From then on, they played as one. Saford holding himself back, Clayton keeping a steady dependable rhythm. They chugged along with the grace and precision of a grandfather clock. They sang along with the singing cabinet. They learned the words and melodies of new songs and sang with voices as pure as heaven's own oxygen.

Little Clayton could really sing! Up until now, Saford had been the lead singer, memorizing words and singing loud with his big mouth. But when Clayton heard Jimmie Rodgers, the singing brakeman of Meridian, Mississippi, yodel his way through those bluesy records at Miss Bessie's, Clayton heard his calling. He yodeled so high he pierced the sky:

T for Texas, T for Tennessee
T for Texas, T for Tennessee

T for Thelma, that woman's a-killin' me
O yodel-lay-he-ho, lay-he-ho-a-lay-heeeeeee!

Miss Bessie busted with pride.

•　•　•

The Halls were an extended musical family. One of the twins' first cousins claimed years later that he had ninety-one cousins who made music. Clayton and Saford inherited that same banjo-shaped chromosome. Rafe Brady was gifted, too.

Good ol' Rafe Brady. What a fiddle player. What an entertainer. What a character. Others would say "What a drunk," but I don't like to speak of Rafe that way. Sure, he liked his rotgut, sometimes excessively so, and he was known to pull a drunk or three. For this story, it's a good thing he was a drinking man, because if he hadn't been, he never would have passed out in the woods and allowed the twins to steal his prized fiddle.

Rafe was the twins' first cousin. His mama was Mamo's sister Margaret, whom he called "Babe," because Rafe called everybody "Babe" or "Baby." He was a few years older than Clayton and Saford. He had a few older illegitimate brothers, but his mama had married Dowell Brady by the time Rafe came along. He never buddied up with the twins when they were little, but once Saford started learning the fiddle, he'd saw one off with them.

"Now, Baby, you watch me and you'll learn something," he'd tell the twins.

Then he'd play the fiddle behind his back or between his legs and dance a jig like a monkey.

Rafe was dark-skinned, too, and told people he was part Cherokee. His thick black hair swept upward like a mountain road climbing a peak. By the time the twins approached puberty, Rafe was in his late teens and had already acquired some bad habits, the worst of them the dual lust for liquor and fiddle music. He carried a fiddle with a rattlesnake rattle stuffed inside, and he wore a baggy coat with a half-drained liquor bottle in one pocket. He told people he had the rest of the rattlesnake in the other pocket so the liquor was snake repellent. He could often be found playing fiddle outside the tobacco warehouses in Mount Airy, where roughneck workmen pitched pennies at him. He played all the old tunes—"Hop Light Ladies,"

"Sally Ann," "Soldier's Joy," "Duck's Eyeball," and some that didn't have names. The workers ate their dinner from tin pails and smoked unfiltered cigarettes. When they went back to work, Rafe picked up the pennies and unfinished butts, which he smoked.

One of Rafe's buddies was Jumpy Shinault, an older dude who may or may not have done prison time for slicing up somebody in a knife fight. Jumpy was a fair guitar picker, which is why Rafe hung around with him (and because Jumpy liked liquor, too). He played a beautiful, big, black Gibson with steel strings that made every flat-picked note stand out like the prettiest girl in school. Rafe and Jumpy would disappear into the woods for days and play music and get drunk. When they got hungry, they'd break into Granny Hall's smokehouse and cut raw slices off a curing ham and eat them. Clayton and Saford bird-dogged the shabby duo as they staggered into the woods. Clayton had his eye on that black Gibson. Saford wanted to play Rafe's fiddle.

The twins hid out and waited until Rafe and Jumpy got too drunk to make a tune—which doesn't give them an excuse for propping their instruments against a tree and throwing rocks at them, but that's what they did. Fortunately, their aim had been adversely affected by the liquor. When Rafe and Jumpy finally passed out, the twins made their move. They liberated the fiddle and guitar from their rock-throwing owners and beat it back to Granny Hall's cabin.

In Saford's little hands, Rafe's fiddle looked as big as a canoe and sounded like a foghorn when he dragged the bow across the strings. The low G note went *hummmmmmmmmmmmmm* and seemed to shake Granny Hall's cups and saucers like an approaching summer storm. Clayton flicked the steel strings of Jumpy's black Gibson and they rang like church bells. They sounded like real pros on "Going Down the Road Feeling Bad" and "Get Along Home, Cindy." The twins played those glorious instruments for three days and nights, right until Rafe and Jumpy sobered up enough to go hunting for them.

Rafe came around, crying about his lost fiddle.

"Baby," Rafe said to Clayton—or Saford, he couldn't have told them apart—"somebody done stole my fiddle."

Clayton said they had taken the instruments while Rafe slept because a couple of drunks were throwing rocks at them. Rafe thanked them both profusely for saving his fiddle from people like that. Then it was back to the tin fiddle and the Montgomery Ward guitar for the twins.

Time to come clean. I left something out a while back when I quoted from Mom's cute little bio for the twins' "150th birthday" invitation. Here's the bio again, restored to its original state:

> Saford and Clayton were born May 4, 1919, in Patrick County, Virginia, to Judie Elizabeth Hall. They lived with their mother, their sisters Lee and Roxie, their brothers, Thamon, Mack, Romie, Samson, Simon and Asa, and their grandparents, Henry and Susan Hall, in a small cabin in the The Hollow community of Ararat.

I omitted the part about the grandparents. Granny Hall you knew about. Pappy Hall, you didn't. So there was a man in the house, but only briefly. I am sorry to have misled. I wanted to wait until the time was right before telling you about Pappy Hall. Don't feel deprived—Clayton and Saford didn't know about him at first, either.

By the time the twins met him, Pappy Hall was half-dead and blind, which was the only way Granny Hall would take him back. They were separated, never divorced. Granny Hall had tired of his drunken, sorry ways and tossed him out. Pappy Hall had built himself a cabin. "Heh-heh! Ol' Susanny'll never darken that door," he said when he finished his little shack, as if Granny Hall ever in a million years considered setting foot inside.

. . .

Mamo and her sisters took care of their daddy. They took him food and doctored him when he was sick. The twins knew none of this. Then, one day, Mamo showed up at the cabin with this half-crazy old buzzard with cottony eyes, jug-handle ears, and a bushy mustache that resembled a dead rat.

"What's he doing here?" Saford demanded to know.

"He's your Pappy," Mamo replied, which confounded poor little Clayton.

This daddy business was ridiculously confusing. First, they had to contend with boys taunting them with claims that some dudes named Dan and Fitzhugh were their daddies...or daddy...whatever. Now, here comes Mamo with some drawed-up bag of bones, blind as a possum and drunk as a month of Saturday nights, and we're supposed to believe he's our daddy?

"Not your daddy," Mamo explained. "Your grandpappy. He's my daddy."

Turned out Granny Hall was the one who had sent Mamo to fetch Pappy Hall. She was going to look after him until he died, which didn't appear too far off. Henry Clay Hall was nigh on eighty years old and fairly feeble when Granny Hall took him in. He still drank, although he could hardly see a liquor bottle in front of his face. He was originally from Yanceyville, North Carolina, and would have been the right age to have fought with a local regiment in the Civil War, but if he ever served a day, no one ever heard tell of it. That's shocking, because in Virginia, we build statues for any long-dead Confederate relative who so much as shoveled horse manure for J. E. B. Stuart (even if we can't tell you what our own dads and granddads did in World War II or Korea). The fact that nobody knows beans about Pappy Hall's service record is pretty conclusive evidence that he lacked enthusiasm for the Southern war effort. His youth would forever be a dark hole in the Hall family mythology, as if the line began only after he found his way to the foothills of Virginia, The Hollow being the perfect hiding place not only from a rich man's war but from most of life's trials and responsibilities.

He had been a carpenter at some point. Even as an old man, Henry Hall possessed estimable woodworking skills that he plied by building cabins and carving wooden dough boards he called bread trays. He built coffins, too, for which there was a high demand during the 1918 influenza epidemic. He probably built a coffin for little Simon, the twins' brother killed by an accidental bullet.

He met a pretty girl named Susan Montgomery, a tiny slip of a thing from up on the mountain, with long black hair and dark brown eyes. Somewhere along the way, the two courted, became lovers, and had a family. Somewhere else along the way, Henry took to drinking and never stopped, not even after Susan banished him from their home. He didn't do much to raise his children. He left them alone to fend for themselves, a parenting philosophy that produced a family of desperate, lovely girls who did whatever they could to feed and clothe themselves and the babies that never stopped coming.

That's when Susan became Granny Hall, whose sole purpose of existing was to fend for her pretty daughters and bastard grandchildren who wore babies' gowns.

When Henry became too feeble to care for himself, she took him in like one of those helpless, fatherless children. With Pappy Hall back, the twins witnessed the roots of their family's dysfunction firsthand.

"Susanny!" Pappy Hall hollered from his bed. "When I go to meet the Great Almighty, you ain't gonna bury me in the Montgomery graveyard, are ye?"

"I suspect I will," she said.

Pappy Hall was mightily offended.

"When that eastern sky splits open," he said, "I don't want to rise with them leather-eyed Montgomerys."

The Montgomerys probably didn't think much of the idea, either.

. . .

The twins were about ten years old when they were ordered to tend to Pappy Hall while Mamo and Granny Hall worked outside the cabin. This particularly perturbed Saford, who couldn't sit still long enough to care for a decrepit old man. So he made the most of his time with the helpless geezer—he taunted him and teased him. Every morning when he fed Pappy Hall his breakfast gruel, Saford held the spoon in front of Pappy's face, giggling as poor, half-blind Pappy groped at the spoon with his mouth like a baby bird. Saford would just hold that spoon out there, moving it ever so slightly away until Pappy grabbed the spoon and shoved it, and part of Saford's hand, into his mouth.

Pappy Hall continued to make bread trays, mostly by memory and feel since he couldn't see well enough to know what he was cutting into. The twins would lead him into the woods and help him find poplars, from which he'd chop out a large block. Then they would drag that block on a tarp all the way back to Granny Hall's, where Pappy Hall would whittle and smooth the wood into a concave tray, perfect for rolling out biscuit dough. After he'd made enough trays to peddle, he'd strap himself on the back of an old mule and seek his way through The Hollow, selling his wares.

When he died, Granny Hall did like she told him. She buried him on the hill above her cabin in the Montgomery Cemetery, among her own kin. Mamo had the hardest time with the loss of her daddy, as sorry as he was. Maybe she had waited on him more than the others, or maybe she understood how life can just get away from you and things happen that you're not proud of, but you're still a human being. Anyway, she draped herself over his coffin and sobbed uncontrollably.

Granville Gwynn, the Methodist minister, preached a eulogy that has forever lived in family lore.

"Poor old Pappy Hall," Preacher Gwynn began. "Never did no harm to nobody. Never did no good to nobody. No good to himself or nobody else. But the Good Book says, 'In my house are many mansions,' and how do we know that Pappy Hall doesn't have one of those mansions right now?"

And he was so right. How do we know? We don't know how this whole circus called life turns out. Pappy Hall might be taking a nip of corn liquor from a golden chalice. If a preacher didn't know for sure, then two little bastards didn't know, either. When your mama never marries your daddy, and when your grandmother dresses like a widow even though your grandpa ain't worth killing, you learn not to judge people too harshly.

. . .

The bullies of Chestnut Grove School were merciless. They still called Clayton and Saford names. "Hey, Dan! Hey, Fitzhugh!" The twins could handle the younger boys in a fair fight. The bigger boys were a problem.

But they found a way to handle the ruffians and they owe Mack all the credit. No, Mack didn't beat up the bullies for them. He tormented the twins, too, the way big brothers will, and he also used physical intimidation to impart discipline on his rambling baby brothers. Fast approaching twenty—which was about thirty-five in Hollow years—Mack was almost twice the size of the twins. The trouble started when he caught Saford smoking a homemade cigarette he'd rolled from some of Granny Hall's tobacco stash. Granny and Mamo dipped a little snuff and took a drag off a pipe or cigarette every now and then, so Saford figured he'd give it a try.

When Mack caught him, he commenced to thrashing little Saford. He didn't see Clayton nearby behind a rock, where he was about to get sick from swallowing his own plug of tobacco before Mack could catch him with it. Clayton watched the beating for only a moment before that brotherly defense mechanism kicked in and he ran to Saford's aid. What unfolded changed the law of the Hall fraternal pack.

Clayton blindsided Mack and nearly leveled him. Mack was stunned for a second or two, then he grabbed Clayton and nearly throttled him. That's when Saford hurled his tiny body against Mack's backside and knocked him over. Mack barely got to his hands and knees before both twins were on him, pounding him with little fists, kicking him in the ribs, and generally making Mack miserable.

It took a minute, but Mack was finally able to throw both boys off. He stood up, unhurt, but definitely beaten and a little shook up.

"I'll fight either one of you," he said as he staggered away, "but I won't fight a pair of varmints!"

* * *

Personally, I have never fought anybody, except in the second grade when I tangled with a boy I'll call "Skippy" on the playground at Lambsburg Elementary School. I pushed him to the ground (a development that was so surprising I even bragged about it to my teacher, who, equally shocked, never punished me). A year or two later, my buddy Randy and I wrestled each other in a classroom while the teacher was out, and I—in a move that was as tactically brilliant as it was just plain miraculous—ended up on top of him. I had him facedown and wrapped in a bear hug, as much for my own survival as for strategy, but didn't dare try anything more because Randy would've pummeled me had he escaped. Like Cold War superpowers, we were trapped in mortal deadlock, until I finally let go and fled the room before he could whip me.

I never saw a fight that I couldn't flee. Two older, bigger bullies terrified me so badly in the sixth grade, I quit the safety patrol rather than have to see them at the flagpole every afternoon when I was assigned to take down the American flag and fold it like a paper football. I never really fought with my baby brothers, Ricky or Billy, either. Ricky was three years younger, and our rivalries played out in highly competitive games of Wiffle ball and Nerf basketball, both of which Ricky could beat me in because he was that good (and because I was not above throwing a game every now and then when he was little, just to keep him from whining about getting beat). Billy was younger by eleven years, so he was much too little to scrap with, although that rarely stopped Ricky from terrorizing him.

You may think me a wimp, but I saw myself as a cagey diplomat. By the time I was in intermediate school, I had befriended most of the school bullies. They all fought one another, sometimes viciously right there in the cafeteria, the school courtyard, and ball fields, but I was above the fray. They ended up in the principal's office, doubled over to provide ample targets for hard licks from a wooden paddle (this is the South, after all; we believe in God, guns, and whippin' children). I stayed neutral. Like Switzerland.

I would've been eaten alive by the bullies of The Hollow, circa 1929. But I never had schoolmates call me a bastard to my face every day of my life, either. If so, I might not have had such a peaceable nature. Clayton and Saford, to hear them tell it, fought all the time, not because they enjoyed it, but because they had to.

Clayton might have been the peaceful one, had he gotten the chance. He might have been the conciliator, but that was never an option. He was a bastard. And he had Saford as a twin.

Saford would start a scrap with anybody. He'd get into a tiff with an older boy who'd called him a name and next thing Clayton knew, he was in the fight, too. One boy kidded Saford about his hand-me-down shoes, which were a couple of sizes too big and looked like clown shoes. Saford quarreled with the boy, who then resorted to the tried-and-true tactic of calling Saford "Fitzhugh" to his face. "Fitzhugh! Fitzhugh! Aw, wassamatter, Fitzhugh? Don't know who your daddy is?"

"Quit calling me Fitzhugh!" Saford shouted as he took off after the boy, only to run smack into a pack of bullies and a mess of trouble. The bigger boys had the drop on him. They threw Saford to the ground, kicked him in the rump, and rubbed his face in the dirt.

In a flash, there was Clayton, good little Clayton, to the rescue. Smaller and skinnier than his older twin, Clayton fought with a rage that doubled his size and evened every battlefield. He did to that pack of beasts what he had done to Mack. He waylaid the first one with a body block. He decked the second with a vicious haymaker. He never laid a glove on the last boy because he was halfway to Booger Branch by the time Clayton was finished with the first two.

One of the boys hurled Clayton to the ground and started working him over. Instantly, Saford tackled him. Clayton got up and punched the boy in the belly. Saford hopped on his back and chewed on his ears. The fight was a schoolyard version of cougars attacking a deer in the woods.

The twins were often outnumbered, and they never let their guards down. They climbed trees next to the road and waited for the beasts to lumber past. They dropped, guerilla style, from the treetops and beat the bullies senseless. They took on three, four, five bullies at a time. Entire families of thugs were vanquished in minutes. The twins were terrors, yet beloved by the girls for their good looks and respected by the boys who admired their dashing schoolyard heroics. Clayton and Saford never ran from a fight, and they even sought out a few. They were tough little bastards.

The thing about being twins is that you have an eternal ally and an eternal foil. Somebody's there to watch your back, right before he stabs you in it. Every day was a competition. Every report card, every ball game, every footrace, every song, was a duel. Saford relished his role as instigator. He initiated the scraps, either by punching Clayton when he didn't expect it or by bragging that anything Clayton could do—play the guitar, throw an underhand curveball, recite multiplication tables—Saford was superior. Not only superior, but articulate enough to explain to Clayton point by point where he came up short.

Not that Clayton wasn't smart, because he was. Somewhere in a pile of notebooks and printouts on my desk is one of his old report cards from Chestnut Grove School. I borrowed it from one of my grandmother's photo albums. (Those photo albums are amazing. There's about a half-dozen of them, each crammed with eighty years' worth of photographs, letters, newspaper clippings—even the occasional *National Enquirer* headline—arranged in absolutely no order whatsoever. They're page-turners on par with any Raymond Chandler novel. You have no idea what to expect on the next cellophane-sheeted page. There's me dressed in a Carolina blue tuxedo with my junior prom date in 1983. There's my parents' wedding photo. There are the twins again, dressed like Chicago gangsters, only they're armed with fiddle and banjo instead of tommy guns. Oh look, there's some long-dead relative pointing a pistol at a puppy's head. There's me as a baby. . . .)

I can't find that report card. If I could find it, I'd be able to relay if it was a 99 or a 100 Clayton got in arithmetic. He scored high marks up and down the curriculum. Even his penmanship was exemplary—it got even better once he signed his autograph enough times. Clayton was no dummy. He just didn't brag. Saford did. Sometimes, Saford's bragging would get so deep under Clayton's skin that he'd bear down extra hard to try to beat his older twin.

Their natural rivalry made them better at everything. They were better in school than their older brothers had been. They even became better musicians, each trying to outplay or outsing the other. They were rivals, but they needed each other.

"If we stick together," Saford liked to say, "can't nobody do nothing to us."

Saford was right. As long as they hung together, the twins were invincible. You messed with one boy, you messed with two. The bullies of Chestnut

Grove finally left them alone. Their big brothers moved on to more important concerns, such as making whiskey, then getting married, raising their own babies, and finding honest work. The twins had it made. They stayed in school, picked apples in the summer, and made music every night until Mamo sent them off to bed. They lived a better childhood than a pair of fatherless twins could expect to have in the rough hills of Virginia circa 1930.

. . .

And I haven't even told you about the White Plains fiddlers competition yet. That's the greatest story ever. That story is such a part of family lore that when my mother wrote an article about Clayton and Saford for the Carroll County Genealogy Club's family history book in 1994, she dedicated six full paragraphs to the White Plains fiddlers competition. World War II got two paragraphs (one for each twin's service).

Mom started it like this:

> The little entertainers moved on to greater rewards in their musical careers at age ten when they set out on a journey to White Plains, North Carolina, to enter their first competition. For their debut their mother and grandmother had made each of them a new outfit from some black and white striped material. When they donned their new outfits, it quickly became apparent that their mother and grandmother had not communicated well to each other the directions the stripes were to go. The shirts had stripes going across while the knee britches had stripes going up and down. This situation would only get more humorous as the day went by.

Clayton said they looked like little convicts in the suits with the stripes running wrong directions. It was probably a Saturday. I imagine it was summer, since the boys walked all day in knee britches and bare feet. "Ankle Express," Clayton called it. The trip from The Hollow to White Plains, a community just past the "big town" of Mount Airy, was twelve miles. I don't know how they heard about the fiddlers convention, nor do I have a clue how they knew the way to White Plains. Rafe Brady might've had something to do with it.

Saford toted the fiddle he had earned by selling salve. Clayton carried a cheap guitar. They walked barefoot down Wards Gap Road and arrived in Mount Airy just as the boiling noon sun blistered South Street on the factory side of town. They passed a greasy spoon where a crowd of rough-looking workers from the furniture factories milled about. One of the roughnecks saw the silly-looking twins with their instruments, and he called them over. He asked where they were headed, and they said to White Plains to enter a contest.

"Play me a fiddle tune and I'll buy you both a Co'Cola," the roughneck said.

Even though they didn't know a Co'Cola from a whiskey sour, Saford and Clayton scrubbed off an old-timey number, and the men clapped and whistled. The roughneck kept his promise and escorted the boys into the diner and pulled two Coca-Colas from the icebox in those beautiful six-and-a-half-ounce bottles that were shaped like voluptuous women. People have always said that Coca-Cola got its name because it used to be made with cocaine. I don't know if those bottles were laced with little-c coke or not, but when Clayton took a big slug of carbonated Coca-Cola, his head nearly blew off. The strongest thing he'd ever guzzled was buttermilk. Fizz and bubbles hit the back of his throat and Coca-Cola shot out of his nose, and maybe even his ears and eyes, too.

He dropped his bottle like it was poison and hollered, "Throw it down, Saford! It'll blow you up!"

Saford flung his bottle, too, and the twins ran like whipped puppies, leaving behind a group of tough men who probably for years told their kin about those pitiful hillbilly twins who were scared off by their first sip of Co'Cola.

The twins would've kept right on running all the way to White Plains if it hadn't started raining. They made it to a bridge across Stewarts Creek and scampered beneath it for shelter. Within minutes, gentle Stewarts Creek ran fast and brown. Clayton noticed the water rising quickly. They were about to be washed away. Before you could holler "four feet high and risin'" the twins crawled out from under the bridge and beat it down the muddy road.

The rain was blinding, which was a good thing because that meant they couldn't see the blue dye from the stripes in their mismatched suits running down their legs and arms.

They arrived at the White Plains schoolhouse, soaked, cold, and blue all over. Dye had stained their limbs in the colors of bruises. Clayton told Saford he looked like a "drownded mouse." Clayton poured rainwater from his guitar like it was a watering can. He strummed a chord that sounded as melodious as a basket of rotten peaches splattering onto a hardwood floor. Saford's soggy bow went limp as a noodle. They were a sad sight, all right. Garnett Warren, a big-shot fiddler player with one of the bands expected to win the competition, took such pity on them that he let Saford borrow his bow. Poor little fellers, he must've thought. This'll be the highlight of their life. Let them leave here with at least a taste of dignity.

The scene inside White Plains School resembled a hillbilly Lollapalooza. People packed together hip flask to hip flask, some flatfooting to the music, most just hollering at the musicians. Bands assembled in crescent patterns so they could see and hear one another over the clackety-clack of the dancers. Fiddlers sawed breakneck versions of "Sally Ann," banjo players flailed double-time gallops, washtub bassists thwacked their taut twine tied to broom handles. The music was invigorating, and the crowd—especially the twins—loved it. The boys had heard their mother sing unaccompanied ballads and they had been transformed by Mrs. Boyd's 78 phonograph records, but they had never heard music played like this or heard an audience go hog wild. By the time the twins took the stage, their arms and legs stained blue with dye, that crowd was primed. People went bonkers. They damn near blew the roof off the joint. Clayton was flabbergasted. They love us and we haven't played a note yet! Wait till they hear us!

Saford laid Garnett Warren's fiddle bow against the rusty strings of his tin fiddle. He sawed off a four-potato kickoff and tore into "Going Down the Road Feeling Bad," an appropriate summation of their trip so far. Clayton beat a perfect rhythm on his warped, dead guitar, which sounded as hollow as an African drum. It didn't matter. The crowd was delirious or drunk or both. They loved the twins and the best was yet to come.

The big finale was Clayton's rendition of "Blue Yodel Number One," which he had learned off a Jimmie Rodgers phonograph record. He chunked chords on his dead guitar, Saford fiddled backup fills, and the two of them sang harmony.

> *T for Texas, T for Tennessee*
> *T for Texas, T for Tennessee*
> *T for Thelma, That woman's a-killin' me*

Then came the good part.

> *O yodel-lay-he-ho, lay-he-ho-a-lay-heeeeee!*

When in doubt, throw in a yodel. The crowd erupted as if a Wild West show had taken the stage, which it sort of had. More like vaudeville, actually—identical twins looking like clowns in ridiculous costumes and blue war paint. They exited the stage beneath a deluge of applause. Saford returned the fiddle bow to Garnett Warren, whose bemused band had the misfortune of following this kid act. Old men patted the boys' shoulders and asked them for their autographs. Saford didn't know what an autograph was, so he respectfully declined.

They won. The result was a foregone conclusion. The judges based their votes partly on musical skill, partly on crowd response. The twins were awarded a blue ribbon and a cash prize of $2.50 each, a sum that nearly equaled two weeks of apple-picking wages. They packed their winnings into a five-cent matchbox and started for home just around midnight. They ankled it up the muddy road and crossed the creek where they had almost been washed away. They turned up South Street and passed the diner where Clayton's head had nearly exploded from a sip of Co'Cola. They followed Wards Gap Road back into Virginia and into The Hollow where they crashed into Granny Hall's cabin at four in the morning.

The twins woke up Granny Hall and Mamo as they dumped the winnings on the kitchen table, all five dollars of it. Granny Hall didn't speak. Mamo leaned over the coins and bills. "Where in the world did you get all that money?" she asked suspiciously.

"We won it making music," Clayton said. He showed them the ribbon.

What Granny Hall and Mamo couldn't stop looking at, though, was the money. As years passed, the value of that prize rose and fell like the stock market, depending on who was telling the story. Sometimes it was three dollars. In one version told to the *Carroll News* in 1989, inflation had pushed the amount to twelve dollars. Sometimes they were ten years old when they won the contest, other times they were twelve. They won first place in duet singing and fiddling, unless it was the version in which they finished first and second. Details, details. None of that really matters. What matters is what Papa Clayton told the *Carroll News* in '89:

"Buddy, I want you to know that when we got back home we was rich. . . . They had never seen that kind of money before. We told them we won it making music."

To which Saford added:

"Winning was like going to Hollywood. They couldn't get over it. They thought we were professional musicians."

Soon enough, they would be.

In 1938, at the age of nineteen, the twins and their mother lived in Bassett, Virginia.

—MOM'S BIO OF CLAYTON AND SAFORD IN A CARROLL
COUNTY GENEALOGICAL BOOK, 1994

Bassett is like those old soldiers I remember from Boys State. You wouldn't know it to look at it today, but it's had one heck of a life and could tell ten thousand stories if those empty factory buildings could talk. Bassett is still a fine little town. More than 1,300 people call it home, down more than half from its postwar boom years. Bassett High School's Bengals football and basketball teams are still competitive and still play for championships against larger schools. Low-slung along the Smith River, what's left of the business district is bisected by train tracks that used to carry the town's chief export—furniture—to exotic locales across the continent. The trains don't run through here like they used to and all the furniture bearing the Bassett name is imported, mostly from China. So, when I drove into town looking for the Hell's Holler section, I had to imagine Bassett as it was, circa 1937, when the twins were barely eighteen years old and had moved here from Patrick County.

Clayton and Saford worked in the finishing room on the very top floor of the three-hundred-thousand-square-foot, three-story main factory. The twins applied dark stains to bare wood pieces and inhaled noxious fumes ten hours a day. The room had a high metal ceiling and a floor crowded with barrels of stains, hoses, rags, and sprayers. The work was hard but enjoyable enough for two boys who needed money. In fact, the twins would have been happy enough working, living, and staying in Bassett, and this story very well could skip ahead nearly fifty years to 1984 and they'd still be here, winding up their long careers at Bassett Furniture. Retirement would allow Clayton more time to watch his grandsons play high school baseball. Saford would spend retirement playing fiddle every Saturday night at square dances in Ararat or Stuart or some other wide spot in the road. Then they'd grow old, die, and both fade away like most of us will do. But that's not what happened.

Let me explain how the twins got to Bassett in the first place. Last time we saw them, they were barefoot little boys agog over their winnings from a backwoods fiddlers convention. They were almost professional musicians. Now, we find them as teenagers, making thirty cents an hour smearing stain on table tops and killing their lungs in the process. What brought them to Bassett? Humiliation, that's what. That's what they told me, anyway.

. . .

By the time the twins were teenagers, their big brothers Thamon, Mack, Sam, and Romie all worked in Bassett—and for Bassett—at one time or other, opening a pipeline from the orchards and whiskey-making woods of The Hollow to the promised land of Henry County's new economy. When the twins reached Blue Ridge School, Mamo could afford new shirts and britches for her youngest sons, although most of their wardrobe was still made up of hand-me-down rags and shoes that were too big. They played music better than they ever had. Music lovers in Patrick and Carroll counties knew of "those Hall boys from below the mountain," and many families invited the boys to dinner in exchange for some flashy picking. When they arrived at Blue Ridge School in the ninth grade, they played old-timey tunes during the school's morning vespers in the auditorium. Saford fiddled "Golden Slippers" and Clayton sang Mainer Brothers songs for classmates. They loved the Mainer Brothers, J. E. and Wade, a pair of North Carolinians who scored hit records such as "Curly Headed Baby" and "Maple on the Hill," with J. E.'s band, the Mountaineers. Brother duos were popular in North Carolina and other parts of the South—the Mainer Brothers, Monroe Brothers, Callahan Brothers, Delmore Brothers, and the Blue Sky Boys (who were actually the Bolick Brothers but had more imagination than that). Brothers were, and still are, natural musical acts. Their voices blend in God-given harmonies that strangers can't fully duplicate. It's also easier to find practice time when your singing partner shares your bunk.

Not that Clayton and Saford always lived in perfect harmony. They still liked a good scrap now and again. On Sundays, Clayton and Saford strapped on fat boxing gloves and staged a boxing match in their sister Lee's front yard. Neighbors, friends, and kinfolk rooted them on. Teenage girls swooned over the good-looking identical twins with pitch-black hair, olive skin, ropy biceps, and calves that bulged like baseballs. The Sunday afternoon fights followed the same script each week: Clayton would pop Saford a good one right in the nose; Saford would respond with a sniffling, teary, "Now, baby, I told you not to hit my nose"; whereupon Clayton would drop his arms in apology only to catch a cheap-shot uppercut to the gut that would drop him to all fours. They'd fight a little more, then make up, and retire to the shade of a giant catalpa tree where they'd take out their instruments, make music, and drink lemonade. That made for about as good a time as a young man could have in The Hollow and not run afoul of the law.

In time, they formed musical bands with some of their guitar-toting pals. The first actual musical outfit was called the Blue Ridge Buddies, which looked and sounded like a real band.

The Buddies were Clayton, Saford, Rex Willis, and Clarence Marshall. Clayton and Saford's bandmates were boys from the top of the mountain who had thought they were hot pickers until they met the twins. Rex, a handsome boy with bright blue eyes and sandy hair, played a hollow-bodied Kalamazoo guitar. Clarence, a moony-faced lad with a toothy smile as big as a whitewashed fence, was Rex's buddy, and he picked a Kalamazoo banjo. They had met during a party at somebody's house, where they discovered they all liked the same kinds of songs, everything from old-timey tunes to the new Western numbers on the radio about life on the prairie. They even dressed Western-style for their publicity photo. In the classic picture that my grandma has, the boys look like they were auditioning for the role of "faithful sidekick" in a Bob Steele movie. Dressed in their cheap dime-store cowboy hats, they looked as imposing as a band of cap-busting six-year-olds. They wore white shirts with light blue checks and rolled-up sleeves. They knotted red bandanas around their throats and slung their instruments over their shoulders with leather straps.

They had the name and the look, and they even had a theme song. Set to a tune that sounded a little like "If You're Happy and You Know It, Clap Your Hands," it went:

> *How do everybody, how are you?*
> *The Blue Ridge Buddies have come to you*
> *We hope to make you smile, as we play for you a while*
> *Yes, we've come to sing and play our songs for you*

The Buddies were a polished band. They played all over Patrick and Carroll counties, from schoolhouses to house parties. Clayton and Saford's mastery of the Mainers' hit records gave them a leg up on the competition. Their version of "Curly Headed Baby" was the high point of every show:

> *She's my curly headed baby*
> *Used to sit on mama's knee*
> *She's my curly headed baby*
> *She's from sunny Tennessee*

Clayton and Saford tossed in a yodel at the end of the chorus, having learned that a good yodel wins over the crowd every time.

The Blue Ridge Buddies were so good, they hitched rides to Winston-Salem and played outside the tobacco warehouses and textile mills. During summer vacation, they stayed in Winston-Salem for days, making enough money to pay the three-dollar weekly rate at a boarding house.

By that time, the twins had devised a comic stage show, complete with cross-dressing, a staple of the kerosene-circuit medicine shows that passed through Mount Airy. Men dressed like shrewish housewives and nagged their "husbands" in comic sketches that tickled Clayton and Saford. Clayton knew cross-dressing was comic gold, so when the band started playing Saturday night shows in the Blue Ridge School auditorium, he worked up a sketch in which he'd wear a dress that was much too short for his five-foot-seven frame and he'd strut bowlegged on stage with freckles painted on his face and his front teeth blacked out. The effect on an audience was as subtle as a two-by-four to the funny bone.

"Woman, go into the kitchen yonder and fetch me a drink," said Saford, the "husband."

Clayton the henpecker grinned a wide black-toothed smile, and the audience snorted themselves silly. He responded that he would not fetch Saford any refreshment anytime soon. Saford pulled a cap buster on Clayton and fired, prompting a dramatic, flailing death spasm in which Clayton spun and tumbled backward into Saford's arms and was dragged away with his toes pointing outward.

OK, so politically correct sketches and snappy punch lines were not yet the sixteen-year-old twins' forte. Still, the time had come to take this show on the road.

Rex's daddy heard that a new radio station in Winston-Salem was auditioning bands for broadcasts, and he told the Buddies they should try out. The boys hitched a ride with Arnold Sowers, who hauled lime to Winston-Salem in a Ford half-bed truck. Saford, Clayton, Rex, and Clarence clambered aboard with their instruments and settled in for the open-air, forty-mile ride down U.S. 52.

Now, lime is a white powdery compound made from burning limestone. People used it—still do—to make plaster or glass; they even spread it in their gardens. That's not important. What's important is that Arnold Sowers had swept the lime from the truck bed, but he hadn't cleaned between the bed's wooden floorboards. A few miles into the trip, the whooshing wind that whipped the Buddies' bandanas and mussed their combed-back hair began to kick up a dust storm and sting their eyes.

"Hey, there's lime blowing everywhere," Saford hollered. Blowing lime swirled from the cracks and coated the boys and their instruments. They rode all the way to Winston-Salem, eyes scrunched and mouths clenched against the squall of lime. Arnold Sowers pulled up in front of the building for the *Winston-Salem Journal* and the *Twin City Sentinel*. The owner of the two newspapers had started the radio station and lent it their initials, WSJS, which stood for *Winston-Salem Journal-Sentinel*, as call letters. The Buddies fell out of the truck looking like dusty millers, white as ghosts.

A guard directed them to the paper's newsroom, where the new radio studio had been built a year earlier. The Buddies shuffled dustily into the studio, hoping their appearance wouldn't lead to their eviction from the premises. They were warned not to touch anything and for God's sake don't sit down in those filthy britches. The grumpy sound engineer positioned them in a crescent pattern around a single microphone and snapped at them to play something. Saford sawed off the start to "Curly Headed Baby," and he and Clayton sang it as good as the Mainers, especially Clayton's roof-scraping yodel.

When the Buddies finished the song, the engineer was grinning. The Buddies had gotten the gig. They were going to be on the radio.

* * *

A weird thing happened in The Hollow during the Depression: Most people's lives got better. Just when all those New York guys started jumping out of windows and the movie houses began showing clips of starving people standing in breadlines, folks in the country made some gains on their previously well-heeled northern neighbors. They'd all been poor forever, so what was it to them if the stock market crashed? Sure, many rural folks suffered and had to leave home to find work, but for most, the work they found was better than any work they'd ever done. Other improvements followed. Houses, which included more than a few ancient cabins, were increasingly electrified. Indoor plumbing made cooking and bathing easier. Commodes rendered the midnight walk to the outhouse obsolete, which was especially gratifying on those cold nights when all you had to keep you company was the Sears and Roebuck catalog. Not everyone embraced the modern technology; Mamo would claim years later that her newfangled electric oven never baked biscuits as good as her wood-fired cookstove did. Nobody got rich. But, for the most part, The Hollow's hard-scuffling populace made strides. Nothing hastened this forced march into the modern age like that high-tech piece of furniture, the radio.

Radio was the '30s versions of the Internet, DIRECTV, and Xbox all rolled into one. Farm boys and city boys alike were obsessed with radio, like today's tech geeks with their laptops. They learned how to build their own receivers and never missed their favorite shows. Radio brought the rest of the world to places like The Hollow. You could get the news from Cincinnati, listen to a ball game from St. Louis, and hear the National Barn Dance from Chicago. Folks in The Hollow who could afford them bought deluxe Philco radios, the "cathedral-style" models with arched tops that looked like big-city churches sitting on a dresser. Those beautiful sets reeled in the voices and songs from exotic locales—like Nashville. That was home to WSM, the all-powerful home of the Saturday night Grand Ole Opry, which was beloved by millions of listeners, including a pair of bastard twins in The Hollow.

Radio changed the country, and by that, I mean *country* country. Clayton and Saford grew up learning the ancient mountain ballads from their mother and timeless fiddle tunes from guys like Rafe Brady. By their teens, they heard the Delmore Brothers and the Blue Sky Boys sing polished harmonies, Uncle Dave Macon's comic banjo bashing, DeFord Bailey's bluesy harmonica, and the fancy fiddling of Arthur Smith. The music was as invigorating to young boys from The Hollow as Elvis Presley would be to American teens a generation later. Radio, phonograph records, and cowboy pictures shaped the music of the Blue Ridge. Old-timers despised the hot licks of "them radio musicians in NAYSH-vul TIN-uhsee" that leeched into the playing of mountain boys. The young folks dug it, though.

The Blue Ridge Buddies grabbed their tiny piece of the airwaves by landing that gig on WSJS in Winston-Salem. Their neighbors thought it quite an achievement, too. Everybody told the Buddies they sounded great on the radio, even though they surely never heard them. WSJS broadcast at only a couple hundred watts and could barely be heard outside the Winston-Salem city limits. The Buddies' buddies were just trying to be supportive, and no one was more supportive than Dr. Gates.

. . .

Arthur C. Gates had taken a liking to Judie Hall's baby boys. He saw a potential in them, some kind of magic, that often goes unseen in poor children. Dr. Gates had gotten to know the boys well because of his work with their mother and grandmother, The Hollow's medicine women. Even though he was a bona fide doctor with a diploma from the Medical College of Virginia in Richmond and a briefcase full of modern medicines, he had come to rely on Granny Hall and Mamo to provide care for The Hollow's weak and infirm. Those women were still the closest thing to a doctor as most old-timers ever met.

After graduating, Dr. Gates had returned to his native ground in Patrick County determined to wrest his neighbors free from the superstitions of the previous century. These people drank slimy potions to kill worms rather than learn how to cook meat properly. They treated children's coughs with sips of whiskey instead of cough syrup. Dr. Gates was bent on teaching the locals the virtues of modern medicine. The shelves in his home office were laden with small medicine bottles bearing handwritten labels. He'd hold a clay jug of cough syrup atop his shoulder like it was a gallon of liquor and gently tip it, pouring thick syrup into tiny bottles that he'd pack into a hefty leather bag. He dispensed scores of bottles right before the winter season of bad colds and influenza. Science was displacing superstition.

Dr. Gates might've come home as the cocky, college-trained doctor with the pretty, elegant wife from Richmond, but he quickly came to appreciate Granny Hall's country expertise. Susan had delivered five hundred babies in Patrick County and had treated at least that many sick and suffering adults. Not even Dr. Gates could say that, yet. Her bedside manner was impeccable. One time she helped a mother deliver a breech baby after twenty-four hours of labor. Mother and child could have died—probably would have died—had it not been for Granny Hall.

Dr. Gates admired Granny Hall immensely and once told a friend, "She can do anything I can do."

He also respected the fact that the Hall women had raised a family without a whiff of help from a man. Yes, the older boys were a little hot-tempered and uneducated, but they were no worse than any boys in The Hollow who'd grown up with daddies. The twins, though, were his favorites. They were personable and respectful, bright and outgoing. They were also gifted musicians, which is why Dr. Gates regularly invited them to join his family for supper and stay over at his house. He lived close to Blue Ridge School, so the twins wouldn't have to ride the bus to and from home each day. Mamo agreed to let her sons stay with Dr. Gates, since it ensured they would stay in school.

The only payment Dr. Gates required was music. He wanted his own sons to be pickers. Dr. Gates invited other bright boys over, including the twins' younger schoolmate Ralph Epperson. Ralph was one of those techno-geeks, consumed with radio. He didn't just like listening to the radio, he wanted to know how the blasted thing worked. He caught the radio bug in a most unconventional way, which, this being Patrick County, naturally involved a mule. Ralph borrowed a pair of headphones with two wires attached, climbed atop a bareback mule, and rode it beneath a low-hanging telephone line. He clipped one of the headphone wires to the line and touched the other wire to the back of the mule, completing an electrical circuit that allowed him to hear a conversation through the headphones. Newton had his apple, Ben Franklin his kite, Ralph Epperson his mule.

The twins always obliged the Gates family and their guests with a slew of tunes. Dr. Gates chomped his cigar and bellowed, "Boys, that's wonderful! You keep practicing, stick to your studies, and you'll make something of yourselves. You might even make it on WSM!"

For now, they'd settle for WSJS.

. . .

Trouble always followed Saford around. About the time the twins were high school juniors, Saford started running around with some boys who were mostly interested in chasing girls and drinking illegal liquor. Clayton wasn't averse to taking a sip or two, but having learned how to hold his Coca-Cola, he mostly stuck with that. He pestered Saford about the rough crowd he was hanging with. He didn't care for them, and he told Saford they'd bring him nothing but misery.

"Why are you following them boys?" Clayton would ask. "You know ain't nary a one of 'em no good."

"They're fun to hang around," Saford would say, perturbed. They were more fun than the company he was used to. That hurt Clayton.

For the first time, Clayton could feel his twin brother drifting away from him. Saford flew off the handle at the slightest provocation and fought other boys at the drop of a hat. If Mamo asked him where he'd been all night, Saford figured Clayton had tattled on him.

"Why don't you just let me live my own life?" he snarled.

One night, a fellow came looking for Clayton to tell him Saford was stirring up trouble down in Mount Airy. Saford hit all the beer joints on Main Street that filled up on Saturday night with factory workers looking to let off a little steam. This particular night, Saford had started early, flipping tables and grabbing waitresses at the Bluebird Café. The management had tossed him onto the sidewalk, but the night was still young.

Clayton raced to Mount Airy in a borrowed Chevrolet, and when he got there he heard that Saford was last seen on the verge of starting a brawl at Doc's Drive-In on Lebanon Street.

Doc's was a notoriously rough place, especially on Saturday nights when it always closed with police showing up. They didn't call it "Doc's Drag-Out" for nothing. The squatty cinder-block building looked like a jailhouse, only less hospitable. Inside, a permanent smoke cloud blinded visitors. Conversations were loud and grew louder by the hour and by the glass. Saford could get in real trouble in a place like that.

Clayton entered Doc's and slid silently between chairs and tables, hunting for his twin. He didn't dare say a word to anybody. He noticed some rough-looking dudes eyeballing him as he made his way to the bar. The conversations seemed to die table by table as he moved past. As he approached the bar, he walked right into a .44 pointed directly at his head.

"I told you if you ever came in here again, I'd blow your goddamned head off," the bartender drawled.

Clayton stopped and threw up both hands.

"Whoa, now," he said. "You got the wrong man."

"Like hell I do," the bartender said.

Clayton kept his hands up. He kept his wits, too.

"Now, look, I know what you're thinking," he said. "You think I'm a troublemaker. But the guy who was in here before, he was drunk, right? Well, I ain't. And I didn't come in here looking for a fight or to cause nobody any trouble. I'm just looking for my brother, and I want to take him home before he gets hurt."

He turned his head slightly toward the rest of the room.

"Does anybody know who I'm talking about? Kindly a short feller. Looks a lot like me but more ornery."

"I think I seed him passed out outside," somebody said.

The bartender lowered the .44 just a little. Clayton dropped his hands slowly and kept them right in front of his chest as he backed his way out of Doc's. He found Saford around back, passed out across the backseat of some dude's car. The dude stood by the driver's side door, a shit-eating, rotten-toothed grin cracking his face.

"I believe he's had too much beer," the dude said.

Clayton carried Saford to the borrowed Chevrolet and headed back up Wards Gap Road. Saford, the old instigator, had done it again. What to do with him?

* * *

Clayton and Saford had accepted that they didn't know their daddy and probably never would. Questions about their old man still came up on occasion, especially from the new friends they made at Blue Ridge School who didn't know the twins' family history. Clayton simply replied, "I never knew my daddy." Saford told people it wasn't any of their damn business who his daddy was.

That anger is probably why Saford had the hardest time when the Smith kids arrived in Patrick County. The Smiths were good people, fine, mountain middle-class folk, which meant they weren't rich but they weren't poverty-stricken. The Smiths had lived in North Carolina for several years, but returned home to Patrick County when a couple of the children were teenagers. Two girls and a boy attended Blue Ridge the same time Clayton and Saford were there. Soon, people started asking questions.

Principal Charles Fultz was one of the first to notice the new kids. Their long faces, prominent noses, and black hair reminded him of another family. He asked Saford for confirmation.

"I don't mean nothing by this," Principal Fultz said, "but are y'all related?"

Saford had never seen the Smith kids before this, but he figured that if he admitted as much, then Principal Fultz and everybody else at Blue Ridge would start wondering why the Smiths and the twins looked so much alike. Saford wanted to stop the tongue-wagging before it started.

"Yeah, I believe so," he answered Principal Fultz. "I believe we're cousins."

"Well, I thought so," Principal Fultz replied.

Saford's ruse didn't work for long. Every day after that, he looked the Smith kids over closely, searching for a resemblance. For his part, Clayton didn't see what all the fuss was about. Everybody in Patrick County's related some way, ain't they? So what if the Smiths look like we do? Maybe they are our cousins. Big deal.

It became a really big deal. Somebody told the twins that the Smith kids' daddy was named Dan. Somebody else mentioned the Smith kids had an older brother who had moved away long ago. His name was Fitzhugh.

Dan and Fitzhugh! That's what the bullies of Chestnut Grove had called them when they were little. Somehow the mean boys had known that either Dan or Fitzhugh had sired the twins. All the old hurts, the old taunts, returned. Saford, ever proud, was especially sensitive to perceived slights.

"What's the matter? My coat not look good enough to suit you?" he'd bark at a kid who might have gazed a little too long at his hand-me-down coat held together with holes.

"My shoes too big? My socks don't match? My shirt's worn out? Whatcha gonna do about it?"

Clayton was always there to help finish the fights Saford started, and he restored a tenuous peace. Clayton didn't care if people talked. In fact, he wasn't so sure that Saford wasn't making too much of all this business with the Smith kids.

"We'll show them," Saford told Clayton. "We'll go to Bassett and get jobs and make more money than those jerks have ever seen."

We? Without much say in the matter, Clayton was shanghaied into moving to Bassett. Like their brothers before them, the twins quit school and never looked back.

Dr. Gates, their mentor who had seen so much potential in them, was furious.

"You're throwing it all away, boys," he lectured them. "You'll never make it in this world without an education."

The world would have to take them as they were. Their minds were made up.

Not long before they left, the twins saw the Smith kids walking down the road away from Blue Ridge School. A car pulled up beside the Smith family, its door flew open, and the children climbed in. Clayton and Saford saw the driver from behind, and they could make out only the back of his balding head. That's the only glimpse they ever caught of Dan Smith. The car moved on down the road, the family headed for home.

. . .

"Let me do all the talking."

Saford was going to talk his way into jobs for the both of them. The twins arrived in Bassett in the spring of 1937. Most of the young men of The Hollow had relocated to Bassett, including their brothers, at least for the workweeks. On weekends, the men returned to The Hollow to give their wages to their families, maybe drink a little 'shine, fight, lose their money, and come back to Bassett to start the whole cycle over again.

Mack had told the twins to go see the finishing room foreman about jobs. The finishing room always had work, due to the fact that people hated it. Clayton and Saford went up to the third floor of the factory and met with the foreman, John Carter, who took one look at the skinny, shrimpy twins and chuckled.

"Where'd y'all leave your cradles at?" he drawled in a deep baritone.

"We can do anything you got to do," Saford snapped back.

Carter didn't tease the boys. He didn't have time. The factory was sending scores of pieces of bare wood furniture to the finishing room every day. He needed help. He sent the twins down to the main office, where they filled out the proper forms and were immediately put to work. They were placed in a company house in Hell's Holler, a rough section of town where plain weatherboard houses stair-stepped up the hill by a creek that ran past the factory. Hell's Holler was home to poor mountain trash that blew into Bassett from neighboring counties. Boys from Franklin County were particularly rough. Rent was three dollars a month, which was taken out of the bimonthly paychecks, along with the light bill, water bill, and other assorted expenses. It didn't take long for Clayton to realize that Bassett Furniture got most of its money back.

The pay was good enough, though. Thirty cents an hour for a workweek that reached sixty hours. Finishing work was the hottest, nastiest, smelliest, and dirtiest job in the plant, which is why the people hired to do it were black men and poor white trash from places like The Hollow. The twins hadn't been around many black people, hadn't seen many, really. One thing they learned was that in the finishing room, there were no black people or white people—only stained people. The twins sprayed varnish onto tables, not bothering to wear gloves or masks, because none were available. Next, they'd tote the furniture into the "rub room" where it was polished with rags. At the end of the day, workers washed their hands with soap, water, and paint thinner, but the dark stain never completely came off. Stain outlined their fingernails and seeped into the cracks of their knuckles. You could always tell a finishing room worker by his hands.

Six months into their new lives, the twins got a new roommate—Mamo. All her babies were grown up and had left Granny Hall's cabin. Instead of tending to the growing brood of grandbabies tugging at her apron, she decided she'd take care of her real babies. She cooked for the twins, washed their clothes, and babied them, even though they were men. The twins were real mama's boys. Mamo's boys.

. . .

With its two movie houses, cafés, and a bowling alley, Bassett laid more fun at the twins' doorstep in one night than The Hollow had in eighteen years. Back home, boys drove or walked to Mount Airy to find a good time. Bassett, though, had it all. It had a music scene.

The town produced fiddlers, banjo pluckers, and guitarists like dresser drawers and bed frames. Pickers played on front porches and in barbershops.

In the late-night hours following a full day at the factory, the twins quickly established themselves as the hottest pickers and singers around. Pops Maxey's barbershop was a good hangout spot because Pops played fiddle between haircuts. A cousin named Haze Hall lived in Bassett and played banjo—all their cousins played something. Bassett thrummed with music.

They met Wayne Fleming, a sixteen-year-old dropout from Mount Airy, who played a slide guitar that he laid face up in his lap. The twins had never seen anybody play like that. They had much in common with Wayne: They had all quit school to go to work, they liked music more than work, and Wayne had earned his first guitar the same way Saford had procured his first fiddle, by selling salve. The three young men formed a little group that played at the company store on Saturday nights, making a joyous racket that kept people singing, dancing, hollering, and drinking until early morning.

But the best music the twins heard was on the radio, where, from Winston-Salem, you could pick up WAIR, the rival to WSJS that broadcast live bands every day. The very best of the lot was Roy Hall and His Blue Ridge Entertainers, a hillbilly outfit that played a half-hour show every weekday at lunchtime. After the noon lunch whistle blew, the twins climbed the metal stairway that led from the factory grounds into Hell's Holler. Mamo had lunch ready, and the twins gobbled down baloney sandwiches and listened to Roy Hall's broadcast.

Roy was an OK singer, a little nasally with limited range and just a passing familiarity with pitch. The twins had heard better. *They* were better. Roy Hall's singing wasn't his strong suit, though. Putting together a top-flight band and leading it was. The Blue Ridge Entertainers were incredible. Bill Brown played slide guitar, just like their new buddy Wayne Fleming. Clato Buchanan was a decent banjo picker. Bill Brown and bass player Wayne Watson sang some nice duets. But the undeniable star of every broadcast was the fiddle player, a young dude by the name of Tommy Magness. Every day at noon, Magness kicked off the show with a pair of high drones that sounded like a train whistle. The band fell in like a line of freight cars, chugging at a quicker tempo than other bands the twins were used to. After a few more "bells and whistles" (which Tommy made by plucking his bottom E string and dragging his bow across the middle two strings), Tommy Magness took off on a wild double-shuffle melody that barreled into a flashy finale. He played fast and wild, almost leaving the band behind. The tune was called "Orange Blossom Special," and Saford had never heard anything like it.

"How does he do that?" Saford asked every day. Clayton allowed that he did not know. He couldn't even hear that fast. Clayton was playing a little fiddle now, too, in addition to banjo and guitar. For his part, Saford had learned to play anything with strings. The Hall twins were good. But they couldn't play like this band.

Saford broke out his fiddle and tried to play "Orange Blossom Special." He couldn't do it. Tommy Magness was a monster. Saford figured he'd never be able to play like him.

Roy Hall's broadcasts were sponsored by Dr Pepper. The band kicked off every show with a Dr Pepper theme song, set to the tune of "She'll Be Coming 'Round the Mountain":

> She'll be drinking Dr Pepper when she comes
> She'll be drinking Dr Pepper when she comes
> She'll be drinking Dr Pepper and we'll all go out and he'p her
> She'll be drinking Dr Pepper when she comes

Clayton and Saford had never tasted Dr Pepper, but if Roy Hall and His Blue Ridge Entertainers swore that its blend of real fruit flavors made it the perfect daytime beverage, it must be good stuff.

That was their routine during the fall of 1938 and winter of '39. They'd listen to Roy Hall and His Blue Ridge Entertainers during the day, and then play music around town at night.

. . .

The twins lived in Bassett for more than a year, perhaps even as long as two. They stayed long enough to save a little money from their jobs, although Saford went through wages the way a drunk goes through corn liquor. Mamo stayed with them in Hell's Holler. Around this time, the twins composed their first song, a suitable ode to Mamo called "When Mother Prayed for Me." The song's melody was slow and Western-influenced. The words were oddly nostalgic for a couple of twenty-year-olds who hadn't seen much of the world, yet they captured the tenor of their rough-and-tumble existence:

> When mother prayed for me
> Down on her bended knee

A blinding tear rolled down her cheek
When mother prayed for me

She held me in her arms
Her eyes lifted heavenly
When she asked God above to shine down his love
When mother prayed for me

She had good reason to pray. Saford hadn't taken long to fall in with the rough types, just like he had in Mount Airy. He knew more than a few bootleggers and might have owed some of them money. Tough characters always came up to Clayton and asked, "Are you Saford Hall or the other one?" That worried him. One time as he walked into a diner, Clayton was sucker-punched by some dude who hollered something about staying away from his woman, or he'd kill him. Clayton was just about tired of these mistaken-identity ambushes.

Trouble finally broke loose one night at a downtown café. Clayton walked in and saw Saford in a loud argument with three big dudes around a table topped with several empty beer bottles. The men grabbed Saford by the arms and were about to hoist him outside when Clayton intervened and asked what the devil was going on.

"You're coming with us," one of the big dudes said to Clayton, as he escorted the twins to the backseat of a new Ford sedan with the engine running.

The car rumbled into the countryside, as Clayton wondered what Saford had gotten them into. The car stopped two miles north of town on a dirt road that ran along the top of a steep bank. The night was black as a barrel of stain. One of the thugs got out and ordered the twins to follow. The guy buried his hand in a coat pocket. Clayton didn't want to know what he might be hiding.

Clayton slid out quickly and in less than a heartbeat he grabbed the thug's right arm and slammed the door on it, hard. The guy hollered and Clayton slugged him in the cheek and knocked him down the steep bank. The other two dudes moved fast to get out of the front seats, but they were too slow. Clayton grabbed the guy in the passenger seat and tossed him down the bank. By now, Saford had climbed out of the car and had waylaid the driver. Before the thugs could recover, the twins hotfooted it down the road.

The old instigator had struck again.

"Saford, what did you do?" Clayton asked.

"I didn't do nothing!" Saford exclaimed.

They ran, huffing, puffing, and, finally, laughing. They didn't stop until they got back to town and home to Hell's Holler. The funny thing was that Clayton had kind of enjoyed himself. He liked finishing the fights Saford started.

. . . .

The twins' workday routine never varied. The only difference day-to-day was Roy Hall's song list—would they play "Cotton-Eyed Joe" today or "Katy Hill"? One day while they ate their sandwiches and listened to the radio, Roy Hall interrupted his own program with terrible news. Tommy Magness was leaving the band. Tommy Magness! Leaving the Blue Ridge Entertainers! Saford was crushed. Roy blathered on about how Tommy had a wonderful opportunity and the rest of the boys would sure miss him but would somehow find a way to manage. Tommy would stick around for a few more show dates before heading off to Nashville. Clato Buchanan was moving on, too, though not to Nashville, which meant that the Blue Ridge Entertainers were about to lose their fiddle and banjo players. Roy promised the listeners that he would find replacements who would make fine additions to the band and pick up right where Tommy and Clato left off.

"I sure wouldn't want to be those guys," Clayton thought. Replace Tommy Magness and Clato Buchanan? Impossible.

. . .

Mamo always dreaded seeing a lawman. Deputies had hounded Mack and some of her other boys for years over the production and distribution of liquor. Every time Mack had a run-in with the law, Mamo had to bail him out of jail. She had no cash, so she was forced to sell off some land Granny Hall's family—the Montgomerys—had left her. Mack's three stints in jail had devoured all the real estate she owned, save for Granny Hall's cabin and the surrounding fields and woods. Lawmen cost her a ton of money, Mamo thought.

So, the day two large men in wide-brimmed hats and white shirts pulled up outside the house in Hell's Holler in a big black car, Mamo became a tad unnerved. Oh Lord, what have these babies done now?

The twins were in the house with her, listening to Roy Hall's radio program from Winston-Salem. Tommy Magness was still with the band, but they knew his days were numbered. Outside, the broadest, toughest-looking of the two strangers strode up the porch steps like he owned the place and banged hard and fast on the screen door. Mamo answered, reluctantly, and found herself looking eyeball-to-holster with a .44 strapped to the big man's hip.

"Hello, ma'am," he said. "I'm looking for the Hall twins. I've been told they live here. Are they home now?"

Mamo hesitated for a second, then looked at the .44. Roy Hall's radio program could be heard from the kitchen in back of the house.

"Just a second," she said.

She went to the kitchen and told the boys in a hushed voice that a man was at the door to see them. He wore a big hat and had a gun, she said.

"I think he might be the sheriff."

Clayton's head spun reflexively toward Saford.

"What have you done?" he demanded to know. The machinery in Saford's head fired up.

"Well, I don't know," Saford said. "I drank a beer last night at the café."

Clayton was incredulous.

"They ain't gonna get after you for that."

"I ain't done nothing," Saford said, his voice frosting with defiance.

Mamo decided she'd better not keep the man waiting, lest he get suspicious. She invited him into the house and told him that her boys were eating their dinner and would have to get back to the factory in a few minutes. The man assured her he wouldn't keep them long.

The twins stood up when the tall, wide-shouldered man entered the kitchen. They stood there in their filthy blue work shirts, their faces and hands spotted with black stain. His shirt was whiter than any snow that had ever fallen. Over his left breast were stitched the words "Dr Pepper." Across his right breast was his name.

"Hello, boys," the man said. "My name is Roy Hall. And I sure have had a time tracking you two down."

Roy Hall had come to Hell's Holler and was standing in their house! In their kitchen! But wait. This couldn't be Roy Hall. Roy Hall's program was on the radio that very minute. They could hear him singing "Come Back Little Pal" as they all stood there.

Roy explained it all. That was a transcription they heard on the radio, a recorded program that aired on days when the Blue Ridge Entertainers were on the road or taking a day off. Roy had taken this day off to come to Bassett to look for the famous Hall twins. When word started getting around that Tommy Magness and Clato Buchanan were leaving the band, people had told Roy about a brother duo that just happened to specialize in fiddle and banjo. The Hall twins had garnered some positive attention and acclaim from their days playing on WSJS. Trouble was, nobody knew whatever happened to them. Somebody at WSJS had heard they were working in Bassett. Roy drove to Bassett, asked around town about the Hall twins, and now here he was standing in their kitchen while his voice sang from the radio.

He'd heard a lot about them, he said. Now, he wanted to hear them for himself.

"So," he said, speaking with that same nasal baritone the twins had heard on the radio. "Get out your instruments."

Finally, it hit them. This was an audition to join the Blue Ridge Entertainers.

Clayton dragged his Kalamazoo banjo and Saford's fiddle from under the bed. Neither instrument had a case. Roy asked if those were the best instruments they had. They sheepishly nodded.

He told them to wait there while he went to his car.

Roy came back with another tall man he introduced as Wayne Watson. Each of them carried a case. Roy sat his on the floor and popped out a shiny black Gibson guitar. Wayne opened his smaller case and lifted out a fiddle with a finish so smooth—smoother than any work the boys had ever done in the finishing room—that it shined like gold. Roy checked the tuning pegs, plucked the strings one by one—E, A, D, G—and passed it to Saford.

Great God Almighty, Saford had Tommy Magness's fiddle. The same one he'd played "Orange Blossom Special" on a thousand times. Saford was afraid he'd start shaking and drop it.

"Play me something," Roy demanded.

Clayton strummed mighty chords from the black Gibson, Saford sawed on the grandest sounding fiddle he'd ever heard, and they played "Curly Headed Baby," their old standby.

> She's my curly headed baby
> Used to sit on mama's knee
> She's my curly headed baby
> She's from sunny Tennessee

Saford sang lead on the up-tempo verses, while Clayton provided a high tenor that swept the cobwebs off the ceiling. Then came the best part— a yodel, naturally—only this time, Saford yodeled a harmony, which blew Roy Hall away. He had never heard a brother duo as tight as the Hall twins.

Roy asked for another. They went with another favorite, the Mainers' "Maple on the Hill," with Saford singing lead and fiddling breaks after each loping verse.

> In a quiet country village stood a maple on the hill
> Where I sat with my Geneva long ago
> As the stars were shining brightly we could hear the whippoorwill
> As we sat beneath the maple on the hill
> I will soon be with the angels on that bright and peaceful shore
> Even now I hear them coming o'er the hill
> So good-bye, my little darling, it is time for us to part
> I must leave you 'neath the maple on the hill

Satisfied with their singing, Roy requested a couple of instrumentals. Their picking was fine, but it was their singing and the fact that they were twins that won him over. Roy Hall invited the Hall twins to join His Blue Ridge Entertainers to replace Tommy Magness and Clato Buchanan. The brothers were dumbstruck. Join the Blue Ridge Entertainers? Replace Tommy Magness? Quit their jobs? Mamo didn't think much of the offer, especially the job-quitting part.

"We have to take care of our mama," Saford told Roy.

Roy Hall pulled out his wallet and fished out a crisp fifty-dollar bill.

"Reckon that'll take care of her for a month?" he asked.

"A month," Clayton said. "That'll take care of her a whole year!"

Mamo warmed up to the offer at the sight of the fifty. She told the boys not to worry about her. She'd be fine.

Roy Hall had to get back to Winston-Salem for a show date. He instructed the twins to take the train from Bassett and meet him at the WAIR radio station the next day. He would reimburse them for their travel expenses when they arrived. Clayton and Saford promised they'd catch the train as soon as they picked up their last paycheck from Bassett Furniture the next day. With that, Roy Hall said he'd see them in Winston-Salem.

. . .

That's when the trouble started for the twins. The next day, they went to John Carter, the finishing room foreman who had hired them, and told him they were quitting and moving to Winston-Salem to play music with Roy Hall on the radio. Carter was unimpressed.

"Aw, y'all ain't gonna play on no radio," he drawled. He ordered them back to work.

Saford informed Carter that they were done with the furniture business. The twins were quitting and they wanted the money they were owed. Carter wouldn't budge. He said they couldn't quit until the end of the week, so they might as well get back to the finishing room and work out the string.

Clayton was horrified. They were supposed to meet Roy Hall in Winston-Salem today, but they wouldn't have train fare until they cashed their checks. They weren't about to ask Mamo for that fifty-dollar bill, and she probably wouldn't have parted with it anyway. If they didn't make it to Winston-Salem, they'd blow their big chance.

Carter locked up the time clock and the time cards. The boys couldn't punch out. Certain that they would miss the noon train to Winston-Salem, the twins made tracks for the depot, determined to get on that train. Inside the depot, a middle-aged woman sat behind a desk covered with papers, files, and a telephone.

"Let me do all the talking," Saford told Clayton.

Saford strode up to the woman's desk and started with his sob story. He began with the tale of Roy Hall coming to Bassett to offer the twins a job on the radio. His voice rose in pitch and tempo when he got to the part about trying to get his money from the boss man.

Clayton cut in and finished his brother's sentences.

"We ain't got the money...," Saford began.

"To get the train tickets for Winston-Salem," Clayton finished.

"See, we're supposed to be on the radio..."

"With Roy Hall and His Blue Ridge Entertainers."

"If we don't get the money for a ticket..."

"Then we'll miss the train..."

"And we won't make it on the radio..."

"With Roy Hall and His Blue Ridge Entertainers!"

The woman's head turned from side to side like she was watching a tennis match as one twin started a sentence, then the other chimed in. Finally, she found an opening and interrupted. Who were they supposed to meet in Winston-Salem? Did they know where he could be reached? Perhaps he could send them money for tickets?

Within a few minutes, the lady was on the phone with the management of WAIR radio in Winston-Salem. They got a message to Roy Hall, who sent word that he would wire them the money for tickets. He also told them that as long as they made it there by the end of the week, everything would be OK.

"Don't worry about anything," said the nameless woman behind the desk who saved Clayton and Saford's music career. "He'll wire the money to me and I'll have your tickets Friday. We'll get you on the right train to Winston-Salem."

Overjoyed, Clayton and Saford thanked the woman profusely. As they turned to leave and head to their house in Hell's Holler, Clayton noticed the web of telephone lines and cables that lined the depot's walls and ceiling.

"Now, which one of them wires does the money come in on?" he asked.

* * *

Clayton and Saford packed their few belongings in a single duffel bag. They still didn't have cases for their instruments. They piled their earthly possessions onto a train car and said good-bye to the woman who had taught them those old mountain songs when they were boys, who had first propped the fiddle under Saford's chin and held his hand as he played his first note, who first tuned a banjo for Clayton. The twins told Mamo they'd send money as soon as they started making a regular wage.

Mamo told them she'd be fine. She'd stretch that fifty-dollar bill until it hollered.

The twins left Bassett on a train that no longer runs, leaving behind jobs in a factory that no longer makes furniture. They hadn't changed much from the hillbillies they'd been when they arrived. They were still bare wood, as unpolished as any dresser or table that they'd ever worked on in the factory. They were about to receive a coat of polish from a different kind of finishing room all together, one run by a boss man named Roy Hall.

For the next three months, the twins joined the band in Winston-Salem, North Carolina, for a daily show on radio station WAIR. The sponsor for the program was Dr Pepper.

—MORE GOLD WRITTEN BY MOM FOR THE CARROLL COUNTY GENEALOGICAL BOOK, 1994

The twins were in a real band. They met the great Tommy Magness. They were bona fide professional musicians.

By the middle 1930s, WAIR had opened its airwaves to local musicians, black and white alike, to perform country and gospel music. Roy Hall landed a gig there in 1938, the same year two bastard twins in Bassett, Virginia, first heard his program. Even then, North Carolina was the media source for rural Virginians just fifty miles north. The Tar Heel state owned the talent, too. The list of bands traversing the Piedmont in the '30s reads like a freewheeling caravan of hillbilly music hall of famers. The Mainers played on Winston-Salem and Greensboro radio stations. The Blue Sky Boys were from nearby Hickory. The Monroe Brothers recorded in Charlotte. North Carolina's well of musical talent was as deep and rich as a silver mine, but the profit margin was shallow. All these bands played over the top of one another, bumped into one another on the road, and played the same kerosene-heated schoolhouses in the same little towns. The market was saturated.

That's why Winston-Salem didn't turn out to be the gold mine the twins had expected when they got on that train in Bassett. Winston was a smoking town, so to speak, home to Camel cigarette manufacturer R. J. Reynolds. The twenty-one-story Reynolds building dominated the skyline and was the tallest building south of Baltimore. But man cannot live by cigarettes and Dr Pepper alone, so the Blue Ridge Entertainers struggled financially, even though Roy's group played on two radio stations—WAIR and WBIG. In fact, the band was so popular on WBIG, it received more than ten thousand pieces of fan mail during a three-week popularity contest in 1939. WBIG awarded Roy a trophy with his vote total engraved on it. Seventy years later, that very trophy showed up on eBay.

Clayton and Saford's first taste of the big time was bittersweet. Not long after they arrived in Winston-Salem, they got some sad news. Back home in The Hollow, Granny Hall had died.

She was nearly ninety, having entered the world during the California Gold Rush year of 1849 and leaving it in early 1939, just as Europe disintegrated into war. She had worked as long as she had been able, almost to the last year of her life, delivering a fourth generation of Patrick County babies. Her breathing became increasingly wheezy and difficult, and she took to her bed that winter. Dr. Gates checked on her regularly at the cabin, examining her and keeping her informed of the goings-on around The Hollow. There was nothing he could do for her. She fretted over her children making such a fuss over a dying old woman. She could feel life stealing away, like her body was hollowing out. One morning, she told one of her granddaughters, "I've got the death rattle." That night, she was gone.

As soon as they got the news, Saford and Clayton hopped a ride to The Hollow for the funeral in the Montgomery Cemetery, where Susan Montgomery Hall was laid to eternal rest next to Pappy Hall. Clayton and Saford sang "Amazing Grace" as their own mother wept nearby.

> Amazing Grace, how sweet the sound
> That saved a wretch like me
> I once was lost, but now I'm found
> Was blind but now I see

At least Granny Hall lived long enough to see those little grandbabies grow up to become professional musicians.

Back in Winston-Salem, the twins went to work. They studied the Blue Ridge Entertainers' songbook and learned their parts. They jumped right into the WAIR broadcasts, having learned their way around a microphone from their youthful excursions to WSJS. They knew where to stand, so as not to drown out the soloist or overmodulate their vocals. Their new coworkers Bill Brown and Wayne Watson were childhood buddies from western North Carolina. The musicians slept five to a room in a boardinghouse, ate meals together, and rode to show dates crammed tight in one car, five dudes wedged shoulder to shoulder, everybody smoking unfiltered cigarettes, their instruments packed in the trunk. A sign on the back read "Roy Hall and His Blue Ridge Entertainers, playing on WAIR Radio." When Wayne finally procured a reliable upright bass to replace the washtub bass he usually played, he strapped it to the car's roof.

Shortly after the twins arrived, Tommy Magness left to work for Bill Monroe, who was starting his own band. Tommy was a friendly young man, only a couple years older than the twins. He was a stocky-built, nice-looking chap with a pudgy baby face. His Georgia drawl made him sound older than he was, and he came across as a bit bashful, even though his fiddling was anything but. His version of "Katy Hill" actually outran the rest of the band, who desperately and failingly attempted to keep up. Saford had never seen anybody's fingers work that fast. Most fiddle players he had known played not too slow, not too fast—they played "half-fast," which sounded like "half-assed." Tommy played really fast. He was the best fiddle player Saford had ever seen.

In the short time they were together, Saford played guitar and soaked up as much of Tommy's style as he could. For his part, Tommy demonstrated how to work the bow and finger different notes with each bow stroke. He even showed Saford his pièce de résistance—"Orange Blossom Special." The tune had a unique shuffling bow pattern, completely foreign to Saford, in which Tommy rocked the bow across two strings at once and occasionally caught a third string on every other stroke. The sound was electrifying to Saford, who tried like mad to get the pattern down, but he couldn't match Tommy's skill. Then, quicker than a verse of "Katy Hill," Tommy was gone. The twins doubted they'd ever see the likes of him again.

Saford was no Magness, but his repertory of old-time fiddle numbers could carry any square dance. Every night, the band had a show date—which is what every working band called their live performance. Clayton made a good accounting of himself, too, playing a rapid-fire two-finger banjo style that kept pace with the fast instrumentals. The twins' strength was, as always, their singing. They sang a slew of numbers each night, their harmonies as tight as Dick's hatband. Their singing and looks earned them new fans among the young ladies in the crowd.

. . .

But music was work. The band played a thirty-minute set on the radio every day, then piled into the "Push Model DeSoto"—so-called because the band often had to push-start it to crank it. They headed for towns all over mountainous northwest North Carolina, the pretty part, but also the part with the crookedest roads—and the most musicians. The Blue Ridge Entertainers hurtled up the mountains to play a place like Asheville only to discover that the Mainers had played there the night before, the Callahans the night before that, and the Blue Sky Boys were on their way tomorrow. The crowd was small, the pay low, and the DeSoto wouldn't crank after the show.

But it sure as hell beat the finishing room. The twins never forgot that. Every time Roy assigned Saford some tedious task, such as researching music copyrights for the next week's radio programs, a job that took hours, Saford needed only to remember the finishing room's poison fumes and unwashable stains. The music business was more work and more tiring than he'd imagined it would be, but at least he didn't have to walk around with his hands shoved in his pockets to hide his black fingernails. He wasn't trapped in The Hollow, either, picking apples or making liquor. And nobody was asking who his daddy was or calling him a bastard.

Roy Hall was the indisputable leader of the band, but Dr Pepper wrote the checks. As chief sponsor, the soda company paid each member twenty-five dollars a week. That was less than the twins made at Bassett Furniture, but they also earned a cut of show dates. All they had to do was wear their Dr Pepper shirts wherever they played and promote Dr Pepper ceaselessly and shamelessly on the radio and during performances. Roy managed all the money. He took a little bit from each member— himself included—to pay for gas and promotional posters. By the end of the week, none of the band members was taking much cash home to the boardinghouse. Roy Hall had a shelf filled with trophies won at fiddlers conventions and radio stations, he had made records for the Bluebird label, he had sackfuls of mail that he liked to pile on the ground for the band's publicity photographs, and he had a kick-ass band that boasted great singers and players. But other bands had all those things, too. He needed to turn things around, and fast. What he needed was a pick-me-up...and he got it from a soda pop. Dr Pepper was opening a bottling plant in Roanoke, Virginia. The owner wanted a hillbilly band to promote his beverage on a powerful radio station called WDBJ.

Roy received a telegram from a fellow named Wright in Roanoke. Someone in Roanoke had heard Roy Hall's group in Greensboro and recommended them to WDBJ. The Blue Ridge Entertainers' previous experience with the company made them a superb candidate for the new gig. Dr Pepper officials requested that the group send a transcribed audition disc to the Roanoke offices immediately.

The Blue Ridge Entertainers cut a disc at WAIR, which consisted of about fifteen minutes' worth of tunes, comedy bits, and copious Dr Pepper plugs.

A few days later, Roy got another telegram. The Dr Pepper bosses liked the audition. They requested that Roy Hall and the Blue Ridge Entertainers report to WDBJ studios on Kirk Avenue in Roanoke within two weeks. Management was offering a contract of $500 per week—a weekly salary of $100 for each band member.

If he'd had an airplane, Roy would have flown to Roanoke. The boys played their remaining North Carolina show dates in early April, finishing late on April 13, 1940, after which they loaded up all their clothes and instruments into Roy's DeSoto and Bill Brown's Ford. The twins were returning to Virginia but moving to a city they knew less about than they had Winston-Salem. The DeSoto wouldn't crank, so the boys all got out and assumed their usual positions behind it. They pushed it until it was rolling fast enough for Roy to pop it into gear and fire up the motor. If it hadn't started, they would've pushed it all the way to Roanoke. Anything for $100 a week.

. . .

Roy Davis Hall had left the cotton mills of western North Carolina in 1937 when he was thirty years old and started a new life as a musician. He had learned guitar on the front porches and in the kitchens of houses strung along the factory village of Marion, North Carolina. The town was thick with musicians, men who worked like dogs all day in the Clinch-field Mill, then picked up guitars, fiddles, and jars of home brew at night. Clyde Moody, a terrific singer, was from East Marion. Fiddle-playing Steve

Ledford was from up the road in Spruce Pine. Zeke Morris and Hicks Burnette were musicians and songwriters from nearby towns. Dobro man Jack Stewart was a regular at Roy's picking parties. With musicians as abundant as cotton bolls, Roy got good quick.

By the time he turned thirty, he'd already packed in enough living to fill three lives. He was born in the North Carolina mountain town of Waynesville in 1907. The Halls were a large family, and as soon as the boys were old enough to take care of themselves, they struck out on their own. The family moved to Marion in the 1920s where Roy's daddy, Wade, took a job in the cotton mill. Roy left home at fourteen and worked hard-labor jobs throughout the wild western Carolina mountains. He made his way across the country, working as a lumberjack in Washington and on a fishing boat in the Pacific. He returned to North Carolina in his twenties and operated heavy machinery for road-building crews blasting tunnels through the mountains. He ran a store and got married and divorced. By 1935, he had come full circle and was back in Marion working at the Clinchfield Mill.

Like most Depression-era factory towns, Marion was a rough place after dark. The local saying was "ain't no kin after six o'clock," which meant you were as likely to get into a drunken knock-down drag-out with your brother or cousin as you were with a stranger. Marion had been at the vanguard of the labor union movement of the 1920s. Workers at Clinchfield and Marion Manufacturing went on strike in 1929, only to have their efforts crushed by company bosses and hired guns.

By the '30s, the textile labor movement was dead, but Roy had his own way of outsmarting bosses. He was a good baseball player, and he managed a team of mill hands that played other local textile teams. Roy was catcher, an important position because he could call for what he wanted the pitcher to throw, move infielders around, and basically control the flow of the game. Catchers are leaders. When Roy's team was set to take on the squad from Valdese, the best team in the textile league, one of his bosses made Roy an offer: "Roy, if you beat them boys, we'll spend two days at my place on the lake and we'll have a fish fry and we'll just pull one"—as in, "pull a two-day drunk." The offer was basically a joke, because Valdese was expected to clobber the poor old Clinchfield Nine.

Roy had a game plan that didn't involve batting practice. Instead, he instructed his older brother Jerry and teenage brother Rufus to pack up dozens of bottles of home-brewed beer and take it to the Valdese ball field early on game day. The temperature that afternoon approached ninety degrees, so Jerry and Rufus packed the beer in an ice-filled washtub and sold it to the Valdese club at the low, low price of two bottles for a quarter. By the time the Clinchfield club arrived, the Valdese boys were three-and-a-half sheets to the wind. They couldn't hit, pitch, catch, or stand in the batter's box without wobbling. Roy's team pummeled Valdese, 10–0, earning Roy a weekend party at the lake on the boss man's dime.

Roy looked for angles and opportunities. Music looked like a good line of work to get into, except that he couldn't play. He swapped an old pistol for a guitar and began following his music-playing buddies to dances. He'd go hear the Callahan Brothers or the Morris Brothers, or pick on Clyde Moody's front porch. Roy's younger brother Jay Hugh learned guitar, too, by playing Roy's guitar at night when Roy worked the late shift. The Hall boys were fast learners. They played dances and sang together and were presumptuous enough about the music business to write to the RCA Victor recording company to see when exactly the company would like for them to come make records. Incredibly, the company invited the untested brother act to come to Charlotte and record for its Bluebird label. On February 16, 1937, Roy and Jay Hugh Hall recorded twelve songs in Charlotte.

The results were phenomenal. Even though they were influenced by other smooth-singing brother groups, the Halls' cotton-mill rawness tore through. Armed with just two guitars and an occasional mandolin, Roy and Jay Hugh played and sang with reckless abandon. They recorded the requisite love song and sacred number, but that first session was dominated by gritty songs from a pair of mill workers. "McDowell Blues," "Spartanburg Jail," and "Hitch Hike Blues" were all rough around the edges. The best song they recorded was their first one, the party-till-you-drop number "When It Gets Dark":

> *I don't know whether it's so or not*
> *But they tell me this town's red hot*
> *When it gets dark*
> *When it gets dark*

Sounded like Marion. The song is fantastic, mostly because of Jay Hugh's twangy tenor harmony and manic guitar solos. Rock and roll was twenty years away, but Jay Hugh had that same kind of wild spirit.

. . .

Not long after the session, Roy and Jay Hugh left Marion, even though they owed hundreds of dollars to friends who had loaned them money to help them gain a toehold in the music business. The Hall Brothers, as they were known on record and in person, played on the radio in Asheville, North Carolina, and Spartanburg, South Carolina, until Jay Hugh left to join Wade Mainer's group, Sons of the Mountaineers. Roy formed his own band. Recognizing his shortcomings as a musician, he built a band that he could take farther than he could get on his own. He would be the boss man who gave orders, the catcher who called the pitches. Roy hired Bill Brown on slide guitar, Wayne Watson on bass, Clato Buchanan on tenor banjo, Bob Hopson and Talmadge Aldridge on guitars, and a young fiddle player he'd met in Spartanburg, Tommy Magness. The Blue Ridge Entertainers were born.

Roy was a perfectionist when it came to the band's look and attire. Tommy, a rough-around-the-edges north Georgia boy, didn't have proper dress clothes, so Roy bought him a new white shirt and dark pants. Roy had first heard Tommy at a date in Charlotte, where he had impressed Roy with a new fiddle tune he'd learned either from the radio or from other fiddlers. Tommy played the fire out of it, ripping through it like a locomotive, shuffling his bow so fast it made smoke rise from the strings. Roy had never heard the tune, which had been composed by a pair of brothers from Florida, Ervin and Gordon Rouse, who played it all over the Southeast but had never recorded it. When Roy hired Tommy, he wanted to record that tune—"Orange Blossom Special."

In November 1938, in Columbia, South Carolina, Roy Hall and His Blue Ridge Entertainers recorded eighteen songs for Vocalion, the same label that a year earlier had issued bluesman Robert Johnson's only recordings. The Blue Ridge Entertainers waxed the Rouse Brothers' soon-to-be fiddle standard "Orange Blossom Special," the first time it was ever recorded. Tommy played it fairly stiff that day, with fewer train-whistle doodads and a tighter, grinding shuffle. After a couple of breaks, Roy and Bob hollered out call-and-response verses—"Bob, where you going?" "I'm taking that Orange Blossom Special to Spartanburg, South Carolina!"—and then Tommy took off again, like a crazed conductor driving the musical train down the track. The band thought it had a surefire hit record—that was, until the Rouse Brothers heard about it.

When music historians wrote about the careers of Roy Hall and Tommy Magness many years later, they always included the unfortunate fact that

Roy never got to release his version of "Orange Blossom Special." They found a note buried in the files of record producer Art Satherly, the head artists and repertoire guy for the American Record Company, which owned Vocalion. "Hold release, Rouse Brothers refuse to sign contract," the note read. On the recording session ledger was written another foreboding note: "Don't release—Pub. promises trouble." Translation: The Rouses' music publisher was threatening legal action if Roy released "Orange Blossom Special." So he didn't. The Rouses finally put it out in 1939, which was their right. Roy and Tommy's version was relegated to the archives.

Roy never seemed bothered by the haggling over "Orange Blossom Special," especially since the Blue Ridge Entertainers were getting tons of work, both on the radio and on the road. He'd made dozens of records by that point, which generated a little additional income. Things got even better when Roy was introduced to the Dr Pepper people by Marty Lyle, a radio announcer at WSPA in Spartanburg. The soda company wanted to sponsor the Blue Ridge Entertainers, but it needed them to move to Greensboro to radio station WBIG. Soon, they switched to WAIR in Winston-Salem. Tommy and Clato left the group. Roy took a trip to Bassett, Virginia, to find the Hall twins. Times got lean, the DeSoto ran rough, and then, just when it looked like this little ragtag band would dry up and blow away in North Carolina, the telegram came from Roanoke. In April 1940, Roy Hall made the shrewdest decision he'd made since he traded that pistol for a guitar. If he couldn't be better than all the other bands, he'd outfox them, the same way he did the Valdese baseball team. He left the cutthroat competition of North Carolina and took his band to the virgin musical frontier of Roanoke.

ROANOKE

Saford and Clayton, 1940

The band flourished in Roanoke.

—MOM AGAIN, FROM THE CARROLL COUNTY
GENEALOGICAL BOOK, 1994

Kirk Avenue is a skinny one-way street that stretches from downtown Roanoke's City Market to Second Street. Kirk is more of a side street, but it's a route I'll take on foot if I'm heading back to my office from downtown. I go that way so I can sneak a peek inside the front door of 124 Kirk Avenue, a three-story gray-brick building on the street's shady south side. Through a glass entrance on the right, you can look down and see four letters inscribed in the terra-cotta flooring: WDBJ.

WDBJ operated here for more than twenty years. In the 1990s, the old second-floor studios were converted into a high-dollar apartment by the current owner. The building was constructed for a little more than $100,000 in 1936 to house Roanoke's fast-growing radio station. CBS engineers came to town to help design its three studios, ensuring the rooms would be completely soundproof and free from vibration. Live performers dominated the station's daytime schedule, with classically trained organists sharing airtime with bandana-wearing fiddle bands. This was Roanoke radio, circa 1940, when a band of good ol' boys from North Carolina came to town and first strode over the terra-cotta WDBJ in the breezeway. Right here, at 124 Kirk Avenue, is where life changed for a pair of hillbilly brothers from The Hollow.

• • •

The band left Winston-Salem in an all-night, two-car caravan and crossed into Virginia well after midnight, just hours after their final show date in Winston-Salem. On the Virginia side, the road began to curve back and forth like a drunk trying to find his way home from the corner bar. The boys passed through Henry and Franklin counties, bypassing the twins' old stomping grounds in Bassett, and eventually broke through the wall of the Blue Ridge and twisted downward into a valley that seemed as wide as the ocean. On the valley floor, hugged by mountain ridges on all sides, lay the city of Roanoke.

Roanoke, the Magic City. It earned that nickname in the 1880s because of the way it seemed to appear from nowhere after the railroads came through. Before the boomtown of Roanoke, there had been the village of Big Lick, named for the marshy salt licks that had attracted wild animals—and the Indians and pioneers who hunted them. After the Norfolk & Western and Shenandoah Valley railroads crossed their lines there in 1882, Big Lick exploded overnight into a rowdy, brawling town that drew wild men the way it had wild game. Workers who labored in the railroad shops came in all shapes and shades—they were Greek, Lebanese, Irish, German, and African, not to mention the Big Lick holdover Brits and Scots. Saloons and houses of ill repute provided off-hours recreation for the men who made up the bulk of the population. Decent ladies were mostly absent during the boom years. Big Lick began to change its image in 1882, when it renamed itself the more lyrical Roanoke, from the Roanoke River that flowed through the valley.

By 1940, Roanoke had matured and settled down into its conservative middle age. The railroad still provided most of the work and political power, as railroad bosses often became mayors. Banks, hospitals, and hotels dominated the skyline. Roanoke was still a hopping place, with streetcars, automobiles, and pedestrians all jockeying for the right of way on Campbell Avenue beneath a web of telephone and telegraph wires. The heart of downtown was the City Market District, where vendors hawked vegetables and live chickens inside the City Market Building, a long, low brick structure with a spacious second floor suitable for dances and basketball games. Entertainment was easy to find in Roanoke. Five downtown movie theaters stood within three blocks of one another. For all the city's vibrancy, however, Roanoke only had one major radio station—WDBJ, which had signed on in 1924 when a young electrician named Ray Jordan fiddled three tunes for a broadcast that was heard by a rich gentleman across town who owned the only radio receiver in the valley. By 1940, Ray Jordan was the boss, and WDBJ was saturating the mountains of southwest Virginia with five thousand watts of radio magic.

. . .

The caravan followed its directions into town along Franklin Road in the predawn hours of Sunday, April 14, 1940. Roy missed the turn for Kirk Avenue, but Bill took it, only to hear Clayton holler that he was going the wrong way on a one-way street. Since it was still early, Kirk Avenue was empty and they avoided a head-on collision, but it was not the grand entrance they had hoped to make in Roanoke.

Bill proceeded the wrong way down Kirk Avenue, and Clayton immediately pointed out the gray-brick building with the large neon sign hanging vertically on the front, its bright red electric letters reading top to bottom "WDBJ." Bill parked, Roy pulled up (having circled around and finding the proper way on Kirk Avenue), and the Blue Ridge Entertainers caught a few winks in their cars before going inside to discover what Roanoke had in store for them.

The band did not know that, two weeks earlier, the *Roanoke Times* had announced the Blue Ridge Entertainers' impending arrival with great fanfare inside the Sunday newspaper. A banner headline on the April 7, 1940, edition read "WDBJ to Sign On At 6:30 A.M. Beginning Monday, April 15." The subheadlines read "Early Risers to Receive Service" and "Blue Ridge Entertainers Take Program April 22." Adorning the article was a photograph of the Entertainers from their pre-Clayton-and-Saford days, posing around a microphone, a pile of fan mail at the boys' feet. The caption, which misspelled Tommy's name as "Tommy Magnus" (a common mistake), stated in part that the Blue Ridge Entertainers "are widely known in North Carolina and South Carolina and have made a number of RCA Victor recordings."

Now, here they were in Roanoke, without Tommy "Magnus" but with two handsome, talented twin brothers. In the coming weeks, people naturally assumed that the three Halls must be related, but the twins would set them straight. That is, unless they wanted to mess with the folks.

Sometimes they'd tell fans that Roy was their daddy, a mean old cuss who had made them sleep outside in the firewood box as babies. Sometimes Roy was their uncle.

So that's what people called him: Uncle Roy.

Their new radio announcer, Irving Sharp, called him that. A garrulous, paunchy young man with prematurely thinning hair and a wisp of a mustache, Sharp was part of a generation that had cut its teeth on radio, and he had a knack for knowing what audiences wanted to hear. He was a radio triple threat: He could sing, he could play the piano, and he could ad-lib right over the air. He was a cool customer, only twenty five, who easily dropped pitches for Dr Pepper into broadcasts as smoothly as taking a sip of pop. The Blue Ridge Entertainers hit it off immediately with Sharp. Pretty soon, Uncle Roy was calling him Cousin Irving.

. . .

The day they arrived, the Blue Ridge Entertainers toured WDBJ's trio of studios and control room. Studio A was the largest of the three, capable of holding a couple dozen spectators who wanted to watch musicians play on the radio. The only people who ever showed up to sit in the studio were usually either hardcore radio nuts, a few music fans, or curious boys who admired the electrical equipment. Finding a seat was never a problem.

The station provided the band with accommodations in Mrs. Hankins's boardinghouse across town in northwest Roanoke. The boys moved into their quarters on Sunday afternoon and planned out the program for Monday's 6:30 a.m. debut.

On the morning of April 22, 1940, Roy Hall and His Blue Ridge Entertainers played the airwaves of WDBJ for the first time. The five musicians gathered in a circle around a single microphone on a stand. No recording or set list survives from that broadcast, but the format was surely similar to the group's Winston-Salem programs: Roy strummed a G chord to kick-start the Dr Pepper theme song, "She'll be drinking Dr Pepper when she comes." Then Saford tore off on a fiddle tune, like, say, "Under the Double Eagle" or "Down Yonder." Roy sang a couple of numbers, and then Saford probably fiddled another hot one, followed by a song by Bill and Wayne or a duet from the twins, such as "In the Pines." They kept it up, switching between instrumentals and vocals, pushing Dr Pepper between every song like it was some magical elixir. "Drink a bite to eat, neighbors,"

Irving Sharp, their announcer, probably said. As the old clock on the wall neared 7 a.m., they wrapped it up with another fiddle tune, as Irving told the audience he'd see 'em again tomorrow for another half hour of your favorite tunes and remember, "Enjoy life more. Drink Dr Pepper at ten, two, and four."

The show went off well, as expected. What shocked everybody was the crowd of people who showed up at the station. Roanokers had heard that this band was red-hot. Studio A was jam-packed for the Blue Ridge Entertainers' second radio program. The third day, the crowd spilled into the second-floor hallway and into Studio B, where the program was piped in over loudspeakers. The crowd was a mix of old and young: rough-looking men who wanted to hear a few tunes before trudging off to work, teenage boys killing time at the radio station before heading uptown to Jefferson High School, and—best of all—girls in their best dresses who came to see this hot band and who tried to catch the brown eyes of those handsome twins.

Roanoke had its share of hillbilly bands, many of them inspired by the same cowboy movies that Clayton and Saford had loved. Bands with names like the Texas Troubadours played regular shows on WDBJ, mixing cowboy songs, fiddle tunes, and a pop number or two. They were good, but they weren't the Mainers—or the Callahans, Blue Sky Boys, or Monroes. After live radio broadcasts, they packed up their instruments and went to work at their real jobs. Nobody in Roanoke played music as a full-time career. Then Roy Hall showed up.

The Entertainers hadn't booked any shows before arriving, not knowing the territory. On their second day at WDBJ, somebody sent a postcard inviting them to perform midweek at the Garden City school auditorium, a short drive south of Roanoke. The night of the show, the DeSoto with the bass fiddle strapped to the top wheeled down a quiet street toward the school and parked, and the boys toted their cases a good hundred yards to get to the venue. Hordes of people loitered outside around the schoolhouse, hanging around doorways and peering in windows. At first, the band thought somebody had goofed—did somebody book us the same night as a basketball game? Why are so many people here?

They were there to see the Blue Ridge Entertainers, of course.

The musicians were a sight in their black hats, white shirts, and dark jackets, all of them wearing wide neckties. They always dressed to the nines, even for the radio. "Never know who might show up," Roy would tell them. This night, it appeared that all of Garden City and half of Roanoke had shown up.

They took the stage and set up Roy's primitive public-address system: one microphone with two speakers, which folded neatly into an easy-to-carry case. The auditorium was packed with a couple hundred people, not counting those trying to sneak a peek from a door or a window. The set list has been lost to history. I know a hundred songs and fiddle tunes that Roy Hall was famous for playing—"Wabash Cannonball," "Turkey in the Straw," "Come Back, Little Pal," "New San Antonio Rose," "No Letter in the Mail Today," "Come Back, Sweetheart," "Sunny Tennessee," "Rubber Dolly," and dozens of others. But I have no idea what they played that night. All I can tell you is that they did not disappoint the overflowing crowd. By the weekend, postcards poured into WDBJ from every community within signal range. The Blue Ridge Entertainers were invited to play every schoolhouse, clubhouse, and outhouse in Virginia, West Virginia, and North Carolina. Roy answered every legitimate request. His demands were simple—the band would get 60 percent of the door. He would also sell his songbooks and maybe some records. The venues were eager to have the Blue Ridge Entertainers. The band would not lack work for the next two and a half years.

   . . .

Everybody called Dorothy Wilbourne "Dot." She lived on Massachusetts Avenue, right across the street from Mrs. Hankins's boardinghouse where this band of young musicians had set up camp. She hardly noticed her new neighbors, but Saford soon took a liking to her. She was a pretty, tiny, spunky girl—a wonderfully gifted musician, singer, and dancer who performed acrobatic routines during dance recitals. She also happened to be fourteen years old.

Saford was twenty, which didn't seem to matter to Dot's mom. In fact, Lottie Wilbourne was probably the first person to meet the new boys across the street. She was definitely the one who introduced Dot to Saford.

Saford the showman, the show-off, was hard to overlook. Dot wasn't impressed. For one thing, he was too old for her, and for another, she already had a boyfriend who was closer to her own age. Saford had his share of girlfriends, too. Everybody in the band did. By the time they'd been in town two weeks, Roy Hall and His Blue Ridge Entertainers were the biggest celebrities and most eligible bachelors in Roanoke. Dozens of well-dressed, heavily made-up girls crowded the band's engagements and elbowed their way into the radio studio. Girls sent cards and letters—addressed simply either to Saford or Clayton, WDBJ, Roanoke, Va.—and requested songs and inquired about marital status. When the weather warmed up in the spring of 1940 and the band began playing outdoor jamborees, girls ambushed the twins armed with cameras and lipstick, begging the boys to pose for photographs. The twins always obliged. They made no secret of their love for the ladies. In their bio for one of Roy Hall's songbooks, they signed off with the admission "They especially like brown eyes."

Roanoke was a smorgasbord of potential girlfriends. Because the band played shows six nights a week, the musicians used the rare night off to go out on different types of dates entirely. On more than one occasion Saford asked two girls out on the same night. When that happened, he'd just pawn off one girl on Clayton, who protested at first, then relented when he realized this was an easy way to meet girls.

"What'll we talk about?" Clayton wanted to know. "I don't even know this girl."

Saford shrugged off the question. "That don't matter," he said. "Just tell her how pretty she is and let her take care of the rest of it."

* * *

Soon, however, Saford was smitten with Dot, whose mother encouraged the couple to spend time together and get to know each other. Roy wasn't happy when Saford started spending more and more time across Massachusetts Avenue at the Wilbournes'. For one thing, Saford was getting sloppy with his music. He skipped practices and was late for shows. The other problem was more worrisome: Dot was jailbait. Roy knew that if his fiddle player and primary drawing card got mixed up in a sex scandal with a child, the whole mess would be bad for business.

Dot had become a fixture, however. She started showing up at show dates around town, sitting in the crowd (often with her parents; she would've gone to even more performances, but she couldn't stay out late on school nights), watching all those other females with their painted faces and mountains of hair swooning over the twins. She ignored Saford's wannabe lovers as best she could, which was more than Saford ever did for her. He rarely let affection go unrequited.

Dot followed the band to as many shows as she could. During the day, she attended the Catholic school at St. Andrew's church, where she excelled in music and art studies. Catholic school didn't mean a thing to Saford, whose religious training was sketchy at best. He'd gone to various Methodist, Moravian, and, of course, Baptist churches in The Hollow, often with cousins or friends, but he didn't know the difference between a Catholic and a cougar—and Dot seemed part both. She loved music and dancing; she was so good on the piano she taught neighborhood children on Massachusetts Avenue. Saford was ready to convert.

. . .

Soon, Clayton had a girl, too. Reba Holland was a chestnut-haired, blue-eyed beauty, whose brothers had gone hog-wild over the Blue Ridge Entertainers and dragged the family to show dates all over town. Reba was a baby, too, barely fifteen, when she met Clayton at the WDBJ studios. Clayton began spending his free time at the Holland house in the hilly southeast section of town. Reba was the second oldest of four, which included big brother Marvin; little brother Henry, Jr.; and baby sister Elinor. Reba's dad, Henry, Sr., who went by his middle name, "Oake," drove a city bus that included the Blue Ridge Entertainers' neighborhood on its route. Clayton often rode Oake Holland's bus downtown and became quick pals with his new girlfriend's father. The men played catch in the backyard on Sunday afternoons, while the women fried up chicken and boiled potatoes for dinner. Reba's mother, Thelma, liked Clayton immediately because he liked the Bible (either he had paid attention in Sunday school, or he was doing anything he could to impress his gal's parents). He was a good boy.

The only thing that irritated Clayton about the Holland household was Elinor, the annoying baby sister. It seemed that every time Clayton and Reba were about to sit close to each other, at the last possible second Elinor jumped between them. When the lovebirds finally did get some time alone, either on the couch or on the front porch, here came Elinor again, usually carrying a cat she called "Kitty Ninju."

"Pet Kitty Ninju," she said to Clayton, flopping the mad gray kitty onto his lap. Clayton didn't care much for cats, especially one that had been dropped on his privates.

Elinor was also a little extortionist.

"I want fifty cents so I can get some ice cream," Elinor demanded of

Clayton one afternoon while he and Reba sat on the Hollands' living room couch, "or else I'll tell Mama y'all are out here kissing."

After Elinor pulled this stunt a few times, Clayton began filling his coat pockets with quarters, dimes, and nickels (when the price of admission to your show dates is thirty cents, you end up with lots of change). Whenever Elinor attempted to blackmail, Clayton just pointed her to the coat tree in the corner.

That was about the only complaint Clayton had. As he and Saford prepared to celebrate their twenty-first birthday in this rollicking railroad town, the twins were popular and successful, and, to beat it all, they had girlfriends. Not bad for two bastards from The Hollow.

· · ·

The Blue Ridge Entertainers' radio programs were a hoot. The music was good, and Roy and the announcer, "Cousin Irving" Sharp, quickly developed an on-air repartee that played off their folksy personas. In an age when radio announcers aimed to impress audiences and station managers with their oratorical skills and erudite delivery, Cousin Irving stood out like a bicycle horn in an orchestra. He was spontaneous, a good improviser, and utterly unflappable. He loved to yuck it up with the band and laughed heartily and sincerely at unplanned jokes. Roy even set aside portions of each broadcast for Irving's solo numbers on a Hammond B-3 organ or piano (or sometimes both in one song). For a city like Roanoke, which was becoming increasingly sophisticated and modernized but still allowed its citizens to raise cows and chickens, Irving Sharp was the pitch-perfect voice that appealed to the ears of both railroad magnates and mill hands.

Irving started each program with a monologue that went something like:

> Well, howdy, friends and neighbors, it's Dr Pepper Time, another half hour of your favorite music as played by Roy Hall and His Blue Ridge Entertainers. Friends, the weekend is coming up and you don't want to get caught short when it comes to having enough Dr Pepper on hand. Dr Pepper comes in an economical six-bottle carton, perfect to get you through the weekend. Pick up a couple cartons. It won't set you back and your family will never enjoy anything more than Dr Pepper. It's refreshing and with its pure blend of fruit juices, it'll keep you wide awake and alert through whatever you've got planned.

Remember, friends, Dr Pepper, it's good for life. Dr Pepper Time start-
ing out with "Cotton-Eyed Joe." Saford on the fiddle, let 'er go, boys,
let 'er go. . . .

And they were off. They drove swiftly through a set, following the same
pattern each day—fiddle tune, Roy's featured solo, a duet by Clayton and
Saford, a spiritual number, Irving's spotlight, a recitation of upcoming
show dates—pausing long enough here and there to sling Dr Pepper like it
was snake oil.

"Uncle Roy, tell the good folks how Dr Pepper is the perfect weekend
drink," Irving would say.

"Well, Cousin, they can pick up a handy carton today, then one tomorrow, and it'll only set 'em back four bits," Roy would summarize.

They never had a problem filling airtime. If a set list came up a little
short, the engineer would give the signal to "stretch" the program by moving his hands apart as if he was stretching a piece of taffy.

"What are you doing, Robert?" Irving would say to the engineer, on air.
"You look like you're pulling molasses."

Irving, knowing his cue, would then pick up a sheet of Dr Pepper "facts"
and read them with Roy like they were reciting a call-and-response church
liturgy.

> IRVING: "We'd like to say to our little buddies that it'll be
> Dr Pepper Time again tomorrow, same time."
> ROY: "It sure will, and I'd like to say to those little buddies that
> Dr Pepper is good for life."
> IRVING: "And I'd like to say to those little buddies' mothers
> and fathers that they never have to worry about giving
> Dr Pepper to their children because they'll enjoy it, and,
> besides that, it's good for 'em."
> ROY: "The equivalent of Dr Pepper is equal to three and
> one-quarter ounces of pure orange juice."
> IRVING: "Dr Pepper is a blend of pure fruit juices, and you
> know how good pure fruit juices are for you."
> ROY: "It has a lemon base!"

They wrapped up every broadcast with a fast-break chorus of "Take Me
Back to the Blue Ridge Mountains":

Take me back to the Blue Ridge Mountains
Where I long to live and die
Take me back to the Blue Ridge Mountains
To that wonderful home in the sky

The Blue Ridge Entertainers' radio shows made Roy Hall enormously popular over a wide area of Virginia, and they sold Dr Pepper by the truckload. Listeners drank Dr Pepper at ten, two, and four and any other time Cousin Irving told them to. Within months, Roanokers were drinking more Dr Pepper per capita than anywhere else in the world. (The funny thing was that Cousin Irving never really developed a taste for the blend of sweet fruit flavors. He plugged Dr Pepper because it was his job. He did haul a cooler in the back floorboard of his car—but he kept it filled with beer.)

The radio broadcasts did more than just sell soda pop, though. They sold Roy Hall and His Blue Ridge Entertainers to a public that craved his kind of music. The band's sound was distinct: a sweet mix of blues-laced mountain music and country swing.

Clayton and Saford were stars, and their identical good looks made them a novelty among Roanoke bands. More important, their musical talents were astounding. They could play any instrument with strings and their harmonies went together like mashed potatoes and chicken gravy. Clayton stuck with the banjo, but was soon mastering the fiddle and the bass. The twins were the biggest difference in the sound of Roy Hall's band compared with his earlier North Carolina lineups, and they were as responsible as anybody for the Blue Ridge Entertainers' newfound glory in Roanoke.

So were Monk and Gibb.

Monk and Gibb were comic characters invented by and played by Clayton and Saford. Every Blue Ridge Entertainers' show featured comedy segments from those wild and wacky Hall twins. Clayton and Saford played stereotypical hillbilly characters in stereotypical ways, with blacked-out front teeth and faces dotted with freckles. Saford, in the timeless role of Gibb, wore a ratty derby hat and a ridiculous pair of oversized britches hitched up with stretchy suspenders. He carried a couple of weights in his pockets, so that when he pulled on his suspenders, his britches dropped to his knees, revealing polka-dotted boxer shorts, then popped back up. When the skit called for Gibb to play guitar, he put it on with a strap that had the words "Huba Huba" (instead of "Hubba Hubba") on it. As Monk, Clayton dressed like a Wild West outlaw and hammed it up on stage. Saford had always been the primary showman of the two, but when it came to comedy, he was the straight man to Clayton's natural-born cornpone silliness.

GIBB: "Hey Monk, where was you a goin' so fast when you run past my house the other day? You was mortally a-flyin'."
MONK: "Man, I was headed to the doctor."
GIBB: "The doctor!"
MONK: "Yeah. See, I laid on my little downy bed on the back of my flat..."
GIBB: "You mean you laid down on the flat of your back?"
MONK: "That's what I said. I was on my little downy bed on the back of my flat and I musta fell asleep with my mouth wide open 'cause I'll be dogged if a rat didn't mistake my mouth for a rat hole, and I want you to know that I swallered that rat!"
GIBB [head bobbing around, eyes bulging]: "You swallered a rat!"
MONK: "I did, and that's when I come a-flyin' by your house a-headed for the doctor. . . . I mean to tell you, I was pickin' 'em up and settin' 'em down. I cut the corner goin' so fast I scooped up sand in my hip pocket."
GIBB: "Well, what'd the doctor say?"
MONK: "That doctor looked down in my mouth and he said maybe I could swaller some rat poison, and I said, 'No thank you! Ain't you got no other way?' And he thought a minute and said, 'Have you got an old Tom cat?' And I told him I did. And he told me to get me some cheese and set it on my chin and set old Tom on my chest and when that rat smelled them cheese he'd come after it and old Tom would get that rat!"
GIBB: "Oh boy! Did it work?"
MONK: "Well, I done like he said and got me some cheese. I laid on my old downy bed on the back of my flat. I set them cheese on my chin and set old Tom on my chest. Well, directly that rat got to smelling them cheese and I could feel him coming up. He was using my ribs as a stepladder. Ol' Tom could smell that rat and he started swishing his tail side to side."
GIBB: "Oh Lord! What happened then?"

MONK: "That rat went after the cheese. And the cat went
after the rat!"
GIBB: "And did he catch that rat?"
MONK: "Naw, man! I swallered rat, cat, cheese, and all!"

And to think they wrote this stuff themselves. The crowd lapped it up
like it was free Dr Pepper.

. . .

On Sunday afternoons—the band's only day off from radio programs—
the Blue Ridge Entertainers played on top of Mill Mountain, a 1,200-foot
summit crowned with a green park that provided dazzling views of the
plucky city and the blue mountains that ringed Roanoke like a fortress.
Automobiles traveled bumper to bumper up the twisty mountain road
that doubled back on and over the top of itself, forming a figure-eight
loop by which hundreds, perhaps thousands, of people made it to the top
for the Sunday hoedowns. Dot and Reba were always there to cheer their
boys on.

The Blue Ridge Entertainers took the stage wearing dark jackets, white
shirts, and wide colorful ties. Roy set up his public-address system and for
the next three hours the band cut loose with what music lovers of 1940
considered modern country music.

Clayton and Saford sang several duets, including a couple that they came
up with on their own. Their song "Little Sweetheart, Come and Kiss Me"
was a big hit with the crowd. The up-tempo ditty might not have been all
that original—it was even set to the melody of another song, "East Virginia Blues"—but the tune swung like a hammer and sounded like gold.

> Little sweetheart, come and kiss me
> Just once more before I go
> Tell me truly you will miss me
> As I wander to and fro
>
> Let me feel the tender pressings
> Of your ruby lips to mine
> With your dimpled hands caressing
> And your snowy arms entwined

The lyrics were poetic and sweet—and possibly written by someone else, even though Roy Hall's songbooks clearly stated "Words and Music by Hall Twins." Long after their careers were over, Clayton and Saford fessed up that the words to some of those songs might have been "inspired" by other sources. Roy Hall had taught them how to copyright material that existed in the public domain. Roy, like A. P. Carter before him and Roy Acuff later, had learned that real money in the music business wasn't made by risking your neck on country back roads trying to get to every schoolhouse with a stage and a woodstove, or even by making records. Publishing rights were where the real money was. The "Orange Blossom Special" debacle had taught him that. Roy could have sold thousands of copies of that record, but he would not have gotten rich because he didn't own the song's publishing rights. Starting then, he began copyrighting songs, even those sent to him by other writers.

Roy told the twins that any time anybody sent them a poem or some song lyrics in a letter, they should copyright the verses if the poor sap who wrote them hadn't done so already. That's surely how they came to copyright a song whose chorus was actually older than they were. Roy reprinted the song in a songbook, under the title "If Trouble Don't Kill Me, I'll Live a Long Time":

I'm troubled, I'm troubled, I'm troubled in mind
If trouble don't kill me, I'll live a long time

A little box of powders, and a little box of paint
Makes all these young girls just think what they ain't
They'll hug you, they'll kiss you, they'll tell you more lies
Than the crossties on the railroad and the stars in the sky

A little bottle of liquor and a little rusty gun
Makes all of these young boys just think that they're grown
I'm troubled, I'm troubled, I'm troubled in mind
If trouble don't kill me, I'll live a long time

From their onstage perch atop Mill Mountain, Roy Hall and His Blue Ridge Entertainers could look out over a crowd of a thousand people who had come to the mountaintop just to see them. Off in the distance, Roanoke spread out across the valley floor like a blanket of jewels.

"Future years may bring us sorrow," the twins sang on "Little Sweetheart, Come and Kiss Me."

That our hearts be little known
Still of care we should not borrow
Come and kiss me or I'll go.

As popular as these Sunday afternoon mountaintop hootenannies were, the biggest weekly music event was the Saturday night Blue Ridge Jamboree at the Academy of Music.

The Academy was a fabulous concert hall built in the early 1890s when Roanoke was booming and the new arrivals from the north brought their love of fine arts—and money—with them. Prominent businessmen built the Academy for $95,000, complete with marble flooring, electric lights, private boxes, seating for 1,500 (including a section reserved for blacks that afforded no access to the rest of the building), and an opulent interior designed by a Frenchman. The acoustics were said to be perfect for every kind of performance, from a grand orchestra to a small choir. The Academy was a musical palace, a repository of art and culture just a few blocks removed from the bars, brawls, and brothels of the rowdy City Market District.

By 1940, though, the palace was a half-century old and showing its age. The roof was leaky, and many of the seats needed repair or replacement. But the old girl was still a musical showplace. Traveling opera companies and orchestras still came, great orators still orated, and now, best of all, the hillbillies were taking over.

Roy made another shrewd business move by getting WDBJ to sponsor a live radio program originating from the Academy of Music. He used his business and music contacts to book big-name acts each week. Within a year, the Blue Ridge Jamboree and the Academy of Music had played host to the Carter Family, the Blue Sky Boys, the Delmore Brothers, the Sons of the Pioneers, and other high-profile groups. Each week, the Blue Ridge Entertainers opened the show for those performers. Around southwest Virginia, Roy Hall's band was just as popular as the top billing.

. . .

In the summer of '40, the twins didn't know, or care, a lick about the looming war. Sure, they'd seen films of the war in Europe on the newsreels that played before picture shows at the American Theater. Everybody knew Hitler was a bad guy, and the twins felt real bad about those poor Polacks who'd been run over by those nasty Krauts, but, hey, what do you want us to do about it? We sent our boys over there in '17 and what did we get out of it? Heartaches, that's what. Those crazy Europeans could fight their own damn wars from now on.

And as for those newsreels showing the fighting between Japan and China, well, who knew what that was all about?

Anyway, the boys in the band were more excited about seeing themselves on the silver screen than watching Japanese planes drop bombs. They'd made their own movie—a clip for National Beer of Baltimore, makers of National Bohemian. The band stood before a whirring film camera in a Roanoke studio, clutching instruments, and sang the National Beer theme song:

National Beer, National Beer
You'll love the taste of National Beer
And while I'm singing I'm proud to say
It's brewed on the shores of the Chesapeake Bay

They sat through many boring war newsreels just to see themselves on the screen.

. . .

Today's platinum-card-carrying crowd might not think of hillbilly music as a particularly glamorous way to make a living, but in Roanoke, Virginia, in 1940, the shows at the Academy of Music were packed each week. Fans crowded the WDBJ studios at ungodly hours to watch the Entertainers put on their program (at one point, they put on two shows, one in the morning and one at midday). Country music allowed the boys to dress well, meet girls, and drive new automobiles.

Pretty soon, the Blue Ridge Entertainers could not accept all the invitations for show dates. Roy called in his brothers Jay Hugh and Rufus and built a second band around them. They were called the Happy-Go-Lucky Boys at first, but after a while people started referring to them simply as the Blue Ridge Entertainers Unit 2. After he and Roy split up in 1938, Jay Hugh had continued playing music with Wade Mainer and his Sons of the

Mountaineers. He was the ostensible leader of Unit 2, so he printed up his own songbooks and sold them at shows. The Blue Ridge Entertainers were now more than a musical group, they were Roy Hall's franchise.

* * *

Clayton and Saford may have been a couple of bumpkins from Patrick County, but each knew his way around a steering wheel. The twins had arrived in Roanoke as passengers, riding shotgun with Roy Hall and his band, but they were determined to take the wheel for themselves. As soon as they had enough dough, they'd buy their own wheels. Roy now kept nearly 70 percent of the door from each show—a higher percentage than most bands received—and he split it evenly with his band, minus a few dollars here and there for gas money and promotional expenses. Roy paid in cash, so Clayton and Saford saved all their bills and coins in cans, sacks, and change purses and hid them at Mrs. Hankins's boardinghouse. Clayton kept most of his earnings in a burlap sugar sack.

After one particularly lucrative gig at a fairgrounds on the twins' home turf of Mount Airy, North Carolina—fifty years later, the brothers would recall that they each took $600 back to Roanoke from that jamboree—Clayton's sugar sack was almost too heavy to tote. Back in Roanoke, he put on his black hat, stuffed his britches legs into his tall black boots, packed up his sugar sack, and strode into Johnson's Chevrolet on Campbell Avenue.

Johnson's was one of those old-timey dealerships where all the new cars were parked in a showroom that faced the street. The black sedans and two-door coupes looked like museum exhibits behind the big windows, safe to look at but not to touch. All duded up like a movie cowboy, Clayton raised the suspicion of one of the salesmen.

"What can I do for you?" the salesman asked the young man in the big black hat and shiny cowboy shirt.

"There's a Chevrolet coupe I like," Clayton said.

"And how are you gonna pay for this coupe you like?"

"I'm gonna pay cash for it. It's cheaper that way, ain't it? No carrying charges or nothing, right?"

The salesman concurred that Clayton was right, but he was still dubious. "And how much cash you got on you, cowboy?"

"This much," Clayton said as he picked up the heavy sugar sack and dropped it on the salesman's metal desk. The bag toppled over, and coins spilled out with a crash. Hundreds of quarters and fistfuls of wadded-up dollar bills earned at scores of Blue Ridge Entertainers shows over the past two years rolled and spun as if a dam holding back a lake of coins had burst. The salesman was shook up by the silvery tsunami.

"What bank did you hold up?"

"I didn't hold up no bank," Clayton explained. "I play with Roy Hall on the radio."

That was the first thing that made sense to the salesman. For the next hour, the two men counted bills and stacked quarters like they were poker chips. Each time they passed an interval of five or ten dollars meant an extra strip of chrome or some flashy feature. Clayton stacked his quarters high, as many as ten deep.

"Don't stack 'em that way," the man admonished him. "I can't count 'em. Stack 'em in fours."

By the time they counted to $500, Clayton had demanded every piece of chrome, mirror, radio, and interior fan be added to his coupe. The salesman told Clayton to come back at two o'clock to pick up his brand-new shiny, black, tricked-out Chevrolet two-door coupe.

"Man, I'll be a hundred miles away," Clayton said. The band was always on the road. That's why Clayton wanted his own car. Roy's car had no air-conditioning and it swelled with five chain-smoking musicians who slurped cold coffee from metal thermoses and played "cow pool" to pass the time on those long trips up the Lee Highway.

The object of cow pool was to see who could count the most cows that passed by on a player's side of the car.

"I tell ya, I'm gonna win this time," good old Bill Brown used to cackle as he tallied up points by the herdful.

A player lost all his points when the car passed a graveyard on his side. That often happened to Bill.

"Aw, I knew I was gonna lose all my points!"

Clayton was ready to ride in the front seat. For the first time, he was going to be independent. Music had just bought him a sleek new car. That old five-string banjo was worth its weight in quarters.

· · ·

Saford bought a car, too, but he went the cheap route. He got a used 1938 Buick and drove it to the Pure Oil station to get it worked on. It was black, with whitewall tires and side mirrors and a big old trunk, but it never ran worth a lick. Saford fiddled with that car as much as he did with Roy Hall.

He didn't go anywhere without Dot, mostly because he adored her but also because he never wanted her out of his sight. There were just too many pissant high school boys catting around.

Roy had never warmed up to Saford's teenage lovebird. He even went out of his way to make Dot feel unwelcome. He was rude and cussed in her presence and said lots of lewd things about other women. He drank liquor in front of her after shows. He thought he could frighten her off, or at least scare her family into keeping her home, but it didn't work. Dot was here to stay, which turned out to be a good thing.

* * *

By the fall of '40, Roy was ready to record again. He hadn't made any records in almost two years, not since he got burned during the "Orange Blossom Special" sessions with Tommy Magness down in Columbia, South Carolina. He should have been nationally famous after that. If he'd owned the rights, he could've sold tens of thousands of records and never have had to worry about money again, but instead, he slogged through the hills and hollers of Virginia and North Carolina, playing schoolhouses for nick-els and dimes while people danced, hollered, and fought. Now, though, armed with a full band and a pair of twin brothers who sang like angels and played like devils, Roy Hall was going to make some damn fine records.

He worked up a good batch of songs, but one in particular was con-founding his abilities. He had heard "Don't Let Your Sweet Love Die" sung by a pair of North Carolina singers, Clarke Van Ness and Zeke Manners, and had liked it. Trouble was, it was more of a pop song than a hillbilly number. He got some sheet music for the song, but being musically illit-erate (as were the rest of the boys), he couldn't make sense out of the gnat-sized notes on the page. The songbooks Roy sold at show dates con-tained just the lyrics and maybe the chord changes. Hillbilly musicians all learned melodies by ear. This song, though, was all written out on a sheet of paper. That summer, Roy swallowed his pride and bad language and took the song to the one person he knew who could read music—Dot Wilbourne.

Dot knew her way around a piano and had even shown Saford a thing or two on the ivories. Roy asked her to help him figure out this elusive tune and show him how to play it. Dot easily tickled the song from the keys and sang a verse and a chorus, which relied upon the same melody.

> *Don't let your sweet love die like flowers in the fall*
> *Don't take away the smile and leave the tears*
> *My heart believes in you, please say you love me too*
> *Don't leave me here to face the lonely years*

Unlike most songs she heard the Entertainers play, Dot actually liked this tune. It was a tender, almost slow piece; simple, but with a rising and falling melody that covered a range of notes. She thought it was pretty—until Roy Hall sang it. Roy figured out a chord pattern to accompany the melody. He gave it a little 4/4 swing and upped the tempo. Dot hated what he was doing to such a pretty song, and she hated the sound of his nasally voice, but it was his song. If he wanted to play it and sing it like that, then heaven help him and his career. She wrote out the music for his arrangement, which so impressed Roy he asked her if she would write out the music for all his songs. Always on the lookout for anything that would give him an edge, Roy figured that he could print the sheet music in his songbooks. People would be able to learn his songs, which increased the likelihood somebody else would record them, which, of course, would mean Roy would earn some royalties.

RCA Victor scheduled several days of sessions for its Bluebird label in Atlanta. Roy had recorded for Bluebird before, so he arranged to take his band to Georgia for a twelve-song set on October 9, 1940, a Wednesday. Leaving Roanoke midweek meant that the Entertainers would miss at least three days of radio programs, so they "transcribed" their shows on WDBJ's record-cutting machines, which turned out sixteen-inch discs that could be played in the band's absence. WDBJ was high-tech, all the way.

With a vault of programs stocked away, the Blue Ridge Entertainers made off for Atlanta in Roy's brand-new 1940 Buick. No more Push-Model DeSotos for Roy. As a publicity stunt, somebody once took a photograph of the band pushing the DeSoto up Bent Mountain just outside of Roanoke. The boys might as well have shoved the old jalopy over the side. They had pushed their last semi-motorized automobile anywhere. They rode to Atlanta in style, jammed into Roy's new Buick, everybody smoking unfiltered Camels, windows cracked, no air-conditioning, everybody well-fed on a road-food diet of hamburgers and fried potatoes.

The Blue Ridge Entertainers arrived at Atlanta's Kimball House Hotel, armed with an arsenal of new and expensive instruments. They'd made enough money in Roanoke to buy first-rate Martin guitars from Kittinger's music store on Church Avenue. Clayton picked up a Gibson banjo. The new instruments improved the band's sound measurably. When they arrived in Atlanta, they did not have a lot of time to tune up, much less rehearse. The Kimball was packed with pickers.

Hotshot musicians roamed the hallways awaiting their turn to cut a record. Fiddlin' Arthur Smith, the great fiddle player from Georgia, was there. Bill Monroe was there, too, with his own band, which included another Georgia fiddler the boys knew well—Tommy Magness. Roy was happy to see Tommy, but Tommy was even more thrilled to see his old boss. He told Roy he was miserable playing music with Monroe.

Monroe didn't want to do anything but rehearse, Tommy said. They stayed cooped up in a house, playing songs over and over, until Monroe was satisfied. Tommy hated to practice. He liked performances where he could show off.

Tommy wanted to come back to Roy.

Roy told Tommy he already had a fiddle player. Tommy said he'd come back and play bass. Roy had a bass player. Tommy said he'd play guitar and sing baritone harmony, drive the car, carry guitar cases, anything to come back to Roy.

Roy considered it. Tommy Magness was the best fiddle player he had ever heard, but Saford Hall was the fiddler for the Blue Ridge Entertainers. Roy was loyal to his men. He wouldn't force Saford aside, not even for Tommy Magness.

But maybe he would take Tommy up on that offer to play guitar and sing. Tommy was elated. He owed Monroe a series of upcoming show dates, but then he was going to tell his boss man he was moving to Virginia.

Saford didn't know any of this. He was too distracted looking at fiddles at a music store near the hotel. In fact, he got so distracted by a dark Stainer violin with a lion's head carved into the scroll that he almost missed the session. Tommy Magness was close to tuning up and playing on Roy's records when Clayton went out and found Saford just minutes before the session started.

The recording took place in a hotel room with acoustic baffling covering the walls to reduce outside noise. A single microphone stood in the middle of the room on a carpet. The band gathered around the mike and played a few measures for the sound engineers, who then ordered the musicians to either step up to the mike or back away from it in order to achieve the proper sound mix. An engineer marked an X on the floor where he wanted each musician to stand for certain songs. Vocalists needed to be close to the mike, banjo players, not so much.

The first song was "New San Antonio Rose," which wasn't so very different from Bob Wills's Western-swing hit "San Antonio Rose" except that this one was "New" (probably to avoid any copyright issues. If only he'd thought to record "New Orange Blossom Special" in '38). Saford kick-started the tune with a sweet fiddle melody. His playing was pretty, ornamented with long bowing, grace notes and little trills at the end of verses that sounded like someone whistling. Roy sang solo, flattening the Texas-bred number into a kind of loping mountain ballad that was the musical equivalent of tearing down the Alamo and rebuilding it in the Appalachians. The Blue Ridge Entertainers cut twelve sides in all, including the twins' original, "Little Sweetheart, Come and Kiss Me," in a couple of hours. The technology of the day did not allow for retakes—once the machine started cutting the record, there was no turning back. They played and sang together, five men making music, no overdubs, no do-overs, no chance to "clean it up in the edit." Yet, this was not old-timey mountain music. This was contemporary country music, played by young men who were still country enough to remember the whine of a cotton mill and the smell of furniture stain.

. . .

On the way back to Virginia, Roy broke the news about Tommy. He was going to play out a string of shows with Bill Monroe, then meet the group in Roanoke. Bill and Wayne couldn't believe the news. They weren't sure how to take it. Tommy was a great fiddle player, but the current lineup seemed to be gelling well, so why mess with a good thing? Besides, Tommy could be flakier than peach piecrust—especially if he was drinking.

Still, Roy knew that the one most surprised by Tommy's return would be Saford. Poor, hypersensitive, paranoid Saford. Roy tried to make Saford understand that Tommy was not coming to Roanoke to take his job. Saford was the number one fiddle player for the Blue Ridge Entertainers, Roy assured him. If Tommy Magness didn't care for the arrangement he could just go back to Bill Monroe or take the noon train to Georgia. Saford reacted to Roy's sincere assurances the way you'd expect. He sulked and worried.

Their popularity was growing quickly. They were invited by many of the major country and western groups of that era to appear in shows all along the East Coast states. The band made two appearances on the "Grand Ole Opry."

—MOM, WRITING IN THE CARROLL COUNTY GENEALOGICAL BOOK

The Blue Ridge Entertainers returned to Roanoke hotter than ever. WDBJ installed extra seats in the studio to accommodate the fans who weren't satisfied just hearing the boys on the radio. Their show dates were standing-room-only affairs. WDBJ's signal took the band to kitchens and living rooms all over southwest Virginia, southern West Virginia, and the Piedmont of North Carolina. Folks in the boonies loved 'em. One night down in Laurel Fork, not too far from where the twins grew up, every man, woman, child, grandmaw, grandpaw, horse, cow, pig, and chicken in the community showed up. The only way to make everybody happy was to play a doubleheader. So the boys performed back-to-back shows for a pair of packed houses.

Roy promoted the show dates during his radio program and by printing up dozens of promotional posters that could be mailed well in advance to the venue. The posters were dominated by a large photo of the band, with the name "ROY HALL" in big letters across the top and the description "With Music and Songs You Love" inscribed beneath. The band always promised "Fun for All" and "A Good Clean Show," so you could take granny and the kids and not have to worry about any dirty jokes.

If none of that was worth the six nickels it cost to get in, there was this little enticement: "A bedspread for the prettiest girl. A cake of soap for the ugliest man."

The prettiest and ugliest winners were both selected by audience vote, usually cast in the form of pennies collected by some band member or an associate. (Roy split the collection with the host, but he usually went home with a few extra dollars in his pocket. That guy didn't miss a trick.) The girl was always pleased to win a lovely handcrafted bedspread or quilt. The dudes, though, were another story. One night in West Virginia, Clayton weaved through the crowd and awarded the ugliest man his bar of Ivory soap. The jug-eared, big-nosed galoot was laughing as Clayton approached, but it was because he thought he was getting a bedspread, too. The guy stopped laughing when Clayton handed him that bar of Ivory soap.

"Friend," Clayton said, "it's just a joke, a friendly joke."

"I don't appreciate being the laughing part of no joke," Jug Ears said.

"Well, it could just as easily have been me as you," Clayton said.

The dude spun and started to walk away, then pivoted back around and growled, "Well, it can *be* you," as the bar of soap went whizzing past Clayton's head.

. . .

By now, the twins could play just about anything made of wood and steel strings. They could switch off, with Saford playing banjo and Clayton the fiddle. Clayton got good enough on the fiddle to win ribbons at fiddlers conventions in Virginia and North Carolina.

As musically gifted as the twins were, they were known as much for their onstage zaniness as for their chops. On stage, Roy joshed with them, calling them "Sifford and Clifford, the Hall Twins" (which sure beat "Satan and Clayton" if you were Saford). He picked them up, one in each arm, like flour sacks, and carried them around the stage. For their part, the twins kept the laughs coming with the tried and true "Rat, Cat, Cheese, and All" routine. Another popular comedy sketch was the "womanless wedding," during which Clayton threw on an old housedress and a wig, carried a bouquet of daisies, and prepared for his special day. Saford usually played the groom. The sketch was basically an update of their ridiculous high-school routines, only more polished and funnier (perhaps). Clayton rolled the hemline up above his knees, so he could show off his bowlegs. The audience howled. Roy played the role of the minister attempting to officiate the ceremony, while Clayton played the fool and did things like dump a sack of coffee onto the stage.

"What's that for?" Reverend Roy demanded to know.

"Well, if this marriage don't work out, the judge told me I'd need to show grounds for divorce. I'm showing my grounds!"

When it came time for Saford the groom to kiss Clayton the bride, Clayton spun toward the crowd and hollered, "I ain't a-gonna do it! He's got tobacco in his mouth!"

. . .

The dances were especially good for Saford's ego. His fiddle carried the night and drove the dancers, proving that Roy needed him, even though Roy had never given him any reason to think otherwise. Then Tommy Magness showed up.

Tommy arrived in Roanoke before the end of the year. Playing with Bill Monroe's Blue Grass Boys had been a tremendous learning experience—Monroe liked to play in different keys, he mixed up his tempos, and, above all, he liked to play fast. His style suited Tommy. His rehearsals did not. Saford acted cool toward Tommy at first. He didn't want to get too cozy with the man who had come to steal his job. He was also a mite sheepish about playing fiddle in front of Tommy. Saford was good, but Tommy was the best he'd ever heard, the best anybody had ever heard. How do you play with a fellow like that looking over your shoulder, silently critiquing you, your style, the way you drag the bow, the way you finger your double stops, probably even the way you set your fiddle under your chin? The whole situation was unnerving.

But Saford soldiered ahead. Roy could tell he was nervous about Tommy's presence. Roy pulled Saford aside and reaffirmed that he, not Tommy, was the number one fiddle player. Tommy knew it, too. It didn't matter how good he was, Tommy was not booting Saford out of a job. Tommy would settle for guitar, bass, washboard, spoons—anything Roy wanted.

Clayton liked Tommy. He was a no-nonsense Georgia boy, who talked kind of slow but lived like Saford in overdrive—funny, quick with a compliment or a joke, the type of guy who enjoyed attention and often got it. He liked the girls and got a little mean when he drank, which, thankfully, he did only occasionally. Roy Hall would harbor no drunks in his band (even though Roy himself would take a nip now and again).

Tommy's wild streak manifested itself in his driving. One night he "borrowed" Saford's old jalopy so he could cruise a few downtown Roanoke joints. The next morning, Saford woke up and realized his car was missing. He caught the bus to the radio station, barely making it in time for the 6:30 a.m. broadcast, and as he rode down Campbell Avenue he saw his Buick—plowed into a streetcar, with one of the Buick's front tires wedged underneath the trolley. Tommy had crashed sometime during the early morning hours. Alcohol was probably a factor.

That was the beginning of a sad chapter for automobiles owned by members of the Blue Ridge Entertainers. Most of the boys had their own rides by now. Freed from carpooling and the sardine-like atmosphere of the backseat, the boys took the wheel and drove like maniacs. They terrorized the streets of Roanoke, wrecking five separate cars in one week, and collecting speeding tickets like baseball cards. Roy Hall drove as fast as any of them. One evening while traveling north on Lee Highway, through the Shenandoah Valley, he was doing eighty to make it on time to a show date in Harrisonburg. The cops pulled him over, and not only did they not let Roy talk his way out of a ticket—the cops in the valley must not have listened to the radio—they hauled him in front of a magistrate. The guy charged him with speeding and fined him fifty dollars. Roy peeled off five twenties, laid them on the magistrate's desk, and said, "I'll be coming back this way at ten o'clock. Please don't stop me."

Roy drove like a daredevil, but he was always in control behind the wheel. After he got married to a pretty girl named Mattie he had met at a show in Franklin County, he'd play a game with the band whenever he hauled the boys to his new house on Shadeland Avenue. He took a shortcut through Eureka Park in northwest Roanoke, where two giant oaks stood at the park entrance, barely far enough apart to squeeze a car through. Roy always accelerated when he approached those trees, flying between them with just a couple of feet to spare on either side, like pitching the end of a thread through a needle's eye. The boys saw their lives flash before their eyes many a night when Roy drove between those trees.

He must have thought he was invincible.

· · ·

In late fall of 1940, RCA Victor started issuing Roy's records on its Bluebird label. "New San Antonio Rose" was first, backed with "I'd Die Before I'd Cry Over You," a song credited to Juanita Moore. The navy blue label read "Roy Hall and his Blue Ridge Entertainers / String band with singing." The records sold as fast as five-cent hamburgers in Roanoke, where Kittinger's music store couldn't keep them in stock. Roy Hall was popular on radio, live, and on record. He was a multimedia juggernaut before the media was very multi.

The twins were getting a good response to "Little Sweetheart, Come and Kiss Me," which would soon be released on a 78. They were intrigued by Western-flavored melodies and cowboy songs. The chord patterns were more complex than fiddle tunes, and the harmonies that those Western guys sang were tight as a horse's bridle. Their favorite Western band of all was, of course, the Sons of the Pioneers.

When Clayton and Saford heard "Cool Water," it was as if they were hearing music for the first time in their lives. They had grown up with cowboy culture, from the movies to the garb, but only now were they getting into the music that Roy Rogers and his former band were making. "Cool Water" sounded like a tour de force to the twins. It was a story of a cowpoke barely surviving a trek through the desert, the mirages playing tricks on him. The singing was multilayered, with rising background vocals and harmonies.

The Sons of the Pioneers' songs "Way Out There," "Tumbling Tumbleweeds," "He's an Old Cowhand from the Rio Grande" were phenomenal. The twins learned those and wanted desperately to sing them during show dates, but Roy wouldn't allow it. He didn't mind Western songs—he had even recorded "Way Out There" with Jay Hugh, although he left out the yodel—but his band had a signature sound: bluesy fiddle and Dobro, twangy vocals, and solid swing. He was taking hillbilly music where he wanted it to go, and it wasn't west.

No matter, the twins kept learning those Western songs. Saford even bought a portable disc recorder and started making his own records. Learning those complex, layered harmonies improved the twins' singing, especially Saford's lead vocals. And singing would be a good skill to fall back on once he lost his fiddle-playing job to Tommy Magness, which he eventually did.

* * *

The band photos tell the story. The first photo of Roy Hall and His Blue Ridge Entertainers that ever appeared in Roanoke, the one published in the *Roanoke Times* to herald their arrival, had Tommy Magness in it, even though he'd been out of the group for more than a year. After they'd been in Roanoke awhile, Clayton and Saford began showing up in the numerous publicity shots that were mailed to newspapers, printed in songbooks, and plastered on posters. The twins posed for their own portraits, Saford clutching a fiddle, Clayton a banjo. In many of the photographs, Clayton wore what appeared to be a string tie or bolo, but it was actually a skinny strap with a hook on the end that fastened to the back of his banjo. He wore his banjo strap like a necktie, almost every day, as a part of his attire.

A number of singers joined the band for brief stints, so there are numerous pictures with Jay Hugh Hall and Woody Mashburn, another North Carolina boy who sang with Roy off and on. Clayton used to tease Woody by calling him "Lucky," because, in Clayton's estimation, "You're lucky to be with a band as good as us." In these shots, Clayton and Saford are smiling broadly, displaying mouthfuls of beautiful long, white teeth that resemble piano keys.

In later photos, we see Tommy, standing with a fiddle tucked under his jaw. Saford crouches in front with a guitar.

In all the years I knew Saford, and after all the conversations we had about music, fiddle playing, the war, Roy Hall, and Tommy Magness, he never spoke of how it happened. How did Tommy take his job? Turns out, Saford surrendered it.

How could he not give it up? You don't hire Tommy Magness and hand him a guitar. The Yankees didn't trade for Babe Ruth and just use him as a pitcher. Roy Hall had a cleanup hitter in Tommy, but he didn't want to mess with the starting lineup. So Saford took the pressure off of Roy and requested the change himself. The whole situation had been tough on Saford. He'd listen to Tommy practice the fiddle before show dates, just to keep his skills sharp, and he knew what the other boys must be thinking: "Why isn't he the fiddle player?"

When they played show dates, folks in the crowd who recognized Tommy hollered for "Orange Blossom Special." Roy told the fans maybe next time. He wasn't going to embarrass Saford. Still, Saford's pride had absorbed enough body blows to stop an ox. Finally, he went to Roy and suggested that Tommy take over as fiddle player. The twins would get to sing more duets as part of the new lineup. Roy Hall wasn't going to hide a vocal talent like Saford Hall on rhythm guitar.

Saford's sacrifice meant that Roy Hall now had the best damn band he'd ever led.

In April 1941, the Blue Ridge Entertainers played the biggest stage of all—the Grand Ole Opry in Nashville. At that time, the Opry was held every Saturday night at the old War Memorial Auditorium, whose roof leaked the night the Blue Ridge Entertainers showed up. The boys met most of the Opry stars, such as Uncle Dave Macon and the show's founder and announcer, George Dewey Hay, the self-anointed "Solemn Old Judge," who was neither solemn, old (he was thirty), nor a judge when he started his radio barn dance in 1925. He renamed it the Grand Old Opry two years later.

The Blue Ridge Entertainers played their hit, "Don't Let Your Sweet Love Die," and let Tommy strut his stuff on "Orange Blossom Special." Roanoke's finest held its own in the hillbilly music capital of America.

Tommy Magness had been a fine fiddle player during his first stint with Roy. After nearly two years of performing with Bill Monroe, he was now a great fiddle player. His tone and timing were sharper, his bowing more fluid and precise. He was a master of what Monroe called the "little bow": Instead of fingering several notes during one elongated pull or push of the bow, Tommy would change directions with seemingly every note. His strokes were short—during fast numbers, his wrist moved back and forth as rapidly as if he were shaking out a lighted match. Monroe had loved that style and had featured it prominently on one of his first hit records, the incendiary instrumental "Katy Hill."

Tommy's fiddling led the Blue Ridge Entertainers into overdrive. He brought a wealth of new tunes to the band—"Fisher's Hornpipe," "Black Mountain Rag," "Devil's Dream," "Lost Indian," "K.C. Stomp," "Fire on the Mountain," "Back Up and Push," "Grey Eagle Hornpipe," "Lee County Blues,"—the boy must've known three hundred tunes! Of course, "Orange Blossom Special" worked its way back into Roy Hall's repertoire. The band had to put in extra time to learn the new material and to get their fingers in shape for Tommy's machine-gun style. Within months, Irving Sharp would comment on the radio about Tommy "really working those fingers and sawing that fiddle half in two."

The boys enjoyed themselves. Tommy and Clayton knocked around town when they had free time. It was through Clayton that Tommy met Tootsie. Her real name was Vada, but everybody called her Tootsie—her brothers, her sisters, and her nieces, which included Clayton's girlfriend

Reba. Tootsie Poindexter was Reba's aunt, the baby sister of Reba's mother. Tootsie was in her midtwenties, with thick black hair and chipmunk cheeks, a real beauty. In a matter of months, she and Tommy were an item. Tootsie and Reba went to most of the show dates around Roanoke to serve a warning to other girls that these boys were taken. Those other girls didn't always take the hint, though.

．．．

After Roanoke shows, Clayton, Reba, Tommy, and Tootsie often grabbed a midnight bite at the City Lunch on Second Street, around the corner from the radio station. The City Lunch was a main hangout for the band, especially during the week, when they'd sip coffee and eat breakfast following the morning radio program. Two Greek fellows ran the place—Jimmy and Victor—and they loved the Blue Ridge Entertainers, if only because they were hearty eaters. During one early morning radio program, Saford happened to mention he was headed to the City Lunch right after the show. Ray Jordan, WDBJ's manager, heard the on-air quip and informed Saford he had just given the City Lunch a morsel of free advertising—except that it wouldn't stay free for long. "That was a plug," Jordan told Saford. "It'll cost you."

One morning at the City Lunch, Tommy spotted a beautiful waitress with reddish hair. He saw her from across the restaurant, carrying a tray of blue-plate specials to a table. Tommy spun around at the lunch counter where he and Clayton sat and looked down, acting as if he didn't want to be spotted.

"My God, it's Ruth," Tommy muttered.

"Who's Ruth?" Clayton asked, apparently too loudly for Tommy, who shushed him.

"That's my wife," Tommy spit out.

Clayton practically shouted, "Your wife!" Tommy punched him in the arm. Clayton whispered, "Your wife?"

All this time, Tommy had been running around with Tootsie while married to another woman. Apparently, neither woman knew about the other. Tommy was only twenty-four years old, but he already had quite the checkered past.

．．．

Tommy Magness was a character whose story ought to begin with some miraculous, spontaneous creation—like a lightning bolt striking a maple tree and leaving behind a baby and a fiddle among the smoldering splinters. Or maybe he met the devil in a bar and swapped some good ol' homebrew for a magic fiddle. But, really, there was no miracle or myth surrounding Tommy Magness. He was just a tater-fed Georgia farm boy who liked playing fiddle more than hoeing corn. His story is pretty much the same as every other mountain music maker's—he grew up in the proverbial musical family—although his path to glory took an occasional dogleg turn.

Tommy was born in the north Georgia hills of Mineral Bluff on October 21, 1916. His daddy favored the banjo and his mama the mandolin. His big sister learned fiddle by watching their mother pick tunes on her mandolin, an eight-stringed instrument tuned the same as a fiddle. When Tommy was old enough to stand, he balanced himself on a chair and held the banjo neck while his daddy plucked the strings. He watched his sister play the fiddle and imitated her by sawing corncobs together like one was the bow and one was the instrument. His daddy was a farmer, but Tommy never took to farm work. As a boy, he'd hide behind the barn and make his own pretend fiddles out of cornstalks and horsehair.

His daddy once made a fiddle for Tommy and his sister, which they eventually fought over and broke. But Tommy upgraded to a better one and was soon good enough to play for customers at Hampton's Hardware in the nearby town of Blue Ridge. He joined a little trio that played around Mineral Bluff and across the state line in Copperhill, Tennessee. Fiddlers sprouted from the north Georgia landscape like tall pines, and Tommy learned from all of them. One of his favorite tunes was the old-timer "Bonaparte's Retreat," a Southern favorite for which he cross-tuned his strings into an ancient-sounding drone.

Tommy believed there was magic in that old tune. As a teenager, maybe earlier, he had traveled with a band to Atlanta, where things didn't go as planned and the fellows went hungry. Desperate and starving, the boys decided to walk home—a hundred-mile trek. As they walked, Tommy took out his fiddle and tuned it for "Bonaparte's Retreat." He stood by the side of the road and began playing. One of his fellow foot soldiers berated him.

"What in the world are you trying to play, with us starving to death?"

Tommy never missed a note. Sure enough, within a few minutes, the parents of one of the fellows drove past and picked them up. There was magic in the fiddle. Maybe it was then that Tommy Magness realized that the instrument could take him places.

He played at talent shows and jumped onstage with radio fiddlers. His family moved to North Carolina, where his mother died, and then they returned to Georgia. When Tommy was sixteen, a young pregnant woman claimed that he was the father of her baby. He left town before the baby was born.

He ran off to North Carolina, where he bounced around from band to band. He worked at a mill and joined a family string band led by Carl McElreath, whose daughter, Ruth, was a crackerjack guitar and fiddle player who won her share of blue ribbons at fiddlers conventions. She was so good that male musicians tried to ban her from competing. Her family obliged and left her at home one day when they headed to Asheville for a contest. Ruth was outraged, so she hired a taxi to Asheville and won anyway. Tommy loved her spunk.

Tommy and Ruth married and had a daughter, Faye. But Tommy would never settle down. He played music on radio stations in Asheville and Spartanburg, South Carolina, where he hooked up with Roy Hall. They recorded "Orange Blossom Special" and moved to Winston-Salem. In 1939, Tommy won a national fiddling championship, whipsawing through "Orange Blossom Special" faster than a locomotive. His victory got him noticed by Bill Monroe.

So Tommy left Roy and became part of Monroe's first edition of the Blue Grass Boys. He recorded with Monroe in October 1940, which turned out to be a pivotal week for Tommy's career. Tommy fiddled "Katy Hill" like a man trying to break the land speed record for fiddling. He sawed the blues as Monroe sang "Muleskinner Blues" and Clyde Moody sang "Six White Horses." That same week, he played twin fiddles with his hero, Fiddlin' Arthur Smith, for a recording of "K.C. Stomp." The next day, he told Roy Hall he wanted to rejoin his band. Talk about a productive week.

When he finally became first-string fiddler for the Blue Ridge Entertainers, Tommy Magness was almost untouchable. In a few years, fiddlers like Chubby Wise and Art Wooten would be better known, but in 1941, Tommy Magness was as good a fiddle player as there was in the country. By the time he was twenty-five, he had made the first recording of "Orange Blossom Special," waxed historic recordings with Bill Monroe, and had won a national championship. Plus, he was a family man; not only did he have a wife and a daughter, but he had a girlfriend, too. He had it all.

His young wife had tracked him down in Roanoke, where she lived awhile and landed the job at the diner. When it became obvious that she and Tommy would not reconcile, she moved back home to Georgia with their little girl. At the time, Tommy had no plans to ever leave Roanoke. He had no plans at all, really.

. . .

To be young and living in Roanoke was more than Clayton Hall could have ever hoped for as a hungry, barefoot boy in The Hollow. He had money, a car, a girl, and music. Roanoke was now thick with bands. Radio stations were popping up all over the state, all of them wanting live music. If there was ever a golden age in Clayton Hall's life, the spring of 1941 was it.

Saford finally seemed content with his lot in life. He was confident with his new role in the band, and he seemed relatively happy and settled with Dot. The two lovers were cut from different cloths, he the fatherless fiddler from the Virginia backwoods, she the refined Catholic schoolgirl who played piano, but the relationship seemed to be working. They had their rough spots, such as the time Saford took Dot and her parents to The Hollow to meet Mamo. The sight of cabins and live chickens was unnerving to Dot and Lottie, and they didn't know what to make of Saford's sixty-year-old mother, who preferred long dresses and black shoes and who wore her hair pinned back in a bun. Dot's daddy, however, took to the new surroundings immediately. Within a matter of hours, he and his son-in-law had sniffed out a still and had sampled copious amounts of good, clear corn liquor. Mr. Wilbourne enjoyed himself to the extent that he had to hang his head out the car window the entire drive back to Roanoke.

Dot wasn't thrilled with Saford after that episode, but he always made it up to her. He bought a Wilcox-Gay record-cutting machine and the two of them made their own records at the Wilbourne house. The aluminum-based Recordio discs were covered with a red lacquer and cost forty cents each. They looked like the colored vinyl 45 rpm records that would become popular years later. Dot played the piano and Saford sang old numbers such as "Molly Darling" and "I'll Love You Till I Die."

. . .

The spring of 1941 was so idyllic for Clayton and Saford that it was hard for them to notice that the rest of the planet was collapsing. The Germans controlled Europe and had bombed the daylights out of Great Britain the previous summer and fall. The Japanese were destroying China and had signed the Tripartite Pact with Germany and Italy, intended as a warning to the United States to stay out of the Pacific. People were dying by the thousands in major cities and upon rocky atolls no bigger than Roanoke. But in Virginia, the mountains glowed with iridescent redbuds, dogwoods, and wild cherries. In the Magic City of Roanoke, two poor bastards from The Hollow had finally caught a break, and they made the most of it. During that gilded spring of '41, Clayton and Saford were truly happy.

It was easy to see why they might want to forget the fact that, just a few months earlier, they had both registered for the first-ever peacetime draft in the history of the United States.

World War II ended all the band's dreams in 1941.

—MOM, PUTTING IT BLUNTLY
IN THE GENEALOGICAL BOOK, 1994

It was an awful wreck. Clayton had taken Reba and her younger brother, Henry, Jr., down to Bassett to visit his brother Mack; Mack's wife, Vera; and their little boy, Jack. Clayton drove home fast. He always drove too fast. He ran off the right side of the road somewhere just across the Franklin County line and overcompensated as he yanked the car back. The car skidded, ran off the road, and flipped. This was 1941, so no one had ever heard of seat belts, and air bags were the stuff of science fiction comic books, but everybody survived. Henry broke his wrist, and Clayton was bruised and banged up bad enough to need crutches, but they all made it. It was a good thing Henry had been the designated chaperone instead of little Elinor. She might not've survived such a spectacular crash.

The silver lining was that the accident spared Clayton from the draft. Saford, though, wasn't lucky enough to be involved in a bad wreck.

The twins both received their notices to report to Local Draft Board No. 2 on February 7, 1941, for their physical examinations. Saford checked out OK. But Clayton, all battered and bruised and on crutches, was sent home. Don't call Uncle Sam, he'll call you. Clayton thought he'd dodged a bullet—literally.

• • •

Saford was ordered to report for induction in June, when he would be shipped off to Camp Lee near Richmond. Before he left Roanoke, he took care of one little loose end. He married Dot Wilbourne in May of '41. He had just turned twenty-two. She was fifteen.

Their courtship had started listing toward the rocks. Dot was a pistol, excited about having an older boyfriend, but not always comfortable with the adult world she had been thrust into. Teenage girls are born to flirt with boys. Boys, however, are born to be jealous. Saford screamed at Dot if he caught her so much as talking to a boy, but if the tables were turned and she saw him flirting with a girl, he got all defensive.

"I saw you talking to that girl from the front of the stage," Dot said to Saford one day when she caught him chatting up some lipstick Lolita at the City Market Building Auditorium. "I didn't like what I saw."

Dot's smart mouth steamed Saford.

"Baby," he said, "you ain't seen nothing yet."

Actually, she had seen quite a lot, because nothing opened your eyes to a man's worst faults faster than going steady with Saford Hall. He was a study in contradictions—funny but mean, loving but hateful, eager to please but just as apt to fly into fits of uncontrollable rage. He liked to show off, sometimes by playing music, other times by beating people up in front of his girl.

After all this time, Saford was still the old instigator, a guy who liked to start a fight. He was just the man Uncle Sam was looking for. On June 18, 1941, Saford (No Middle Name) Hall was inducted into the U.S. Army. He and thirteen other draftees lined up for a photograph that would be published in the evening *World-News*. Most of them smiled, including Saford, who put his hands on the shoulders of the two fellows in front of him. His hair was slightly mussed, but he looked dashing in a striped tie, striped shirt, and dark jacket. That evening, he boarded the train for Camp Lee and entered the army in style.

For the first time in their twenty-two years on this earth, the Hall twins went their separate ways.

. . .

Meanwhile, the Blue Ridge Entertainers played on.

They couldn't let a little thing like a brewing world war slow them down. They had shows to play. Saford would be missed, but Roy Hall had a deep bench. Tommy's red-hot fiddle had lit a fire under the band. Bill and Wayne resumed their careers as duet singers, which had been mostly back-burnered by the Hall twins. Roy's brother Jay Hugh added harmony singing and manic mandolin playing.

Clayton hung in there. Roy threw him a few musical bones every now and then, vocal numbers such as "Long Steel Rail" and "Hung Down My Head and Cried." Clayton and Jay Hugh sounded good together, so they sang duets. Roy made sure to let him know he was still a valuable part of the Entertainers' sound. As summer turned to fall, the band maintained a full schedule, still playing weekly dances and daily radio programs, still oblivious to what was about to happen to the world and to them.

The radio shows were as popular as ever. The band always played a half-hour program at 6:30 a.m. and performed a fifteen-minute lunchtime show three times a week. Host Irving Sharp kept pushing that Dr Pepper. Sometimes he'd run into the studio at the last possible second before the "On Air" light went on, occasionally cussing and spitting. Once, he and Roy showed up seconds before a lunchtime broadcast with their britches legs wet and rolled up from a morning spent fishing in the Roanoke River.

After the familiar Dr Pepper theme song, Cousin Irving launched into his preamble:

> *Hello friends and howdy neighbors, you feeling good? We sure hope you are. It's Dr Pepper Time. Now's the time to kinda relax and sit back, enjoy life, and forget the cares of the day as Uncle Roy and all the Blue Ridge Entertainers get set to bring you the favorite songs you have all been requesting.*
>
> *Now that Dr Pepper sales have really been going up every day, cold weather's coming on. And you, good neighbors, since I begun talking about it last week, have begun to realize that the best thing to do this winter, as every winter, is to try to avoid all the bad colds that you possibly can. Now it's so easy to catch a cold when the weather's damp and chilly, and one good idea I have, and I think you'll all agree, is to stay on the alkaline side. You've heard that many a time, and one good way of doing this is to try Dr Pepper. You drink Dr Pepper at ten, two, and four, and you'll help to avoid colds. Dr Pepper, you know, is a blend of pure fruit juices. You know how good fruits are for you. You get the handy six-bottle carton, and you'll find out what I mean. First tune is "Old Joe Clark." Here 'tis!*

Tommy fiddled three verses at light speed and was through in less than a minute. Irving killed time by reminding listeners that if they felt like dancing, they should push back the dining room table.

> *And speaking of the dining room table, if you happen to be having dinner, Dr Pepper is a mighty good drink with meals or even without meals. So, if you're eating dinner or haven't started yet, Dr Pepper is the thing you want. Right now, it's "Ranch House on the Old Circle B."... Cousin Wayne, Uncle Roy, Bill, all of 'em gathered around.*

After the pretty, Western-style number, Cousin Irving picked on Clayton for not standing with the rest of the band—and for his hair being way too long.

> COUSIN IRVING: "Clayton, you're sitting down, jump up. You go out and get yourself a Dr Pepper, your energy's sagging. That haircut's getting him down."
> [Laughter.]
> CLAYTON [in the background]: "Yeah, man!"
> COUSIN IRVING: "Lord have mercy, you could buy a dog tag...."
> ROY: "He's got a fourteen-gallon hat on top of that hair, too."
> COUSIN IRVING: "Fifteen gallons of hair...Buffalo Bill didn't have a thing on Clayton! [Then, straightening up and getting serious] Right now, it's hymn time on Dr Pepper Time. The old sacred songs always seem to do us a lot of good. There's a lot of cheer and comfort in every one of them. Today, it's 'I'll Be Somewhere Listening' and we hope you like it."

The Blue Ridge Entertainers made more records in Atlanta on October 1, 1941—almost one year after their 1940 session. The band had worked up a slate of six songs—"Until I Return to You," "I Wonder Where You Are Tonight," "I'm Glad We Didn't Say Goodnight," "I Wonder If the Moon Is Shining," "My Sweet Mountain Rose," and "The Best of Friends Must Part Someday"—to go along with a pair of Tommy Magness original fiddle tunes, "Natural Bridge Blues" and "Polecat Blues."

Tommy's fiddle numbers were especially swingy. Even though the songs both had "blues" in their titles, they could just as easily have been called "rags." "Natural Bridge Blues" was colored with moaning slides and lively lopes that soared into a high chorus and swooped back down again. "Polecat Blues" was built on a similar pattern. If old-timey fiddle tunes were corn liquor, Tommy Magness's pieces were like homemade wine: smooth and sweet, but packing a punch. Somehow, a slow-talking, relatively uneducated Georgia boy had become a genius on the violin. And that's how he played it, like a violin.

Tommy had written some lyrics for "Natural Bridge Blues," and he convinced Roy to let his buddy Glenwood Howell sing them for the session. Howell was a fine country singer in Roanoke, who would go on to lead the Dixie Playboys and the Texas Troubadours. But when it came time to record in Atlanta, his voice couldn't hit the high notes in the chorus. The newfangled air-conditioning system freeze-dried his voice, and he froze up, literally and figuratively. After Glenwood blew the chorus, Tommy kept fiddling, Clayton plunked along on the banjo, and nobody sang another note.

For years, nobody knew that the tune had a chorus. Tommy's chorus appeared only on a two-page pamphlet of sheet music:

Natural Bridge is calling me, I'm lonely for you, too
I can't wait until I see all my friends so true
I hear that train a-rolling, I'll soon be on my way
At Natural Bridge I'll settle down, with you I'll always stay

. . .

Despite that little slipup, the Blue Ridge Entertainers completed an outstanding recording session.

Roy Hall recorded fifty-two songs in his career. He wrote songs, covered classic tunes, and, occasionally, copyrighted other people's work. He participated in five recording sessions in four years for three different labels—Vocalion, Conqueror, and Bluebird. RCA Victor, which operated Bluebird, promoted Roy's records heavily, even internationally. The Bluebird catalog advertised his music beneath the banner of "Old Familiar Tunes and Race Records." The band members clearly enjoyed themselves during the '41 recording session in Atlanta. The last number they cut was "Polecat Blues," and you can hear Roy and the others in the background, hollering out funny lines behind Tommy's fiddling.

"That old Polecat Blues!"

"That's an old Virginia polecat!"

Near the end, Roy blurts out, "Anybody want to buy a skunk?"

The boys were having a good old time. It's probably just as well that none of them knew this would be the Blue Ridge Entertainers' final recording session. Roy Hall had made his last record.

．　．　．

They must have known war was coming. The front page of the *Roanoke Times* told of terrific battles raging from Europe to Asia to the South Pacific. France had fallen, and Great Britain was under siege. Japan threatened American interests in the South Pacific. They read all this, surely. They made their living at a radio station, so they probably heard daily dispatches from London. They must have known the army would come for them, too.

But if Roy Hall and His Blue Ridge Entertainers were aware of any of this, they weren't letting it affect their musical output. They still packed houses for show dates, even in the boonies. In the little Virginia town of Ivanhoe, they attracted so many people to the schoolhouse that some fans had to sit on the front of the stage. About midway through the show, Clayton noticed the lone microphone begin to sway slightly, as if the earth was starting to quake. A second later, the front of the stage gave way like a trapdoor. Everyone on the stage toppled cowboy hat over banjo into the boiler room below. Nobody was badly hurt; the band landed right on top of its loyal fan base.

Other than that occasion, you couldn't keep the band off the stage. Roanoke was drawing nationally known hillbilly and Western acts to the Academy of Music for the Saturday night Blue Ridge Jamboree and other special shows. The Sons of the Pioneers headlined a show with the Blue Ridge Entertainers on Easter Sunday, 1941, that packed the Academy to its nineteenth-century rafters. Cousin Irving Sharp was so impressed with the size of the crowd that he took a picture from the stage and included it in a booklet of photos he called a "family album" and sold for seventy-five cents.

Later that year, Roy Rogers brought his hot new Western band to Roanoke. Rogers already had a dozen cowboy movies under his belt, but music was the real reason he was Clayton's idol. He had cofounded the Sons of the Pioneers back when he was an unknown cowpoke by the name of Leonard Sly, and he had been with them when they recorded their best songs—"Tumbling Tumbleweeds," "Cool Water," "Way Out There," and others.

When Clayton met Rogers, he told him how much he loved that yodel on "Way Out There" and that he had tried to perfect it for years. Rogers told Clayton that if he mastered that yodel, he could sing it during a live performance on WDBJ radio. Rogers would even throw in a Western shirt.

Clayton stayed up most of the night strumming "Way Out There" on a guitar repeatedly, practicing the complicated yodel until his yodeler was sore. (For hipster film buffs who dig Coen Brothers movies: Y'all remember the yodeling theme used in *Raising Arizona*? That's the yodel I'm talking about. The first time I heard Papa Clayton do that yodel was the same year I, and every other twenty-something nerd, went cuckoo over the Coens. I was at his house, talking about old tunes, when he picked up his guitar and launched into this "Weeeeeee-ooooooo, yodel-li-lay-he-hooo . . ." and I just about spit up sweet iced tea. I had no idea it was a Sons of the Pioneers yodel.) Clayton showed off his yodel for Roy Rogers on the radio and Rogers was so impressed he really gave him a Western shirt. He also told Clayton that if he ever came to California, to give him a call. Clayton thanked him for the shirt and told Rogers that California was just too far from home. That shirt and a photograph of the Blue Ridge Entertainers with Roy Rogers became prized family heirlooms, even after my mother colored in Roy Rogers's white hat with a pencil when she was a little girl.

. . .

The successful Blue Ridge Entertainers seemed to be living in a parallel universe from the rest of the crumbling planet. As American troops trained for combat and American forces in the Philippines girded for a possible Japanese invasion, back home in Roanoke, Cousin Irving sounded so cheerful as he recited the healing powers of Dr Pepper that you would have thought he never read a newspaper. Dr Pepper couldn't stop a war, however.

Saford wrote to Clayton and told him to enjoy his freedom and avoid this man's army for as long as he could. Maybe you'll luck out, he wrote, and Uncle Sam won't need you.

Saford returned to Roanoke a few times on furloughs. He wore his sharp-looking uniform around town because he liked the way it impressed the girls (including the one he was married to). Asey was in the army, too. The twins hadn't seen much of their older brother since they moved to Roanoke, and Mamo wanted to see her youngest boys, so on one of the furloughs they all got together in The Hollow for a reunion. Their older brothers were too old to serve, and most of them had started families. If there was going to be any fighting, the youngest Halls would be doing it.

Saford and Asey wore their uniforms for Mamo, who would not have known the difference between a corporal and a sack of potatoes. Nor would she have ever found Port Lyautey, Morocco; Normandy; or Germany on a map if you'd given her a year. But over the next four years, this simple country lady would hear about all kinds of places she never knew existed, even if she never did quite understand what her sons were doing there.

Back in Roanoke, Clayton and Saford had their picture taken at a downtown studio. Saford wore his beige army uniform and stuffed the bottom of his necktie between his shirt buttons. A black army hat with an eagle pin sat cockeyed atop his head. Clayton was dressed in the typical white Dr Pepper shirt with a comb poking out of the pocket. He wore his skinny banjo strap around his neck and a white cowboy hat on his head. They photographed well, one twin dressed up like a banjo picker, the other like a soldier.

. . .

Clayton had trouble with blurry vision, which his doctor attributed to cataracts. He had surgery, then spent the night of December 6, 1941, in the hospital. The next day, he saw the world with new eyes.

One of the doctors told him about the Japanese attack on Pearl Harbor late Sunday afternoon. We were at war, and Clayton knew Saford would be right in the thick of it. But it was all so confusing to a poor country boy from The Hollow. Wasn't Saford training to kill Germans? Weren't the British the ones who needed our help? Why do the Japanese have a beef with us? And where is Pearl Harbor, anyway?

Over the following days, declarations of war piled up on one another like brushwood thrown onto a bonfire. Everybody declared war on everybody else. President Roosevelt spoke of "a day that will live in infamy," and Congress declared war on the Japanese. Germany declared war on us. So did Italy. (Italy? What did we do to them?) The whole world had exploded. Young men lined up outside the Roanoke army recruiting center on Campbell Avenue like it was giving away free beer. The time to fight had arrived, and Clayton knew of only one thing he could do.

At the crack of dawn Monday morning, the day after the Pearl Harbor attack, he left his boardinghouse on Church Avenue, marched a block downtown past the post office—and walked into the WDBJ studios and went back to work making music on the radio.

Why give up a gig as good as this? Besides, if Uncle Sam needed him, he knew where to find him. Saford could handle the Japanese and the Germans. Whoever.

The other boys stuck around, too. Bill, Wayne, Tommy, Roy, Jay Hugh, and Rufus all stayed in Roanoke. They figured people needed entertainment and Dr Pepper more than ever to help take their minds off the war, which the United States still wouldn't fully join for several months. The Blue Ridge Entertainers played on.

But soon their numbers would be up.

The band began to disintegrate in 1942. Clayton moonlighted in another group, a cowboy-inspired vocal band called the Wanderers of the Wasteland, a name inspired by a Gene Autry song, which likewise had been taken from a Zane Grey novel and movie.

The Wanderers scratched Clayton's cowboy itch. They sang "Cool Water" and "Tumbling Tumbleweeds" and all those Western numbers Clayton had sung with his brother, who was long gone.

Then he lost his girl. Reba had fallen for a soldier boy named Donald Roman, who had passed through Roanoke on his way to war. Reba's family was impressed with Donald. They adored Clayton, too, but Donald was mature and dignified, an army pilot, no less, headed off to defend his country. Clayton was a hillbilly banjo plucker from The Hollow who didn't seem to be in any hurry to join the fight. He had been a nice high school sweetheart for Reba, but she had grown up and moved on.

Before Clayton knew what had hit him, Reba was on a train bound for Louisville, where she would marry her army pilot, leaving Roanoke—and Clayton—behind.

Clayton was truly alone.

. . .

The Blue Ridge Entertainers made a second and final visit to the Grand Ole Opry at Nashville's War Memorial Auditorium in the fall of 1942 and played "Don't Let Your Sweet Love Die." That record was selling like war bonds, and Roy expected a huge royalty check the next spring.

Back in Roanoke, the band had no shortage of show dates. They continued to play schools and the city's movie palaces, the Rialto and the

American, adding patriotic songs to their repertoire. A big favorite was "There's a Star-Spangled Banner Waving Somewhere," a country-pop number that Roy included in a 1942 songbook. The lyrics could've applied to any member of his band:

> In this war with its mad schemes of destruction
> Of our country fair and our sweet liberty
> By the mad dictators, leaders of corruption
> Can't the U.S. use a mountain boy like me?

"Can't the U.S. use a mountain boy like me?" Yes, Clayton, it sure could.

In October 1942, sixteen months after Saford had been drafted, Clayton received notice to report to Draft Board No. 2 again. He had no wreck-related injuries to spare him from the service this time. He was inducted into the army and was told he would be sent to basic training within two months. He was about to join Saford in the fight of their lives.

. . .

Saford, naturally, thrived in the army.

He was the wiseass, the smart-aleck. Confident and cocky, he talked his way into special training courses, much the same way he had talked his and Clayton's way into Bassett Furniture's finishing room. His scholastic record was less than impressive—made even less so when he reported that seven years of grammar school and two years of high school added up to a tenth-grade education—but you don't need a sheepskin to know how to read a map. Saford excelled in map courses at Fort Bragg. Within a few months, he was promoted to corporal and was enrolled in intelligence and reconnaissance training, where he learned basic tactics needed for scouting, including camouflage, concealment, and mapmaking. Training for "suicide missions" was part of the regimen. He swam across rivers and lived in the forests, figuring out which plants were edible. Turned out that life in the army was a whole lot like growing up in The Hollow.

The army needed men like Saford, poor bastards just crazy enough to try anything once. The boys of the Sixtieth Infantry Regiment had barracks fever. Many, like Saford, had been in the army for a year or more.

They were so desperate to get out and fight they would've mixed it up with their own mamas.

Saford surely knew nothing of the high-level planning that was about to blow the relative peace and prosperity of his recent life to smithereens. He just knew he was going to fight. That was all right with him. He'd done it all his life.

. . .

Saford returned to Roanoke a final time in the summer of 1942. He had stayed in touch with his young bride fairly frequently, writing letters and sending photographs of himself and his new army buddies. Some of the pictures were of Saford and a guy named "Private Warner" and apparently had been made in a photo booth in New York City—Lord knows what Saford was doing in Manhattan, perhaps completing more "training." He wrote on the back of the pictures, "Two sheets in the wind." He appeared to be enjoying himself.

This last trip to Roanoke was just to see Dot. The young couple relaxed at the Wilbourne house, where they played records and sang old torch songs. The world was changing all around them. When Saford left for the train station next to the grand old Hotel Roanoke, he told Dot he didn't know when or if he'd be able to see her again.

A day or two later, Dot awoke feeling like her underwear was on fire. Her private area itched and hurt. She examined herself and thought she saw little critters down there, rummaging around her privates. She begged her mama to take a look.

"Mama, what are these critters on me?"

Lottie Wilbourne nearly died when she saw what her daughter was talking about. She wailed and moaned and spirited her teenage daughter to the doctor's office, all the while cursing that no-account, fiddle-playing hillbilly soldier boy who had done this to her little girl.

. . .

By August 1942, Saford Hall was on his way to war. Dwight Eisenhower, who would soon be appointed supreme commander of the Allied Expeditionary Force in the North Africa Theater of Operations, had received his directive to attack the enemy in the soft underbelly of Africa as soon as practical. A full-force assault on Europe had been ruled out until the Allies had more fighting experience. Saford and the rest of his outfit were sent to Norfolk, Virginia, for amphibious training. Thousands of soldiers invaded and re-invaded the Virginia coast dozens of times in full-dress rehearsals for the landings to occur an ocean away.

Pity the poor people of Norfolk. The city had not endured an occupation like this since Union forces had invaded during the War of Northern Aggression. More than thirty-four thousand soldiers stormed the streets, most of them looking for sex, well aware that this would be their last chance to get laid for a very long while. Main Street provided a buffet of prostitutes and beer joints. Soldiers were arrested by the hundreds for fighting, drunkenness, and carousing. They didn't call the place "Naughty Norfolk" for nothing. Saford mailed Dot another photo-booth picture of himself and his pal Warner after a night of some obvious R&R on the town.

Of course, there was a major military operation to prepare for, so perhaps Saford didn't have as much time for carousing as he would've liked. He was placed in a company of men that had been handed a dangerous, unprecedented assignment: They were to hit the beaches of North Africa ahead of the invading troops, under cover of darkness, by swimming at least two hundred yards to the shore and setting up infrared lights and signals to guide the Allied invaders. Saford and his comrades would perform this feat of derring-do armed only with a trench knife and two hand grenades each. Once the beaches were marked, Allied forces would invade and the battle would begin.

On the misty, chilly morning of October 24, 1942, Saford Hall, one of Judie Hall's bean-fed bastards from The Hollow, set sail from Norfolk on a two-week voyage across the Atlantic Ocean to the shores of North Africa, where the Axis forces awaited. The old instigator was really about to start something this time.

THE
WAR

Mamo's soldier boys: Clayton, Saford, and Asey

Both Saford and Clayton enlisted in the Army during World War II....
Both were wounded, and both received many medals for heroism.

—MOM, FROM THE BIRTHDAY PARTY INVITATION, 1994

I wish I could tell you that Clayton and Saford were heroes. I would love to tell you that Papa Clayton won the Congressional Medal of Honor for saving his platoon and an entire village of Filipino children by single-handedly wiping out a company of Japanese marauders. I wish I could report that Saford earned a Silver Star by silencing a German machine gun nest using only a bag of rocks and a Zippo lighter. But old war stories don't always play out the way they do in the movies. Heroes aren't supermen. Sometimes, they're just good ol' boys who survived, which was certainly heroic enough for those of us who got a chance to be born.

I can verify Clayton and Saford's war stories only to a certain degree of accuracy. Separating truth from myth is messy work. Tall tales and lies come as easy to country boys as howling does to a beagle. In many ways, storytelling is a competition, just like seeing who can skip a rock the most times on a pond or who can pick the most apples in a day or who can throw a ball the farthest. Being twins juiced this natural gamesmanship and the stories. When the twins told their war tales, they surely polished them like the fine pieces of furniture they worked on in the Bassett finishing room. Even if research sometimes strips away the varnish of embellishment, the bare wood stories are still pretty damn impressive.

A better historian than I would have walked the beaches of Morocco and exclaimed "Aha! It was here where the Western Naval Task Force landed, here where the ships sailed up the Sebou River, and here where the Second Battalion of the Sixtieth Infantry Regiment was baptized in battle. And, looky there! The Casbah! Aha, it all makes sense to me now!" But I am not that guy. I stayed home and talked to old men.

I'm the kind of "historian" who records hundreds of hours of interviews then formulates the perfect follow-up questions long after the interview subjects are dead and gone. Lacking the means to hop a flight to Manila, which you can't get to from Roanoke anyway, or the guts to quit my job in order to devote every waking minute to the thrilling adventures of the Ninth and Ninety-sixth Infantry Divisions, I instead slogged back through the swamp of old interviews and read books and combed through war records and memoirs in search of something that sounded like the truth.

Still, when I watch that old video recording of Saford talking about his wartime exploits and I hear him repeat his famous story about meeting Patton, I ask myself: Aw, did that really happen or did he make that up?

After years spent searching for the truth, I've come to ask myself another question: Do I even care if he did? What is it they say at the end of *The Man Who Shot Liberty Valance*? When the legend becomes fact, print the legend.

There's history, then there's his story, which is what Saford told us the same day Ruth gave me the fiddle for my birthday. Mom operated the video camera (it was two days before the fiftieth anniversary of D-Day) and captured it forever:

"I'd like to tell first a little history of our Ninth Division," Saford began, sounding like the narrator of a play giving his one thousandth performance, which is sort of what he was doing.

He spoke nonstop for almost an hour, save for the occasional curveball question I'd lob every few minutes ("Did you ever meet Patton?!"). Saford suffered the interruptions, then picked up the trail that ran from North Africa to Sicily and on to England and France. And, yes, he said he did meet Patton, who commanded the Western Task Force, which included Saford's outfit. During his videotaped monologue, Saford recounted this favorite story about the preparations for the North Africa landings:

> *Patton said, "I'll tell you one thing, anybody that's got any questions, now's the time to ask 'em." I stuck up my hand. I knew when I hit the beach that the enemy would start firing at me and our boats would start firing from about a hundred yards back in the water. I was right*

in the middle. I questioned him. He said, "Yes sir, sergeant, what is your question?"

I said, "Sir, my job is to mark the beach and go on inland and cease that gun."

He said, "Yes, boy. You've been briefed well, sergeant. You are really on the ball."

I said, "Yes, sir. There's one thing I want to ask you."

"What's that?"

"When our boys get so far in shore with their Higgins boats and PTLs and things, hauling personnel . . . the enemy's gonna open up on them, then they're gonna open up and I'm right in the middle. What's going to happen to me?"

He had a habit of biting his lip on the side . . . [then Patton said], "Heh! What the hell's one out of a million?"

It sounds like something Patton could've said. That's the way Saford always told it.

. . .

Saford had never been inclined to pray much in his first twenty-three years, but in the waning hours of November 7, 1942, he had a brief conversation with the Lord. If he wasn't coming back from this cruise, he wanted to make sure he had cleared up a few things with the Big Guy.

He slept a little, then, shortly after midnight, pulled on a black wet suit and gathered his gear. He had sharpened his trench knife the entire voyage from Norfolk, filing the blade until it could slice a hair in two. He even sharpened the knuckles on the knife's handle. When mission hour came, he climbed down from the ship and joined a detachment of other men in a Higgins boat and set off into the oily, moonless night. Fifteen miles through choppy Mediterranean waters lay the beaches of French Morocco. This was it.

The overall North African invasion was called Operation Torch. Saford was part of the Western Task Force, whose mission was to invade Morocco and capture an airfield at Port Lyautey, a few miles inland up the Sebou River. Saford's job was to mark the beaches with infrared signals and lights to guide the invading forces.

About a mile from the invisible shoreline, Saford and his fellow beach markers disembarked from the Higgins boats and climbed into rubber rafts. The men paddled silently until they were within two hundred yards of the beach, at which point they slit their rafts and sank them. With lights, infrared signals, two grenades, and a trench knife strapped to each of their torsos, the men swam in pairs toward the shore. Saford swam alongside a private named Borowski, both cutting through the surf as noiselessly as fish.

The beach was guarded not by Germans, but by the French. North Africa was ostensibly still part of the French empire, but the French themselves were now governed by the Nazi-friendly Vichy rulers. American commanders believed that the French military would turn on the Germans and join the Allies once the landings began. In fact, negotiations between American and French leaders were under way to ensure that the French would not oppose the landings. Out in the surf and closing in fast, Saford knew nothing about negotiations or compromises. He had a mission he aimed to carry out.

He and Borowski made it to the beach, where they rolled in the sand until their sticky wet suits were coated and perfectly camouflaged. Now came the tough part they had trained for at Fort Bragg. The two French guards who patrolled the beach never knew what hit them when a pair of miniature sand dunes rose from the ground, grabbed them from behind, and slit their throats with trench knives that had been sharpened all the way across the Atlantic.

Saford dragged the first man he ever killed behind a dune. He and Borowski located the coastal defenses and returned to the beach to signal the artillery positions to the ship. They marked the beach with the infrared signals and blue flashlights. The Allied invasion of North Africa was about to begin. Soon, the sun would rise behind them and expose them to the enemy.

The landing unfolded agonizingly slowly. Ships lost their formation during the night, landing craft floundered in the crashing waves, and raw, green soldiers seemed not to know what to do once they finally hit the beach.

French guns opened up and the nightmare scenario Saford had laid out for Patton began. Saford was caught in the middle of the shelling. He found a helmet nearby and used it to dig like a groundhog. He buried himself in his sandy foxhole behind a dune and listened to shells roar overhead, flying in both directions.

The shelling went on for hours. When it ended, Saford sat up in the sand and stared right into the sun, bleary-eyed and lightheaded from lack of sleep. He saw a shadowy form of a human silhouette, a brown-skinned, bearded man, clad in a flowing white robe.

"Christ?" Saford muttered.

Just as he realized the man was not Jesus but merely an Arab trader who had come to see what all the shooting was about, he heard someone running at him from behind. A soldier clambered over the dune and stuck his rifle right up against Saford's back, nicking him a little with the bayonet. Saford turned and saw that the boy was American.

"Hey!" Saford hollered. "What are you doing? I'm an American!"

The young, nervous private barked at Saford to shut up.

"They told us you'd say something like that," the private said, keeping his bayonet against Saford's back. Saford kept the chatter up. Using as many English words as possible could only help, he reckoned.

"I know I'm supposed to say 'Hey Mack' and all that stuff they taught us at Fort Bragg, North Carolina," Saford said.

"How do you know about that?" the private asked, confused.

"You're Second Battalion, right? Take me to Major Breeze and we'll get this straightened out."

The major was summoned and the confusion was all sorted out. Within his first six hours of combat, Saford had been first to the beach, had slit a man's throat, had nearly been killed by French and American guns, and had been captured by his own men. And the war had just begun.

. . .

Clayton played his final shows with Roy Hall in mid-December 1942. He wouldn't make music again for—how long? Two years, at least? He had no idea when he'd next see Roanoke or the view from a stage.

Knowing that this was a young soldier's farewell performance, Roy let Clayton sing a couple of songs for his final radio programs.

Tommy kicked up a cloud of dust with "Arkansas Traveler." Clayton kept up with his two-finger banjo style, then he stepped up to the microphone and sang "Hung Down My Head and Cried," which was a pretty good theme song for a boy about to go off to the army.

He and Jay Hugh buddied up for a few duets during the course of the preformance. One of the best was a number they called "Long Steel Rail," which was bedecked with lovely verses sure to put people in the Christmas spirit:

> *The prettiest girl I ever saw was killed one mile from town*
> *Her head was in the driver's wheel and the body was never found*

Clayton and Jay Hugh punctuated each verse with a harmonized yodel that could peel the acoustic tiles off the studio walls. Cousin Irving commended the boys on their selection.

"I like it. It's kinda lonesome sounding, but it picks you up," he said.

"I don't know what we're gonna do with that song," Jay Hugh piped in. "Clayton's got to go in the army."

"Well, I reckon you'll have to find somebody else," Irving figured. He turned to Clayton. "Hi, Private!"

But there was nobody else. Everybody had gone off to war. Saford, Bill, Roy's brother Rufus, and now Clayton. Jay Hugh would be gone soon, as well. The Blue Ridge Entertainers were in their final days.

Late in the session, Clayton was called to the mike again, this time to do "Old Shep," which had been a hit record the year before for Red Foley. The sentimental song about a boy and his dog already sounded quaint and completely out of step with the times.

Clayton punctuated the song with a little Western-style guitar run, a musical benediction for folks to remember him by when he was gone. He probably wouldn't be singing any songs about boys and their old dogs for quite a while.

"I like that little ending you got there," Irving Sharp told Clayton.

"It's a killer, ain't it?" Clayton said.

"It's a killer, all right," Irving said.

I don't know how they said good-bye. I can't tell you if Roy shook Clayton's hand, wished him well, and told him to keep his head low. I don't know if he promised his ace banjo picker that his spot in the band was safe and they'd all pick up right where they left off, making music and playing over the radio, once this awful war was over. I wish I knew if Clayton thanked Roy for all he had done for him and Saford. I wonder if he told him how much he appreciated that Roy had come to Bassett that day and rescued them from the furniture factory's killing fumes, or if he thanked him for leading such a great band and for making them semi-celebrities, not to mention semi-rich. I wonder if Clayton found the words to tell Roy that he had been as good a brother—or a father, even—as he and Saford would ever know, and that his friendship would be forever cherished and never forgotten. I hope he did, because life is short and you never know if you'll get another chance to tell people how much you appreciate them and care about them.

All I know is that Clayton got on a train and headed for Camp Lee on December 31, 1942. Happy New Year. At Camp Lee, his fifteen gallons of hair were shorn and he was dunked face-first into army lingo and rules. Soon after that, he would be on a train to Fort McClellan, Alabama, for basic training before heading west to join his outfit and leave the life he had known two thousand miles behind.

· · ·

Camp Lee swarmed with a commotion that left Clayton discombobulated. Short-haired men in drab uniforms barked at him incessantly. Get in this line, that line. It was like the first day of school at the world's largest schoolhouse, where every teacher was the meanest of all time.

In one line, they shaved off Clayton's hair. In another line, doctors measured him and stuck him with needles in both arms. He learned how to get into formation and endure profanity-laden speeches from fire-breathing sergeants. One sergeant didn't like something about Clayton's looks— maybe it was before his pile of hair had been cut—and he jumped right in Clayton's face.

"Where are you from, boy?"

"The Hollow, Virginia, sir!"

"The Hollow ... the what?" the sergeant stammered.

Clayton learned that it wasn't a good idea to make a sergeant stammer. He was ordered to drop to the ground and perform fifty push-ups.

Clayton got his barracks assignment and was handed a duffel bag of clothes and gear. When he got to his quarters, his arms hurt so bad from the shots and pushups that he couldn't raise them to toss his duffel on his bed, the top bunk. Clayton asked the nearest soldier if he'd help him out.

"Oh, so you're too weak to get in your own bunk," the boy sneered at Clayton.

"Listen, I just need help lifting my bag," Clayton said. "I can't raise my arms right now."

"You lift your own damn bag," the boy barked. Real tough guy. He looked about eighteen. He was as skinny as a hairless rat, and Clayton fig-ured it would take about two seconds to pound him into dust, if his arms weren't sore.

Clayton looked good in his fatigues. After three years of dressing to the nines in jackets and ties, he was dapper in anything. He looked like he belonged in this man's army. That is, until he walked past a lieutenant without saluting him.

"You there," the lieutenant hollered.

Clayton spun around on his heel.

"Private, don't you know how to salute an officer when you meet him?"

Clayton allowed that he did not.

"I could have you on guard duty for a month," the lieutenant boasted.

Clayton tried to reason with the guy.

"Listen, I'm just a country boy. I don't know any of these army rules."

Reason just seemed to make the lieutenant madder. He jumped in Clay-ton's face.

"The next time I see you not saluting an officer, Private, I will bust your rear!"

Clayton saluted as best he knew how and barked, "Yes, sir!"

Everybody in the army was such a smartass.

. . .

After a couple of months of basic training in Alabama, Clayton joined the Ninety-sixth Infantry Division and arrived at Camp Adair, Oregon—about as far from Roanoke as you could go and still be considered part of the United States. The division was led by General James "Smiling Jim" Brad-ley, who told his recruits, "We kill or we get killed."

By the time Clayton joined the Ninety-sixth, the division was full of Mid-western boys, whose funny accents and propensity for profanity shocked the dumbfounded new hillbilly. At twenty-three, he was older than many of the young bucks who had been drafted out of high school or had skipped college in hopes of killing Germans or Japanese. Clayton's maturity impressed his superiors and allowed him to rise quickly through the ranks. He even got a bottom bunk. In a regiment blooming with hot-blooded boys itching to shoot at any shadow that moved, Clayton stood out for his calmness and common sense. The fact that he was good with a rifle didn't hurt, either—a country boy knows his way around a gun the way a city boy knows the bus schedule. By the end of winter, Clayton had been promoted to corporal and made assistant squad leader.

The Midwestern boys treated their new assistant leader exactly how you'd expect them to. They decided to test this Virginia hillbilly and see what he was made of.

One day when the gray Oregon winter had finally melted into spring, Corporal Hall was given the plum assignment of cleaning the barracks, a task he assigned to a group of ten or twelve guys. He sent three men to each of the barracks, ordering them to sweep the floors and wash the windows. But when he checked the first building, all the guys were just sitting around, not lifting a finger.

"Boys, why aren't you working?" he asked. "You've got a lot of work to get done."

One of the fellows chirped something about not taking orders from any dirty old hillbilly. Another piped in with the news that not only was he not going to sweep the floor, he had no plans to do anything he didn't want to do.

Clayton went to the next building and found a scene similar to the first. The guys assigned to clean up the barracks were lying around, reading magazines. Clayton knew then that this wasn't a coincidence. He was being set up by his own men. They wanted to make sure this hillbilly didn't get above his raising. If the barracks didn't get cleaned, they had reasoned, Corporal Hall's superiors would be really hacked off and they'd bust his ass.

Clayton, though, wasn't the type to back off. He figured if he was going to get busted, it might as well be for something that would at least provide him with some pleasure. He went back to the first barracks and grabbed the nearest mutineer by the short collar. Ironically, it wasn't one of the Midwesterners—it was a boy from Tennessee! A kindred mountain man. He shook that boy and he unleashed some of the new vocabulary he had picked up.

"If you don't blankety-blank work I'll blankety your blank and I'll whup every blankety-blank one of you!"

The other privates scattered. One slipped out to find a sergeant. Corporal Hall's gone mad!

Within minutes, a sergeant arrived and demanded to know just what the hell was going on here. Corporal Hall explained that the men had refused to work. The men whined that Corporal Hall had been too tough on them.

The sergeant had no choice but to demote Clayton. You can get away with a lot in the service, but grabbing an enlisted man by the neck and shaking him is going too far, even by the army's standards.

The boy from Tennessee rubbed his neck and croaked, "I believe you were really going to kill me."

"That's some pretty good thinking on your part," the newly anointed Private Hall said. "Where I come from, you'd've ate those words."

"Where do you come from?"

"I come from The Hollow, Virginia," Clayton said proudly.

. . .

One evening, Clayton climbed into his bottom bunk and thumbed through a magazine. Occasionally, a cheap guitar would show up in the barracks, and Clayton would strum it and sing a verse of "Hung Down My Head and Cried" or some other slow number, but he hadn't played in so long, he had lost the calluses on his fingertips.

As he read the magazine, he unconsciously hummed the yodel part to "Way Out There." Just a little "Mmmm, hmmmm, hm, hm, hm..." to prime the pump. Then, the yodel just came natural.

"Weeeeee-ooooooooooh, teedle-di-oh-ti-doo..."

He heard a rustling in the bunk over his head followed by, "Hey, them's the Sons of the Pioneers."

The guy's name was Smith, a Canadian-born soldier who loved Western songs, too. He was surprised to learn that the little hillbilly picker from Virginia liked the Sons of the Pioneers and their songs about tumbleweeds, cowhands, and punching doggies.

Turned out Smith was a fine tenor singer. He knew a fellow named Ramirez in another company who was a good singer, too, and soon the Canadian, the Hispanic, and the hillbilly got together to sing Western songs a couple of nights a week.

The international trio got pretty good. They knew all the Sons of the Pioneers songs—"He's an Old Cowhand from the Rio Grande," "Tumbling Tumbleweeds," and Clayton's favorite, "Cool Water." Clayton sang lead, a departure for him, because he had been so used to backing up Saford. With

Smith and Ramirez harmonizing beautifully on the backup vocals, Clayton strummed a C chord hard and sang:

All day I faced the barren waste without the taste of water—cool water
Old Dan and I, with throats burned dry and souls that cry for water,
Cool, clear water

Just when things were cooking for the cowboy trio, that pesky war intervened again. The soldiers at Camp Adair knew that the Americans and British had the Germans on the run through the deserts of North Africa. Patton chased Erwin Rommel's tanks into Tunisia, where the Allies celebrated their first major victory of the young war. Had the twins bothered to write letters, Clayton might've known that Saford had made it to Tunisia.

The Ninety-sixth left Camp Adair for the arid Oregon hills in June. Most people probably think of the Pacific Northwest as perpetually rainy and foggy, which it often is at its most western points. Central Oregon, though, is called the high desert for good reasons. The landscape is beautiful in its harshness. A hot, dry wind makes it feel like a blast furnace, especially in the summer. In short, the high desert was the perfect place to take an army to learn desert warfare.

The Ninety-sixth and two other divisions met for a series of war games that would test the stamina, readiness, and will of the soldiers. The maneuvers began beneath a blistering late-summer sun as seventy-five thousand men waged pretend war against one another with very real weapons.

By now, Clayton had regained his rank and had been named a squad leader. He thrived in the field. The desert maneuvers near the lumber town of Bend would make or break the soldiers. The twenty-five-mile hikes were difficult, but Clayton persevered. Men guzzled their water too quickly, but Clayton saved his one canteen until his throat burned dry, just like the guy in "Cool Water." The platoons were given a series of problems, which could be solved only by killing or capturing the enemy (or pretending to, at least). Many of the missions were carried out at night, which confused the city boys in Clayton's platoon but hardly fazed a mountain buck who had traipsed mountainsides and walked to house parties on many a moonless night.

A real test came when Clayton's squad was told to destroy a pillbox protected by two machine guns. Clayton sent his men to knock out the machine guns with grenades, then attacked the pillbox with a flame-thrower. The tactic worked like a charm. Score big points for his squad.

So it went for two months. The squad climbed hills in the hot sun and huddled in foxholes during the dry, frigid autumn nights. Men moved at night, dug their holes, and slept a few minutes or an hour before getting up to repeat the process. They invaded communities with the names Alfalfa and Wagontire. They wired bridges with explosives and fired thousands of rounds of live ammunition as artillery roared overhead. Combat surely couldn't be any worse than this pretend fighting in the Oregon desert. The Ninety-sixth Infantry Division was learning to fight, and they were learning fast. They couldn't wait to kill Germans.

. . .

Across a continent and an ocean, on the east coast of Sicily, Saford crouched in a pile of rocks far below the volcanic peak of Mount Etna, an active volcano that could blow any minute for all he knew. He stumbled over the broken molten chunks, failing to find a suitable place to set up his listening post in the dark of night. This time, he was armed to the teeth—his bazooka and his .50-caliber and .30-caliber guns brought him much greater comfort than the grenades and trench knife he had when he landed in Africa. Not even German planes were safe from his firepower.

Still, he was uneasy. The position on the northern slope was too exposed, too precarious. The fact that he was sitting on an active volcano didn't make him feel any better.

"Tell the colonel I can't do anything in this slate," Saford barked into his sound-powered telephone, another high-tech accessory. He packed up his personal arsenal and abandoned his position. Saford's road to Sicily had begun in North Africa. For him, war had not been a game or a concocted series of pretend maneuvers for more than eight months. He had seen the real deal. After the North African landings in November 1942, the Allies marched slowly, but inexorably, eastward, where they met the Germans, were turned back, but advanced again. They were bound for Tunisia, to chase the Germans into the Mediterranean or die trying.

Saford was assigned to the Headquarters Company of the Ninth Infantry Division's Sixtieth Infantry Regiment, reading maps and going on scouting missions, for which his orders were simple: Find the Germans.

There were plenty to be found. Saford went out accompanied by other scouts and Jeep drivers. He crawled on his belly over hills and down sandy embankments, locating Germans and watching their shifting lines through binoculars. It was the perfect job for the sneaky old instigator.

One day, Saford and his driver stopped along a road on the way to Tunisia, where the two of them climbed a steep slope and crawled along the summit on their bellies and elbows. The driver, a young private, looked through his field glasses and practically gagged at the sight: columns of German armor and infantry idling just a few miles away.

The private spat and stuttered. "There's Germans out there!" he nearly shouted.

Saford grabbed the boy by the throat and pulled his face up close to his own.

"Of course there's Germans out there," he said. "Now you listen to me. We're gonna see Germans. We're supposed to see Germans. Why the hell do you think they sent us out here? That's our job. Now, if you're too afraid of Germans, you just let me know and I'll tell the colonel. But you'd better know this—I am not gonna work with a man who's afraid of Germans."

* * *

Saford saw his fill of Germans in Sicily. Almost every day during late summer 1943, Saford ventured ahead of his fellow soldiers into no-man's-land, scouting enemy lines and setting up listening posts, which were positions from which he could watch German and Italian movements and communicate intelligence back to his superiors. The job could be deadly dull or just plain deadly. Saford stayed put for hours, spying on enemy movements, scouting locations of minefields, intercepting enemy communications— basically gathering any type of information that he could take back to headquarters. He was the eyes and ears of a giant, violent beast marching toward the European mainland.

On August 12, 1943, Saford was summoned by a Lieutenant Willoughby. Another green lieutenant, Saford thought. Saford and his buddies at the HQ had taken to calling the never-ending carousel of young lieutenants "cannon fodder"—they were in command one day, gone the next, as if blasted into heaven like mortars. Many times, a green lieutenant found himself in a pitched battle without any clue what to do. Sometimes, one would pull out the army field manual and nervously flip through the pages, only to have somebody knock it from his shaking hands and yell, "The fella who wrote that book ain't here!"

"Come with me," Lieutenant Willoughby said.

"Mmm, hmmm," Saford mumbled, all cocky. "Where we going?"

"We've got a report of Germans near Randazzo. We've got to check it out."

Saford and Willoughby climbed into a Jeep and drove north, back toward the position Saford had left on Mount Etna. Saford was familiar with the terrain, and he suggested to Willoughby that the two of them park and set out on foot.

Willoughby pulled the Jeep over and he and Saford packed their gear and walked across an undulating grassy field, sweating in the early afternoon sun beneath their packs of weapons and grenades. They crested a short hill and saw a shallow ravine ahead of them. Saford recommended they go no farther.

"That ravine is full of Germans," Saford said.

Willoughby was incredulous. They were miles from Randazzo.

"There isn't a German within five or six miles of here," the lieutenant barked.

"Well, I believe there are," Saford countered.

Willoughby paused a beat and scanned the horizon. "You really think there are Germans down there?"

"I do."

"Why don't you go down there and check it out, then?"

Now, it was Saford's turn to resist.

"You want me to go down there?" Saford cracked. "You don't believe there are Germans up ahead, but you want me to go check it out? This is your job, Lieutenant. I'm just along for the ride. I'm just here to tell you where the Germans are. Now, if you're afraid of Germans, we'll go back to headquarters and tell the colonel and have him sort out who's supposed to be doing what."

Willoughby cut him off. "I'm not afraid of any German," he said. "I'll go ahead."

Willoughby set out for the ravine while Saford crept to the base of the small hill. As Willoughby got closer to the ravine, he dropped to his belly and crawled several yards. He shot Saford a quick look. No Germans here.

In a flash, three enemy soldiers poured over the top of the ravine. They overpowered Willoughby before he could fire a shot or pull the pin on a grenade. It happened so fast, Saford had no time to react. Then, he saw it, floating through the air, wobbling in flight like a wounded quail—a grenade, coming right at him.

The grenade sailed over his head and landed directly behind him. The ground rumbled and rose beneath his feet, as if Mount Etna were unleashing a murderous eruption. Saford felt himself lifted heavenward, just before the world went dark.

No Germans, my ass.

Little sweetheart come and kiss me
We may never meet again
We may never roam together
Down that dear old shady lane

—"LITTLE SWEETHEART COME AND KISS ME,"
AS PERFORMED BY THE HALL TWINS

Clayton received the news when he got to Camp White. The Ninety-sixth had taken to its new digs on November 1, 1943, following two months of maneuvers in the barren Oregon desert. The mock fighting and very real marching, digging, and shooting had toughened the hillbilly musician. His feet and trigger finger were well callused and he was an expert shot with his M1 rifle, an infantryman's best friend. His fellow soldiers were just as tough as he was, and the division's glowing performance in the field had earned it a nickname—the Deadeyes.

Camp White was barely two years old, and its bright white barracks stood out against the tall pines and red hills of southwest Oregon. The bunks were soft as goose feathers and the chow a gourmet feast—at least that's how it seemed to soldiers who had spent the last sixty days wandering the desert. The mail service was good and finally connected the men to the outside world.

A lieutenant approached Clayton outside the barracks. He handed Clayton a letter and said in a firm voice:

"Your brother is dead. I am very sorry."

Clayton took the letter and didn't say anything at first. He didn't even look at it.

"Which one?"

"I don't know," the lieutenant admitted. "It's all in the letter."

Clayton looked at the handwriting on the envelope, clearly a woman's. He saw the return address—Massachusetts Avenue, Roanoke, Virginia. The letter was from Lottie Wilbourne. Dot's mother. Saford's mother-in-law.

He could barely bring himself to open it.

The letter began like any other a soldier boy receives from home. Hope this finds you well and in good health. Things are good here...blah, blah, blah...he skipped over the words, looking for the terrible part.

Finally, Lottie got there. She had been listening to the radio and heard the awful news. Roy Hall was dead. He had died in a car wreck. The announcer said that he crashed head-on into one of the trees that guarded the entrance to Eureka Park, one of the two trees he used to speed between when he took the shortcut home. The newspaper said he was dead when officers reached him and that he had slumped over just before the crash. There had been a girl riding with him, a girl named Martha Ferguson....

It wasn't Saford.

It wasn't a brother at all. It was *Roy* Hall. Roy Hall was dead. The emotional swings Clayton had felt during the previous sixty seconds would've staggered a draft horse. He thought he had lost a brother, certain it was his twin, only to learn he hadn't. But his relief at knowing Saford was alive was swamped by the soul-numbing shock that his old bandleader was dead.

Roy had died in May. Clayton had been so far removed from civilization that the news of Roy Hall's death took nearly five months to find him. Lottie's letter had chased him all around the United States before greeting him so grievously at Camp White.

According to the *Roanoke World-News*, Roy had died around 11:30 p.m. on May 16, 1943, a Sunday night. Lottie included a *World-News* clipping from the May 17 afternoon edition, which carried the front-page headline "Roy Hall Dies in Auto Crash in Eureka Park." The story wasted no time before diving into the gruesome details:

> *Roy Davis Hall, popular radio entertainer and leader of the recently disbanded Blue Ridge Entertainers, died of a fractured skull, fractured neck and crushed chest after his car crashed head-on into a tree in Eureka Park, at Carroll Avenue and 16th street, about 11:30 p.m. last*

*night, Dr. Charles M. Irvin, city cor[o]ner, said today. Dr. Irvin added
that he is still investigating the case.*

*Martha Ferguson, of 1020 Gilmer Ave., N.W., who was in the car
with Hall at the time of the accident, was seriously, but not critically
hurt. She was removed to the Lewis-Gale Hospital where physicians
said she was suffering from a fractured left cheek and a broken leg.*

Clayton had no idea who Martha Ferguson was. She wasn't Roy's wife,
he knew that much. Clayton's period of mourning lasted about five minutes before it was time to resume training and drills. He wouldn't know
anything else about Roy Hall's death until he got home on a furlough,
whenever that would be.

. . .

As Clayton's first year with the Ninety-sixth came to an end, he made
plenty of friends, especially fellow Southerners who, like him, were often
fodder for Midwestern boys' jokes.

Houston Humphries was an Arkansas ridge runner whose loping,
ostrich-like gait and molasses-slow drawl earned him the natural nickname of "Speedy." He was popular, mainly because of his ridiculous tales
of chasing razorbacks in the boonies and his magic touch with the ladies.
While stationed at Camp White, he took a furlough to go home and marry
his hometown sweetheart. When he got back, his buddies asked him if
the wedding had come off without a hitch. He told them yes and no. The
girl he was sweet on, her folks wouldn't let him marry her. So he married
another girl down the street.

Another buddy was Virgil Boone, who was from Greensboro, North
Carolina, and had impressed Clayton by knowing who Roy Hall and His
Blue Ridge Entertainers were. Boone knew the band from its WBIG days.
He and Clayton both liked the same kind of music and the same groups.
In a regiment full of loudmouths, Boone was a soft-spoken, friendly fel-
low, someone who kept to himself and didn't brag about how many men
he would kill or women he would screw. Clayton liked that about him.

Clayton was beginning to feel like a grizzled veteran. He walked with a
bit more swagger and confidence, and he talked to new recruits like they
were the baby brothers he never had. Don Huber from Wisconsin was

right out of high school when he arrived at Camp White and heard a man call out "Hello there, young feller!" It was Corporal Hall. He had started calling everybody "young feller."

Smith and Ramirez were still his singing buddies. They sang trio harmony on all the popular Western tunes, sometimes in front of the entire company. Clayton always stole the show. He grabbed a cheap, beat-up guitar and thrashed a bluesy A chord until the rusty strings wailed. Then he sang in a high, twangy tenor:

> And if you see my milk cow,
> Please drive her on home
> I ain't had no milk and butter
> Since my milk cow been gone

The men of F Company, 382nd Infantry Regiment, Ninety-sixth Infantry Division had the "Milk Cow Blues" terrible bad—and they loved it.

· · ·

John Fox did not love the blues. He despised Clayton's playing and singing, and he especially detested fiddle music. Fox was a big, tough son of a bitch from Illinois, real intimidating. He crashed into the barracks one night, tired, perhaps drunk, and ready to fight the first person he saw—which, in this case, happened to be the little fiddle-playing corporal. The big brute demanded that Clayton silence that trashy hillbilly music.

Clayton paused a minute, then resumed playing.

Fox made his feelings plain. He didn't care for the fiddle and he hated all good-for-nothing hillbillies, who, as far as he was concerned, were less than human and had no place in this man's army.

Clayton had had enough.

"Buddy, if you don't shut up, you gonna eat this fiddle," he said.

Fox responded with a barrage of slurs, hitting all the high points of hillbilly stereotypes. Toothlessness was probably mentioned. Personal hygiene and illiteracy are popular subjects. Of course, you can't belittle a hillbilly properly without bringing up inbreeding, which I am sure Fox did not forget to mention.

Now, had Fox known Clayton Hall's story up until this point, perhaps he would have chosen his words more carefully and treated his brother in arms more respectfully. Sadly, he knew nothing about the little guy's rough upbringing, or about the name-calling he endured as a boy, or about his preferred method for dealing with smart-mouthed bullies who called him those names. All he saw was a sawed-off, twangy-talking runt of a solider who didn't even reach his chin.

Fox looked away from Clayton for a fateful second to grin at his comrades, who were laughing right along with him. Before Fox turned back around, Clayton whacked him in the face with the fiddle—hard. Splinters and steel strings exploded from Fox's face. Before Fox could get his wits back, the little soon-to-be-former corporal punched him in the nose.

Soldiers jumped in and separated the two brawlers before things got out of hand, which might've saved Clayton's life, considering how outsized he was. Clayton got busted down to buck private again, but he didn't care. Losing a cheap fiddle hurt him worse than losing his stripes. It was a good thing for Fox he wasn't playing a banjo, or else he might've killed him.

The barracks weren't silent for long. Clayton, Smith, and Ramirez kept their little band together through the spring of '44. While other men played on football and baseball intramural teams, the trio of singing soldiers played and jammed amid their bunks. On weekends they'd head down to the USO show in Medford, where they entertained their buddies with tumbleweed tales and old cowhands from the Rio Grande and sang in three-part harmony. They were so good their commanding officers occasionally gave them a pass from the duty roster so they'd have time for practice.

One night at a USO performance, Armed Forces Radio put the cowboy trio on the air. An announcer told the boys they'd be singing to fighting men all over the globe, which easily eclipsed the Roanoke radio market as the largest audience Clayton had ever sung for. Standing behind the microphone, he strummed a G chord and launched into that famous Sons of the Pioneers yodel. The three young men harmonized on all the verses and even yodeled in harmony.

That was the career peak for the Camp White cowboy trio. Just when the act had gone international, Uncle Sam busted up the party. Word came down that the Ninety-sixth had been designated as an amphibious division, one that would invade foreign lands from the sea beneath screaming skies of artillery fire. The Deadeyes were on their way to California for specialized training, before they would ship off to their ultimate destination. After months spent sweating and shooting in the Oregon desert, the division was not bound for Africa or Italy or anywhere in Europe after all. The Dead-eyes were going to the jungles of the South Pacific to fight the Japanese.

Smith the Canadian joined an artillery company. Ramirez was sent to specialized training. The big radio performance was their swan song. They had stayed together just long enough to yodel their way across the globe, all the way to southern England, where their music was heard on a radio in the barracks near Winchester. An American soldier turned up the volume and listened closely to the cowboy song, a number he knew by heart. One voice in particular sounded familiar to the combat-tested soldier, who recognized his twin's voice from ten thousand miles away.

Saford listened to Clayton singing on the radio. He probably wished he was with his brother, back in the States, singing those old Western numbers. I'm sure he thought he could sing them better than Clayton's new band.

. . .

Saford was, of course, very much alive.

The Germans had left him for dead after the grenade blast in Sicily, and he lay unconscious for three hours before an American patrol picked him up. He awoke in a field hospital, where doctors had treated a grievous wound to the back of his head. Shrapnel had penetrated his helmet and pierced his skull. Army surgeons had patched him up, replacing missing bone with a small piece of steel. Saford lay immobile for days.

The weeks passed and Saford remained hospitalized. He never learned what happened to Willoughby. He never asked. He got word that the Sixtieth Infantry was shipping out—not to invade Italy, as it turned out, but to England, where it would prepare for the major attack against Fortress Europe. Saford was badly discouraged. Doctors would not release him to rejoin the Sixtieth, which meant Saford might be assigned to a new division.

He was having none of it. One afternoon, Saford heard a Jeep idling outside his hospital tent. He gathered his clothes, put on his boots, and headed outside. He jumped in the passenger seat and demanded that the driver deliver him immediately to Sixtieth Infantry headquarters. The driver resisted at first, then peeled away from the field hospital with his stowaway in tow.

Back with the Sixtieth, Saford boarded a ship bound for England. He spent the winter and spring of 1943–44 encamped near Winchester, where he would train, rest, recover, and, on one memorable occasion, hear his favorite songs played over the radio, sung by a familiar voice. Saford, too, had heard the sad news about Roy Hall.

. . .

People heard and repeated all kinds of stories about the night Roy Hall died. Some said that Roy had eaten seven pickled eggs at the Rugby Grocery Store and had had a heart attack before he crashed into the tree in Eureka Park. Others heard that he had stopped at a diner and offered a ride home to a young waitress just getting off the late shift.

Jay Hugh blamed himself for his older brother's death. Roy had called him that fateful Sunday evening and asked if Jay Hugh would help deliver hams to a family in northwest Roanoke. Jay Hugh was tired and told Roy he'd just stay home and would see him in the morning. A few hours later, Roy was dead and Jay Hugh was left to agonize for his remaining thirty years about what might have happened if he had gone with his brother.

Fifty years after the wreck, Clayton and Saford subscribed to the "Roy was giving a girl a ride home and had a heart attack right before he hit the tree" theory. At least that's what they told me. I have no idea if that's what they privately believed. Best not to talk about it. Kind of like having a mama who never got married. It's just nobody's business.

Nobody knows how Roy and Martha Ferguson knew each other. There were so many women around the band in those days. In the black-and-white publicity photos, Roy Hall looks like a paunchy, middle-aged cowboy—not exactly matinee idol material. Roanoke had been good to him, judging by his expanding waistline. Lots of chicken dinners before show dates. People loved Roy Hall and his band. His music sounds so simple and quaint today, it's hard to believe that girls went gaga over it. But they did. It's hard to believe today because we weren't there in 1940 when the Blue Ridge Entertainers arrived with all the fanfare of a traveling circus. We weren't part of the full house at the Academy of Music. They played rock and roll before there was such a thing. If they had all grown up two decades later, they would've played electric guitars and drums.

As if Roy's tragic death wasn't bad enough, Roy's wife, Mattie, had just learned she was pregnant. Roy left behind one and a half daughters— Martha, going on two, and a girl born seven months after his death. Roy's family had hoped for a boy, so he could be named after his daddy. When the baby girl came, Mattie had a plan—she named the child Royce Ann. Roy's brothers and sisters always called her "Roy Ann," but it didn't matter because the baby's big sister had other ideas. Little Martha called her new sister "bee-bee" instead of baby. And forevermore that's who she was—BeeBe Hall.

Over the years, Martha and BeeBe would hear whispers that their father's little indiscretion with the woman in the car wasn't an isolated incident, but their mother never said a bad word about their father, even though she was still young and pretty when he died. She and Roy had been married fewer than three years. Her daughters grew up surrounded by all kinds of vestiges of their father, some pleasant, some not. At Easter egg hunts in Eureka Park, they were confronted by the enormous scarred oak tree that had killed their father. The tree stood for years after Roy's death, before it was finally cut down and the road through Eureka Park closed off because it was deemed too dangerous.

Mattie kept Roy's old songbooks and at least one other document: an unsigned contract from a movie studio that produced B Westerns. Late in 1942, a big car had pulled up to Roy's house, and a fat man climbed out and trundled up to the porch, where Roy was sitting smoking a cigarette. "You're a hard man to find," said the fat man, whose nickname, naturally, was Tiny. He wanted to talk to Roy about appearing with his band in a picture. Roy loved the idea, except there was one problem: Thanks to the war, he no longer had a band.

Tiny left the contract with him and assured him they'd talk again once the war was over and Roy's band got back together. He squeezed back into his car and drove away.

That's the way Clayton and Saford heard the story, anyway. They would have been in the movies, if not for that lousy, stinking war.

Roy's girls remembered that movie contract. They colored, scrawled, and drew pictures on it until one day it was just gone, like flowers in the fall, like a father neither of them knew.

• • •

England seemed like paradise to Saford, despite the many gray, rainy days. The days just seem brighter when you can understand what the natives are saying. The division arrived in southern England in November 1943, where it settled around the ancient city of Winchester. Tens of thousands

of Americans invaded the small towns and villages of the southern countryside. Saford one day told his kin that "you couldn't have sown a rye field
any thicker" than the crowds of American soldiers jammed into the area.

From all appearances, the locals were happy to see the soldier boys. Just
three years earlier, these same people had lived in fear of what seemed to be
an inevitable German invasion. Now, an altogether different kind of occupation had arrived, an army of foul-mouthed, hard-drinking, skirt-chasing,
fun-loving Yanks, and everyone seemed happy.

Saford spent his pound notes on tea, bitter beer, and, of course, pretty
young English girls, with whom he danced the night away at nightclubs.
The debauchery and nightlife of London could not match the unfettered
bacchanalia of "Naughty Norfolk," but not for lack of trying. Army doctors reminded soldiers about the horrors of VD and instructed them to
keep prophylactics on their person in case of emergencies, as London was
a fun town and a man could almost forget a war was going on.

All parties and furloughs must end, though, and by March 1944, Saford
and his regiment were involved in daily maneuvers. They practiced beach
landings on the English coastline, dodged live ammo, and advanced under
the scream of exploding shells. They were preparing for the real deal, the
big invasion, which would make the landings at Port Lyautey and Sicily
seem as easy as ordering fish and chips in an English pub.

They were reviewed by governmental and military royalty—Churchill,
Eisenhower, Omar Bradley, and British general Bernard Montgomery
addressed the troops during training. Upon viewing the mighty artillery of
the Ninth, Churchill proclaimed that the Americans possessed more guns
than had been in all of England during the Battle of Britain. On May 27,
1944, those guns and the men who fired them were put on alert: Prepare to
sail. Operation Overlord was taking shape. The Great Crusade was about
to begin.

In this war with its mad schemes of destruction
Can't the U.S. use a mountain boy like me?

—OLD COUNTRY-MUSIC SONG THAT ROY HALL
AND HIS BLUE RIDGE ENTERTAINERS USED TO PLAY

Saford's D-Day story is not that of movies and novels. The first twenty minutes of *Saving Private Ryan* are not about him or the Sixtieth Infantry Regiment or even the entire Ninth Infantry Division. The Ninth was still sailing across the English Channel on June 6, 1944, in reserve, waiting to hit Utah Beach four days later. By then, nearly 1,500 Americans would be dead, among them nineteen men from the tiny Virginia town of Bedford, just east of Roanoke. Young men who had probably heard Saford play with Roy Hall on WDBJ or perhaps even seen him in person were slaughtered at Omaha Beach in seconds. To this day, little Bedford claims it suffered the highest per-capita loss on D-Day of any town in America, which is why the National D-Day Memorial opened there in 2001.

By the time Saford arrived at Normandy with the rest of the Sixtieth, most of the D-Day objectives had been accomplished. Still, when Saford disembarked at Utah Beach on June 10, 1944, he was greeted by the occasional mortar shell and stray sniper bullet.

"I thought y'all had this beach secured," Saford offered in a smart-ass tone, surely not comprehending the carnage that had occurred a few miles to the east, not knowing that Utah Beach was a picnic by comparison, the beach that suffered the least number of casualties of all the Normandy landings.

Saford joined the other men of Headquarters Company and unpacked the maps of the Cotentin Peninsula, upon which they had just landed. The division's mission was to secure this thumb of French soil and capture the key port city of Cherbourg. Success would allow the Allies to sail rein-forcements directly from the United States to France and flood the conti-nent with soldiers. Failure meant stalemate, which meant quagmire, which meant a war with no end.

After two days of unloading and preparations, the division joined the fight. The men had already heard stories of tough fighting across a diffi-cult terrain. Saford pored over his maps and couldn't understand what the problem was. The ground was rolling farmland, mostly flat, pocked with small towns and villages. From the maps and aerial photographs he stud-ied, he saw that most of the farms were cordoned off by rows of hedges, which he thought might be like American boxwoods and small shrubs. He was wrong.

Saford was now a platoon sergeant, in charge of fifteen men whom he led into the Normandy countryside. There, he got his first look at the *bocage*—which sounded so much prettier than "hedgerows," but was far more imposing to see. These hedgerows were not thickets of boxwoods or flowering forsythia, but walls of earth and stone topped with *trees*, actual trees. The earthen berms alone were four feet high, the trees another four to ten feet taller on top of that. The hedgerows carved the countryside into a crazy-quilt, Cubist chessboard of fields, orchards, and farms, across which infantry pawns must zig and zag if they were to checkmate the enemy at Cherbourg.

The *bocage* were hundreds of years old, built by Norman farmers who had walled off their fields to contain their livestock. They were as perma-nent as any German-built concrete barricade and as formidable as the very Siegfried Line itself. A tank couldn't plow through a hedgerow, and if one tried, it usually flashed its soft, unprotected underbelly to the enemy.

There was nothing Saford could do except venture out and get a handle on what actually lay ahead for the infantry. His platoon had to move fast, because other divisions were making progress up the peninsula as the Ger-mans withdrew toward Cherbourg for a last stand. Armed with M1 rifles, sidearms, and grenades, Saford and another man crept along an embank-ment beneath a slate-gray sky. Eventually, Saford saw that the situation was worse than he thought: The hedgerows were booby-trapped with trip wires and mines.

Just beyond the rows, from inside the invisible field, Saford was stopped cold by the most frightening sound for an American on a battlefield— the sound of German being spoken. He and the other man dropped to their bellies on the upslope of an earthen berm and listened to the guttural shouts of an unknown number of German soldiers running past on the other side of the hedgerow, not more than five yards away. Saford held his breath until the enemy troops moved far enough down the row for him and his companion to escape and tell the advancing infantry what they were up against.

. . .

By mid-June, the regiment was making good progress in hedgerow country, plowing ahead with bulldozers and tanks outfitted with iron forks on the front. The regiment called itself the "Go-Devils" based on a likely apocryphal story about a German commander remarking, "Look at those devils go!" The Germans scattered and fell back, but it was always another mile, another hedgerow, as Allied men dodged machine-gun nests and snipers.

By June 20, 1944, the Ninth Division had Cherbourg surrounded. Four days later, the division attacked with all three of its regiments. On June 27, the city and its port were in Allied hands.

The Ninth rested, and then the division turned away from the port city and looked toward Germany.

That's how the fight for European liberation began for Saford Hall, a platoon sergeant charged with enormous responsibilities, who gathered reliable intelligence day after exhausting day. Three months after landing in France, Saford had seen war from almost every vantage point, including from his belly and from the heavens. He made photographs from airplanes and watched enemy soldiers pass within a few yards of him as he hid in streambeds and ditches. He told his men they would find themselves within "eye-blinking distance of the Germans."

The Ninth Infantry Division broke out from the Normandy hedgerows in July and steamrolled across France, advancing ten, fifteen, even twenty miles a day. The division made such good progress, it outran its maps and its supplies. Saford and scores of other scouts frantically scoped out the territory that lay ahead as they and the men of the Ninth waited for fuel and food. They ate the rations of captured or dead Germans. The Ninth covered 450 miles between D-Day and early September, and it could not afford a day of rest. The trek across northern France and Belgium was not exactly a page out of Fodor's. Determining Saford's whereabouts during these days is difficult, like looking for a needle in a France-size haystack. He was somewhere out front, looking for Germans, who weren't that hard to find. All he had to do was walk in a straight line for a few hundred yards and there they'd be. Saford and the Go-Devils chased the Germans across the Seine and Meuse rivers and followed them into their motherland. With every step east, he traveled farther from his own home, where the apple crops were being picked and where people still sang and played music on the radio. Would he live long enough to return to the life he once knew?

What Saford specifically was up to is left partly to history, partly to imagination. The Go-Devils "ankled it" down muddy roads toward Belgium during July and August, taking towns and villages all across northern France. They met columns of German armor—could these have been the days when Saford and his fellow scouts dived for ditches and held their collective breath as the mighty panzer tanks rumbled past? They forded rivers and streams—Saford's friends remember his vivid accounts of swimming across raging currents to mark bridgeheads for the anxious infantry. Did he swim the Seine? The Roer? The Meuse? The Rhine? All of the above? All I know for certain is that wherever the Go-Devils of the Sixtieth Infantry went—and they went from France to Belgium to Germany—Saford Hall, that fiddle-playing bastard son of The Hollow, was often a few hundred yards ahead of them.

So he would have been among the first Go-Devils that September to hit the Siegfried Line, the seemingly impenetrable wall of defenses Germany had constructed along its border with France. The battered and bloodied Sixtieth was ordered to follow the Germans into the Hürtgen Forest and cut them off from the rest of the western front. To do that, the Sixtieth required its daily ration of intelligence, so Saford plunged yet again into the hellish no-man's-land between warring armies.

He spotted a small, darkened farmhouse in the German countryside, squatting on the edge of a great forest. Dusk fell as he stepped quietly inside to investigate the possibility of setting up a listening post. He walked through a cozy, unoccupied front room into the kitchen and craned his neck to peer through a doorway down a shadowy hall.

At the end of the hallway stood a large German officer, surprised and wide-eyed. The German drew his Luger and fired once, sending a bullet shrieking past Saford's ear. Saford drew his .45 and fired down the hallway, but the German had disappeared. Saford spun on his heels and hotfooted it out of the kitchen. He saw the German through another doorway, and both men fired and missed. Saford ran for the front door and saw the German running away from him, back toward the kitchen. The German turned, fired, and missed again. Saford squeezed off one more errant shot, spilled out the front door, and sprinted into the forest. His little firefight encapsulated the fighting of late 1944—two sides on top of each other, shooting ceaselessly with no end in sight.

● ● ●

Back in San Luis Obispo, California, the army made Clayton and his crew do the craziest things. The soldiers had to climb a thirty-foot wooden tower while weighed down by twenty-five pounds of gear, and then, after they scaled the top, they had to turn around and jump off the other side into a pool of water.

Clayton and the rest of the Deadeyes were amphibious, and all amphibians must know how to swim for their lives. And climb down rope ladders into waiting watercraft, race atop roiling surf without tossing their cookies, and, finally, disembark on beaches ablaze with murderous fire.

By now, the Deadeye training consisted not only of practicing marksmanship with an arsenal of weapons—M1 rifles, Browning automatic rifles, .22 and .45-caliber pistols, and .22-caliber rifles—but also of reading, going to classes, and learning newfangled tactics. The Deadeyes were really going to war.

In California, Clayton got a letter from Elinor, Reba's baby sister. Clayton figured she must have been about thirteen or fourteen by now. She wrote to ask how he was doing and to tell him that everything in Roanoke was fine. Her brother Marvin was in the service and the Holland family prayed daily that the Lord would look after him. Several of her uncles on her mother's side were in the army, too.

Clayton didn't receive a ton of letters while he was in camp, unlike the other fellows, who seemed to get mail every day. He was glad to receive news from Roanoke, even if it was from a seventh-grader. He wrote her back, told her things were going swimmingly in camp, and requested that she say hello from him to all the Hollands back in Roanoke. He included a lapel pin and an insignia patch in the envelope. He told her he looked forward to seeing everybody in Roanoke soon.

On July 22, 1944, Clayton and the rest of F Company rode riverboat steamers down the Sacramento River to the San Francisco pier that would be their entrance ramp to war. Hundreds of residents from the towns along the river lined its banks and waved at the ferries, as tugboats tooted salutes. Upon arrival, the Deadeyes climbed the gangplanks of the USS *Sea Marlin,* wearing their olive drab uniforms and steel helmets, carrying duffel bags. They sailed past the Golden Gate Bridge and into the calm waters of the Pacific, bound for Hawaii, where they would train in steamy jungles in preparation for tropical combat.

A trip to Hawaii sounded lovely to the troops. Hula girls in grass skirts, beautiful weather, sandy beaches—it all made war sound kind of like a vacation, only with live ammunition.

During the voyage, men listened to the music of the Ninety-sixth Infantry Division band topside—no Western songs, unfortunately for Clayton—and watched flying fish from the rails. The Deadeyes arrived at Pearl Harbor in waves. Men poured by the shipful onto flatbed, narrow-gauge railcars dubbed the "Pineapple Express," which carried soldiers past sugar cane and pineapple groves on a two-hour ride to the wood-and-tarpaper Schofield Barracks.

The jungles of Oahu must have felt like the end of the earth to a country boy from Virginia. Training included lessons on how to catch and eat frogs, lizards, and snakes, and how to spot a camouflaged enemy in the trees. Soldiers were taught to swing from vines and to throw grenades, as if World War II were a Tarzan movie.

Eventually, men were granted passes to Honolulu, a brilliant maneuver by the army to remind the boys what they were fighting for. Lines of forty men, mostly sailors, formed outside the whorehouses on Hotel Street. Outside, armed guards kept the lines moving and ensured the men all had their "peace." Inside, young women bestowed many a soldier with a good "lei." On the street, the army maintained a prophylactic station that handed out rubbers like they were cigarettes. Two army-approved dollars imprinted with the word "Hawaii" bought a fellow five minutes of ecstasy with a Honolulu Lulu. Soldiers had their photographs taken with haggard hula "girls" whose ample breasts were covered only with leis.

• • •

Naturally, Clayton loved Hawaii. He didn't want to leave. No wonder, considering what awaited him and the rest of the Deadeyes.

Jungle training continued and the division, which had come of age in the desert air of Oregon, nearly melted in the tropical heat and humidity. Their target was revealed to be the isolated Pacific island of Yap, one thousand miles east of the Japanese-infested Philippines. The time had come to say good-bye to lei-wearing hula girls and beautiful beaches.

Clayton and the rest of the men of F Company climbed aboard the USS *War Hawk* on September 15, 1944, as giant cranes loaded twenty-five thousand tons of equipment and supplies onto ships bound for a tropical hell. Clayton had been promoted to corporal again just before the division set sail from Pearl Harbor. F Company, which had billed itself the "Fighting Foxes," needed disciplined leaders, and Clayton, aside from feeding fiddles to enlisted men and shaking them by the scruff of the neck, was GI all the way. Still, he let his commanders down again.

The voyage hadn't even begun when Clayton got into trouble. The soldiers had been ordered not to touch any cargo that was being loaded, especially if the cargo was navy supplies. If a soldier got caught with so much as a navy raisin in his possession, he would be busted. Just as Clayton boarded the warship, a pallet of apples crashed to the deck. Bright red apples rolled in every direction, and sailors chased after them, picking them up while hollering at the army boys to leave those apples alone—but Clayton didn't listen. A few rolled right up to his army boots, and he scooped them up and stuffed them in every available pocket.

As he nibbled his contraband on the deck, Clayton was confronted by a navy chief petty officer, who demanded to know where the soldier had gotten his apple.

"Out there on the deck," Clayton said casually. "They're rolling around everywhere. Go get yourself all you want."

A little while later, a voice crackled over the loudspeaker:

"Corporal Hall, 382nd, Company F, report immediately to Captain Barron, starboard side."

Captain Barron! James R. Barron was the Fighting Foxes' company commander. He was a tough, no-nonsense, crew cut–sporting Texan whom Clayton had gotten to know well, mainly because Barron was the guy who busted him in rank each time, including this time.

Clayton liked Barron and he believed Barron liked him, even if he did once call Clayton "crazy" for smacking a guy in the face with a fiddle. Now,

Barron had summoned him. Clayton didn't know a thing about a ship except how to board and exit one (even if he had to jump), so he asked a buddy how to get to starboard side. The buddy thought a minute then asked, "Which way are we headed?"

Clayton said, "That ain't got nothing to do with it." Eventually, he found Barron, who had a big smile on his face.

"Corporal Hall!" he said with sarcastic enthusiasm. "Corporal Clayton Hall, from The Hollow, Virginia! So good to see you."

Barron really dressed him down. Here they were, leaving the United States for war, and Clayton could not follow the most simple order he'd ever receive—do not touch navy apples.

As Barron busted him again, Clayton had something to say.

"These stripes don't mean nothing to me," he said. "From now on, I ain't got to worry about nobody else but old Clayton."

Private Clayton Hall returned to the deck and headed straight for the ship's stern. The bastard banjo plucker from The Hollow felt as alone as one could feel on a warship packed with 1,500 men. Honolulu dissolved into the horizon and Oahu sank into the sea, until at last the world he knew had vanished before his eyes. Then Clayton Hall did something he never remembered doing before, not even as a little boy terrorized by brothers and bullies. He cried.

. . .

The trip from Hawaii was long—ten days to the small island of Enewetak. That was to be the staging area for the Yap invasion, for which the troops had studied and prepared during the voyage. Trouble was, once the Deadeyes arrived at Enewetak, they were ordered to forget about Yap because that invasion had been canceled. The Deadeyes had a new mission: the Philippines. The division was seasick not just from ocean travel but from being jerked around. In the past year, the Deadeyes had trained to fight Germans in the desert and Japanese in the jungle, and they had wasted time learning about an island upon which they would never set combat boots. Just who was running this war?

The Deadeyes sweated out their time in boiling heat and humidity while waiting aboard ships for their specific target. Not a comfortable spot could be found above decks or below. Men engaged in calisthenics and weapon inspections until, finally, they learned the specific target—the island of Leyte, right in the bowels of the Philippine chain.

Americans were returning to the Philippines, just as MacArthur had promised two years earlier when the Japanese chased him out and captured the islands less than a year after the attack on Pearl Harbor. The Deadeyes became immersed in crash courses about what to expect and do. More than twenty-thousand seasoned Japanese troops would be dug in. Philippine guerillas had maintained an insurgency against the occupiers. Men should take daily doses of Atabrine to ward off malaria. Halazone tablets were needed to purify water. Other dangerous parasites and diseases were present, so the men were warned to avoid rice paddies and bogs. Clayton and most of F Company boarded USS *LST 1024*, where a scale-model sand carving of Leyte was displayed on deck, revealing the island's topography and landing sites. On board, men stayed up late sharpening bayonets and trench knives. The time had come to fight.

In two days, Clayton would be helping to lead the charge on a beach in the Philippines, part of a mighty armada about to make good on McArthur's promise.

* * *

Could he really do it? Could he really kill a man? When the bullets were flying and the blood was pumping, would Clayton find it in himself to shoot another human being like he was nothing more than a squirrel, or gig him like a frog, or slit his throat? When Clayton drifted off into fitful sleep the night before his first battle, he did not know the answer. He would know it before he slept again.

The men aboard *LST 1024* awoke to reveille at 0400 hours.

The sea was calm but the clear sky thundered with steel and rockets. Shells and bombs pounded the small island of Leyte as Clayton climbed into an amphibious vehicle that would carry him and more than twenty other men to shore. The LVT—or landing vehicle tracked—churned through the surf until it was stopped by a seawall. The men poured out and over the wall and ran in zigzagging patterns to avoid enemy bullets that popped in the sand and water.

For the sixty-some years since the Battle of Leyte Gulf, the opening phase of the Philippines invasion has been officially described as having met "light resistance" from the Japanese defenders. But "light resistance," like other army-speak, is just coded mumbo-jumbo that twists the truth. American soldiers died on the beaches of Leyte, killed by small-arms fire and shell bursts. It wasn't Normandy and the *Saving Private Ryan*–style chaos of beaches strewn with the blood and guts of dead and dying men. But Blue Beach No. 2 on Leyte Island shook with the arrival of war. Two hundred thousand soldiers crashed the island in a matter of hours, and men died.

Clayton's squad pressed on into the palms that had survived the naval bombardment. It needed to advance 2,500 yards inland to make room for all the troops landing behind them. Impeding the squad's progress were thickets of brush and broken trees that looked like they had been felled by a mighty typhoon. Some men fell into deep Japanese-dug trenches and had to climb out the other sides over walls of crumbling sand. All the while, the heat and humidity sucked their strength. Within minutes of hitting the beach, soldiers shed thirty-pound packs stuffed with gas masks, clothes, Bibles. They dropped anything that wasn't a weapon, food, or water.

Clayton plowed ahead and soon was separated from his squad among the brush and coconut trees. Bursts of machine-gun fire from invisible enemy positions sent him ducking and diving. Where were the twenty thousand Japanese? All he saw were dead Japanese soldiers, killed by the navy bombardment, their bodies piled like firewood. Fearful that he might be spotted by an enemy soldier, Clayton dropped to his belly and crawled toward what looked like the foundation of a small building or house that had been flattened by the shelling. With his rifle extended in front of him, Clayton crab-walked on his elbows and knees along the foundation's right side and peered around the corner—and almost bumped heads with a Japanese solider, this one very much alive.

It took only a second to kill him, but the scene seemed like it lasted five minutes. The enemy appeared discombobulated, perhaps even injured. He was dirty and missing his helmet. He was just as surprised to see Clayton coming around the corner of the foundation as Clayton was to see him. He made a panicky reach for something—a weapon, maybe—but Clayton blasted him with his M1 right in the heart. He fell dead instantly.

The war stopped for just a moment. Clayton's hands and arms began to shake and his legs turned to jelly. He looked at the dead Jap and felt his stomach flip. He gagged and heaved. Yes, he could do it. Clayton Hall could kill a man.

After he regained his composure, Clayton reassembled with his squad and reached his destination near a village called Dulag. The men dug their first foxholes and tried to sleep in the rain. Steady, soaking tropical showers made for a miserable first night of combat. If only they had known how easy it had been so far.

· · ·

The Deadeyes had a name for all the dead enemy soldiers they stumbled over as they headed inland.

"Good Jap," they said as they pointed their rifles at bloated, mutilated bodies.

"Good Jap ... good Jap ... good Jap ..."

F Company met no "bad Japs"—live enemies—as it continued to push inland. The entire division progressed steadily on foot and in armored vehicles until the land beneath the soldiers' feet gave way to mud, muck, and, finally, water. Avoid swamps, the commanders had told them. Yeah, right. The only way the men could have avoided swamps was to sprout wings and fly. Clayton slogged through watery muck up to his waist and then his chest, but he and the rest of the men pushed forward.

Trouble was, you couldn't dig a foxhole in the swamp. Clayton crouched in the bog and waited for morning.

The Philippines had become a life-or-death proposition for Japan's fading dreams of empire. American victories at Midway and Guadalcanal had turned the tide against the country. Now, the Japanese were fighting a defensive war, battling desperately to retain what it had and to stave off an inevitable Allied incursion into its homeland. The Deadeyes would learn that a man fighting to protect his homeland was a supremely vicious foe.

The Americans who invaded Leyte Island had already heard a few accounts of bloody Japanese atrocities. They knew that thousands, perhaps tens of thousands, of American prisoners of war had died during the Bataan Death March. Victims had been beheaded, shot, disemboweled, or burned alive. Some of the beheadings had required multiple chops. They heard reports about the inhumane treatment of prisoners, who were summarily starved, beaten, and forced into labor. Allied prisoners of the Japanese faced a nearly one in three chance of dying. Asian peoples fared worse. The Japanese had slaughtered more than two hundred thousand civilians in Nanking, China, and raped thousands of women. By the end of the war, Japanese forces had killed as many as thirty million people, most of them defenseless civilians and prisoners. The Deadeyes might not have known the statistics, but they knew the stories. They had cornered a brutal, bloodied enemy.

The early days on Leyte revealed none of the savagery that lay ahead for F Company. Japanese snipers fired on them, once, on October 23, 1944. Otherwise, they slogged ahead, already running low on K rations and water because supply lines couldn't be established in the swamps. Filipino natives loaded up herds of carabao—Philippine water buffalo—with supplies for the soaked, muddy Americans.

F Company received even better assistance from Filipino guerilla fighters, who provided the Americans with intelligence regarding Japanese positions. They informed the 382nd Regiment that the nearby village of Tabontabon was buzzing with Japanese. A platoon was sent to investigate and returned with information that the village was circled with Japanese emplacements that had been evacuated. An attack on Tabontabon was planned for October 26, 1944. The mission would be quick and easy if the Japanese had truly abandoned the small town.

They had not.

. . .

Sixty years later, Papa Clayton's eyes flashed at the name "Tabontabon."

"That was altogether a new day in our lives," he said. "A new chapter."

The mission did not start well. Relying on outdated maps, the Second Battalion, which included F Company, wandered aimlessly in tall grass until they found their way back through the swamps. Precious hours were lost. Even worse, they did not know that across the Guinarona River, trouble awaited them in the form of an entire Japanese regiment.

This was what they had trained for. F Company crossed the river and took cover beneath the riverbanks, then moved out to search for an invisible enemy. Intelligence had informed them that the Japanese were well dug in just over the top of the bank, perhaps not ten feet away. Artillery had bombarded the tiny village. Maybe nothing or nobody was left standing. The men up front walked into the open where they could see what was left of the town. That's the instant the "new chapter" began.

Humphries, the Arkansas ridge runner, was one of the first to get hit, but survived. F Company walked face-first into a hornet's nest of lead. Japanese machine guns poured merciless fire onto the Americans. Mortars dropped practically on their heads, as though the Japanese knew the precise moment they would walk into view. The well-placed guns threw up an impenetrable shield of crossfire that stopped F Company cold. Humphries was only wounded and was able to backtrack for cover beneath the bank with the rest of his buddies.

Clayton avoided the bullets and crouched beneath the embankment. Men ran along the riverbank and sloshed back across the river. The ground exploded with bullets and shells. The noise made it impossible to communicate verbally. F Company was about to be routed, but the men fought back. Forward troops located enemy gun emplacements and were able to open up on the positions. Clayton, still hugging the bank, pulled the pin on a grenade and lobbed it over the top of the hill. The grenade landed near a stash of Japanese explosives hidden in a foxhole that detonated ferociously. The Japanese firing ceased, and enemy gunners dived for cover. Still, Clayton and company realized their position exposed them to additional fire, and after nightfall that position would prove impossible to defend, so they backpedaled across the river ("withdrew" in army parlance). F Company had met the enemy and had been driven back. But there would be a new fight tomorrow.

• • •

That night, a typhoon of American shells slammed the hapless village. The bombing softened the resistance, at least initially. The next morning, F Company hit the outskirts of the village and split in half. The men saw mind-boggling devastation. Almost every building had been flattened, save for a few dilapidated houses and the Catholic church, from which a Japanese sniper fired upon Clayton's company.

Clayton's squad broke for the church. Their mission was to charge the Japanese lines in the center of town and break the enemy's stronghold. The Japanese had to hold Tabontabon if they were to stop the Americans from controlling all of Leyte. If the Americans controlled Leyte, they could wipe the Japanese from the Philippines. If they did that, they'd be on their way to Japan. The Japanese could not let this first domino fall.

When F Company attempted to roll up the streets, the murderous guns struck with withering fire. Clayton's Second Platoon was pinned down so tightly that whenever a man so much as lifted a rifle or even a radio to summon help, Japanese bullets popped all around. Everything was subjected to

Japanese sniper attacks. Every block disintegrated into maddening, indus-trialized violence. This tiny speck of a town, which would have made Bas-sett, Virginia, seem like a burgeoning metropolis, no longer existed except as a crucible for men to murder one another with staggering effectiveness.

F Company crawled up the street, knocking off a machine gun only to learn bloodily that another gun was protecting it. This went on all after-noon, a slow, inexorable march, one gun emplacement at a time, until two platoons—including Clayton's—made it to the outskirts of the village. But before the men had a chance to breathe easy, they were hit yet again by more Japanese machine guns well hidden in tall grass and shacks. As dark-ness fell, Clayton and his buddies dug in along the decimated streets and blocks of Tabontabon, surrounded by an invisible enemy. A counterattack was expected. Sleep was not an option.

The soldiers had heard about Japanese nighttime attacks—hordes of men running and screaming, charging ahead waving swords and bayonets, firing guns. The Yanks came to call them "banzai charges" for the Japa-nese battle cry *"Tenno heika banzai,"* which loosely translates to "Long live the emperor!" For the Japanese, the charges were a vestige of the ancient Bushido warrior culture, almost always a last-ditch effort to stave off cer-tain defeat. The men of F Company were about to be on the receiving end of such an attack.

Clayton was still digging his foxhole when the whispery skiffs and clicks of entrenchment tools and shovels were interrupted by a most curi-ous sound—the peal of church bells from the steeple of the lone standing church. Men stopped digging and heard more bizarre sounds—the clar-ion call of bugles from the village outskirts, followed by piercing human howls.

The Japanese attack was on. Men dived into foxholes as bullets and hand grenades ripped the ground. Flares fired by American mortar companies lit up the sky as if noon had arrived twelve hours early. Dozens of Japanese soldiers ran toward F Company, firing from the hip, throwing grenades, and shouting like Rebel soldiers during Pickett's Charge. American machine guns poured bullets by the thousands into the zealous attackers, who were mowed down the way a scythe slices through a summer hayfield. Still, they came. Clayton's squad set up crossfires, firing at angles, eliminating clear lanes for the attackers to charge.

After the flares burned out, Clayton could still see the forms and silhou-ettes of Japanese running toward him. He would never forget the sight of enemy soldiers who were so close, he could see them illuminated by bursts of machine-gun fire and tracer bullets. Clayton smelled the sickening stench of burning flesh and realized it wasn't coming from dead, shot-to-pieces Japanese in front of him, but from the scorched hands of a young private in the next foxhole trying desperately to change a machine-gun barrel that had melted.

The firefight went on for ten minutes before the surviving Japanese high-tailed it back to the tall grass. All night long, F Company could hear Japanese soldiers dragging dead and wounded comrades into the weeds. The next day, a private in F Company recorded in his journal that he saw "twelve good Japs," but he suspected that many more dead had been dragged away.

The next day, the Deadeyes moved freely as bulldozers rumbled through the village and shoveled dead Japanese soldiers into enormous pits for unceremonious burial. Clayton had survived his first real battle of the war.

Thank goodness there was no lull in the fighting. Clayton might have broken down into guttural sobs if he had had time to think about how dramatically his life had changed. Just two years earlier, he was in Roanoke, playing the banjo, singing on the radio, and dating pretty girls. Life was joy. Now, he was miserable as he sat in a foxhole, dodging grenades, soaked to the bone with nary a pretty girl or banjo for miles around.

. . .

A week after the fight for Tabontabon, Clayton's battalion headed north toward the village of Dagami. Along the way, Clayton ran into a couple of his old buddies from, of all places, The Hollow. Rex Willis, Clayton's former teenage friend and bandmate from his first group, the Blue Ridge Buddies, was in the Ninety-sixth Infantry Division's 381st Infantry Regiment, as was another childhood pal by the name of Bill Smith. Clayton had not seen his old friends in several years, and he had to laugh when he considered the odds against three country boys reacquainting themselves in the steamy jungles of the Philippines. The reunion didn't last long, because Rex and Bill were soon grievously wounded in the battle of Mecham Ridge.

Mecham Ridge had been named by the Americans for Lieutenant Colonel Jesse Mecham of the First Battalion who had died early in the campaign. The Japanese owned the high ground, from where they harassed advancing

Americans in early November. All Clayton's battalion had to do was knock 'em off, which it did with brutal effectiveness. Clayton's men climbed the hill toward pillboxes, underground emplacements from which the Japanese poured fire on the Americans. Clayton's squad destroyed the enemy's protective guns and pitched grenades into the doomed soldiers' lair. The killing never stopped. Nearly eaten alive by leeches and mosquitoes, Clayton and the rest of F Company dug in for the night and fought off another crazed charge. By morning, he could have used dead bodies as steps and climbed the hill without touching the ground. In the daylight, American tanks smashed pillboxes as if they were a little boy's cardboard-box forts. As frightened Japanese soldiers ran like rabbits for higher ground, the men of F Company shot them down dead.

Whatever they had been before—truck drivers, college students, factory workers, or banjo-playing hillbillies who used to dress up like women on stage—these American men were now something completely different. After just a few weeks of war, they were killing machines, men who could kill other human beings as easily as they had done any job.

"Thou shalt not kill," so goes the sixth commandment, which even a bastard boy from The Hollow knew to be the God's-honest truth. But "Thou shalt not kill" doesn't mean what it says. The correct and proper translation, according to the scholars who know their Greek and their Hebrew (which I don't), should have been "Thou shalt not murder," which is a whole different ball game. Murder is when you kill somebody who doesn't deserve it, and we all know the enemy deserved it, whether they were Japanese or German. My grandpappy wasn't no murderer, my generation says. He was a damn hero. If you say different, this means war.

And war means this: Thou has to kill. It's the only commandment to live by.

Clayton's battalion took the hill.

* * *

If there is such a thing as drudgery in war, F Company was right in the thick of it. Move forward. Kill the enemy. Dig a foxhole. Repeat. This was the "mopping-up" phase, which means slaughtering the enemy until there's not enough of him left to clean up with a mop. When it wasn't fighting, Clayton's company dug muddy roads through the mountains, and the engineers built bridges in a combined effort to move troops more quickly to places where enemies needed to be mopped up. As they dug and dragged, the men of F Company occasionally stumbled upon enemy pill-boxes, which they mopped up with explosives, the biggest mop of all.

Filipino boys brought them food and supplies on the backs of lumbering carabao, enormous bovine-like creatures that resembled oxen to a boy from The Hollow who could still see the farmers plowing fields in preparation for corn and tobacco planting. Leyte, however, hardly seemed suitable for any kind of life to flourish.

A wholly different enemy also attacked the men in Leyte's steaming jungles—disease. Dengue fever, dysentery, jungle rot, and other tropical afflictions had felled thousands of soldiers, their bodies drenched with feverish sweats, blood occasionally running from their noses. The sickness and death of Leyte made it one of the biggest hellholes on earth.

In early November 1944, the entire 382nd Infantry Regiment had been taken off the front line—except for Clayton's battalion, the Second. Clayton and his buddies patrolled the hills for weeks, right up until Thanksgiving, when a shipment of canned turkey arrived on sleds pulled by carabao and horses. The thought of a prospective feast was mouthwatering, even if it was just turkey in a can. The stuff had spoiled, however. They buried the thermal canisters of rotten meat and sat down to a meal of C rations and were glad to have it. They had much to be thankful for. They were alive.

* * *

F Company had been on the front line for fifty days. Whenever possible, the men shed their muddy, stinking, wet uniforms and bathed in mountain streams. They were badly in need of a break, but once again they were called out to fight. Japanese ground forces and paratroopers had attacked an American airfield near the small town of Burauen in a daring night-time attack in the early hours of December 7, 1944, the third anniversary of Pearl Harbor.

The fighting was under way by the time Clayton's men arrived. It looked like a mob brawl. Both sides were confused amid the chaos. Japanese soldiers attacked while wearing American uniforms they had peeled from the backs of dead soldiers. Initially, the airfield's only defenders were a ragtag assortment of American engineers, clerks, and truck drivers, who at one point fought off 150 drunken Japanese attackers. Some airfield defenders were killed by their own .50-caliber machine guns, which had either been commandeered by the Japanese or had been mistakenly turned on Americans by Americans. Nobody ever knew for sure.

F Company joined the fight and swiftly helped regain the airfield. Once again, flares illuminated the night sky, giving the Americans a clear view of the rattled, desperate enemy, which F Company annihilated. The Japanese were almost finished on Leyte. Out at sea, the U.S. Navy destroyed the mighty Japanese fleet, despite the brand-new Japanese tactic of airborne kamikaze attacks. Other divisions had won their battles all across Leyte, just like the Deadeyes. The Japanese wasted so many resources—so many lives—in a failed mission to stave off the Americans that they drained their defenses for the rest of the Philippines. The islands of Luzon and Samar would soon fall into American hands, and the Philippines would become the staging ground for the war's eventual climactic fights. Although the war was far from over, dusk was approaching for the empire of the rising sun.

On December 25, 1944, MacArthur declared that all organized resistance on Leyte had ended. Men celebrated with Christmas feasts of beer and C rations. The crack of a rifle sent men scrambling, thinking a Japanese sniper was still on the loose. Turned out it was Captain Barron killing a wild boar, which the company cooks roasted and sliced for a well-earned holiday meal. Somebody did the math and figured that F Company had been on the front line for sixty-six consecutive days. There was more grim arithmetic: twenty members of their company had been killed, nearly 10 percent of the two hundred or so who had landed on A-Day. Young men who had been with the outfit since Oregon were dead, but their names, faces, and voices were still fresh in the minds of their buddies.

War had been harder than anything they could have imagined or trained for. The war games near Bend, Oregon, seemed like a church picnic by comparison. They had seen their pals blown to pieces and had smelled the stench of rotting flesh. When they wrapped up their work on Leyte, the Deadeyes were more than battle-tested, they were cocky sons of bitches.

They must have known, however, that this was just the beginning. They were still far away from their ultimate destination—mainland Japan. If the Japanese had fought this ferociously to defend an island chain a thousand miles from home, how hard would they fight to protect their beaches, their cities, and their very homes?

∙ ∙ ∙

When Clayton was an old man, I asked him about the injuries he sustained during the war.

"Well," he said, then paused. "I was *wounded* in the Philippines."

Message received. This is what happens when you win a war so your grandson will never be expected to fire a rifle at another human being. The grandson will grow up not knowing the difference between a wound and an injury. Injuries happen to rec-league softball players when they trip over second base. Soldiers are wounded. They are wounded by flying bullets and jagged pieces of metal from exploding shells. They are wounded by bayonets and trench knives. Their wounds are often gruesome, too horrible to look at, much less treat, which is why soldiers thanked God every day for the medics who saved life and limb by risking their own. When you're wounded, you earn a medal that could fit in the palm of your hand. You get a tall trophy for rec-league softball. Hardly seems right.

Papa Clayton kept his Purple Heart pinned to his army jacket, that is until the day he pulled the jacket out of the closet and discovered it riddled with moth-eaten holes. This was about the same time he went looking for the copy of his discharge and found it torn to pieces and stuffed inside his daughter's piggy bank. (This was also about the time my mother colored in Roy Rogers's white cowboy hat with a pencil.) He mailed the ripped pieces to the army along with a letter explaining what his little girl had done and asked if the army might replace it with a duplicate. A few weeks later, the army mailed back his ripped-up copy—all taped together. (No telling how many American tax dollars were spent on the Army's Department of Taping back in those days.) Clayton filed away his taped-up discharge and hung his medals and ribbons in a frame. His Purple Heart hung between his sergeant stripes and his Bronze Star. The frame also held his army portrait and the typewritten report of how he earned that Bronze Star, but that's getting ahead of the story.

Clayton was wounded—the first time—the day after Christmas, twenty-four hours after Leyte was declared secure. Small teams continued to root out the last of the Japanese resistance. Clayton was on point of a three-man patrol. By the time I got around to asking him he had forgotten who was with him, maybe it was Humphries and Clark. What he remembered was the smell of "them high-powered Jap cigarettes," probably opium, which some Japanese soldiers smoked to embolden themselves for battle and almost certain death. Clayton claimed he smelled smoke almost every time he came in close contact with the Japanese, which happened more frequently than he would have liked. As the patrol hacked its way through the thick jungles on northern Leyte, Clayton thought he smelled smoke—and where there's funny-smellin' smoke, there's trouble.

He signaled the men behind him to stop. He turned to them and mouthed something about "smoke" and to be alert. He stepped forward and hacked a large banana stalk about waist-high with his machete. The top of the plant dropped straight down as if it had been sucked down a hole. In its place stood "The Story of How Papa Clayton Got Shot in the Head."

The last thing Clayton remembered was the explosion of fire. He might have heard the noise from the machine gun, but he wasn't sure. He remembered the flame, then waking up in a field hospital. What actually happened was easy to sort out, because his two witnesses survived.

Standing behind the banana stalk had been a Japanese soldier with a "grease gun," a small, tommy-gun-like machine gun. The gunner opened up and expended most of a thirty-round clip right into Clayton's helmet, which was really too big for his small head and always fell over his eyes and nearly sat on his shoulders. The bullets buzzed between the helmet and helmet liner like killer bees. Bullets spit out from the back and front, and the top of the helmet exploded as if a volcano had erupted. This entire horrifying episode took about three seconds, and Clayton remembered none of it.

Clayton awoke in the field hospital, seriously wounded. He had a good-sized gash on the top of his head, and his neck and chin were badly sliced up. One bullet had passed through his neck and barely missed his jugular. Incredibly, that was it. A machine-gun bluster of thirty bullets fired directly at his head had resulted in a nasty, but treatable, neck wound, a few bad cuts, and a bad headache. Talk about lucky.

Just before he was shipped out to a hospital in New Guinea, Clayton received a get-well present from his buddies—his shot-up helmet. It looked like someone had tossed a grenade in it. It was riddled with bumps and lumps that looked like goiters, and the top was completely blown out.

"What'd y'all do to my helmet?" Clayton asked groggily. "Boy, I'm gonna get whoever done that."

"You don't have to do anything," one of his buddies assured him. "We made a good Jap out of him."

. . .

Clayton didn't keep the helmet, which was functionally useless. Its extra weight in a pack exceeded its sentimental value. He kept a photograph of it, but he lost it, so I never saw that picture. I saw the Purple Heart, though. It's still in the frame where he hung it, right next to the Bronze Star and the photograph of him in his army uniform.

While traveling through this world of sorrow
I'm trusting Lord in thee
That I may safely meet each trial
Oh Lord, remember me

—"REMEMBER ME," CLAYTON AND SAFORD'S FAVORITE
GOSPEL NUMBER WITH THE BLUE RIDGE ENTERTAINERS

Half a world away in the Hürtgen Forest, mail service was spotty. If anyone tried to let Saford know his twin brother had been wounded, he never got the message. Besides, he had a little problem of his own that was more pressing.

The Go-Devils became the Slow-Devils during that grim fall and winter of 1944–45, when the war seemed to stop cold. The entire Ninth Infantry Division was repulsed at the Roer River, where three regiments tried and failed to take the dams. Up north, the British-planned Operation Market Garden had failed in its attempt to outflank the Germans in the Netherlands and northern Germany. It fell to the Ninth Division to attack the Germans in the well-shielded, mystical Hürtgen Forest.

The Hürtgen must have seemed like a setting from the Brothers Grimm, except that instead of teeming with witches and trolls, the forest was flush with Nazis and panzers. The evergreen canopy shrouded the terrain in eerie perpetual darkness. Tanks and artillery were rendered practically useless. Men trudged forward on foot, up the slippery banks and down narrow paths. Saford slogged through the woods in the unenviable search for enemy positions. He moved slowly, tree to tree, looking and listening for Germans.

The solitude of the forest was pierced by the high-pitched whine of incoming mortars. Saford and his men scattered and fell to the ground as branches snapped and shells exploded just yards in front of them. Saford picked himself out of the mud and skedaddled down a hill just as a machine gun opened up. Bullets peeled bark from conifer trees and showered him with dead needles. In barely a minute, he was separated from his squad. He dropped to his belly and crawled toward a streambed as more shells rained down. Saford nuzzled himself against an embankment and waited there for several minutes, which became an hour, which became several hours, which became all night.

At dawn's first light, Saford arose from a sleepless night and climbed over the embankment above the streambed. He had lost his men and lost his way, mere yards from the German front. He took a minute to check his compass and get his bearings, then set out to find his outfit.

After several hours spent wandering in the woods, Saford was exhausted and starving. He had neither eaten nor slept in a day, and he was starting to hallucinate...perhaps the trolls and witches really would get him. Right around midday, he staggered into a sunlit clearing, where he saw a sad, gruesome sight: a dead American and a dead German lying just a few feet apart.

Saford walked over to the dead American and flipped him over. He felt around the dead man's torso, looking not for his dog tags or a last letter home, but for food. By now, Saford had long since gotten over the shock and sentimentality of seeing a dead person. He was an animal now, a wild boar rooting around the woods to survive, even if it meant taking the C rations off a fallen comrade.

He peeled the lid off a can of meat and potatoes with his can opener and proceeded to dig his fingers into the goop. He took the dead man's chocolate bars and cigarettes and looked for a place to sit. Finding no patch of dry ground in the dense, muddy woods, he plopped himself atop the dead German and ate his meal.

. . .

Saford made it back to his outfit, just as it was being pulled off the line and sent to Elsenborn, Belgium, to recuperate. The Go-Devils had been badly mauled during the initial phase of fighting that autumn. Now it was time for other American divisions to dive into the Hürtgen meat grinder.

On December 16, 1944, the Germans launched a surprise counterattack that smashed the Americans' V and VIII Corps and created the infamous bulge in the Allied lines. Voluminous books have been written about the Battle of the Bulge—and this ain't one of them. Those historic last two weeks of December 1944 have been studied extensively and chronicled exhaustively by scholars whose work I cannot supplement, other than to say that, just as on D-Day, Saford Hall was *almost* there. The Ninth was called to reinforce the bulging lines and stand against further German attacks to the north. The Ninth's regiments held at Monschau and the Elsenborn ridge. The Germans attacked again, but they were spent. The Allies closed in and trapped the beaten Nazi foot soldiers in January, cracking the seemingly impenetrable Siegfried Line at last.

By February, the Go-Devils were on the march. In their path lay German-guarded dams along the Roer River. Past them was the mighty Rhine. If they crossed the Rhine, they would win the war.

Four months had passed since the Ninth had first attempted to take the Roer's dams. Frozen in place during the winter stalemate, the division's advance thawed in February, and by month's end all three dams along the Roer were in Allied hands.

The crossing of the Roer, however, had not occurred. The Germans had succeeded in blasting the floodgates of two dams before losing control, which raised the Roer's level a good ten feet. Engineers could not lay the cables necessary for bridge construction across the raging river. Boats were swamped by the violent currents. At one point, somebody rigged a crossbow-like weapon and fired cables over the river to the opposite side. To make matters worse, German shells were still falling uncomfortably close for all those stationed along the riverbank. Something needed to be done quickly.

And that's how Saford got picked to swim across the Roer River.

Several men swam with cables draped around their bodies. Not all made it across. Saford, who had paddled through the brackish waters of Morocco when this whole mess had started more than two years before, slipped into a wet suit that he hoped would protect him from the icy waters of the angry Roer. He rigged the cable around his waist and waded out into the river with another soldier.

Saford paddled heroically against the current, which pushed him downstream with a force of fifteen miles an hour. He kicked and stroked, the cable adding even more resistance to his suicidal swim, until he could see the riverbank on the other side and then feel the rocky river bottom with his feet. He pushed himself against the current and fell to his hands and knees on muddy ground, gasping for oxygen as if he had just run ten marathons. He had made it.

The other man had not.

Saford Hall swam across the Roer River with a cable tied to his waist. I still can't get over that. The Saford Hall I knew was sickly, with weak lungs and bad eyesight. He wasn't even allowed to drive a car the last ten years of his life. He was sweet and meek, an old man who played the fiddle and told corny jokes and sang "I'm Back in the Saddle Again" to the delight of lifelong friends and fans. He did not swim across ice-cold raging rivers beneath rocket-filled night skies. He did not shoot pistols at Nazis at close range or slit men's throats or relieve a dead soldier of his last meal and eat it atop another dead man. Not the Saford I knew.

Which is to say I never really knew Saford at all. Even when he told me these war stories, I still viewed him as my cute little great-uncle who fought World War II like all the other cute little men of his generation—like Papa Clayton, for instance. Maybe it was because he didn't tell me everything, just those well-rehearsed adventure tales that he punctuated with a hillbilly cackle, which always seemed to lighten the gravity of the stories.

He was dead almost ten years before I finally got it. His story was not that of a sweet old man who played the fiddle. It was that of a strapping, cocky, courageous young man, much stronger and braver than I will ever be.

Saford Hall swam the Roer, and maybe the Rhine. He later told some family members that he was briefly captured near the end of the war, but quickly escaped from a makeshift prison camp during the chaos of the Germans' retreat and the advance of his own division.

He was at the famous Battle of Remagen. Well, almost. The Go-Devils crossed the Rhine on the night of March 8, 1945, one day after the Ninth Armored Division had accomplished the unthinkable by capturing the Ludendorff Bridge at the town of Remagen. The beaten, retreating Nazis poured all they had on the Ninth Infantry Division as it crossed the Rhine, the last major natural obstacle between the Allies and victory. Ten days later, the bridge collapsed after a German rocket struck nearby, killing twenty-eight Americans. By then, engineers had constructed other crossings, and the final push was on.

German towns fell into Allied hands like winnings pouring out of a slot machine. The Ninth Infantry Division captured ten towns one day, a dozen the next. Only the most fanatical Nazis stood up and fought. Hitler's well-trained SS resorted to firing antiaircraft guns at the unstoppable Go-Devils. German soldiers surrendered by the thousands. The Third Reich was collapsing.

On April 30, 1945, ten days after Hitler's last birthday, the Ninth Infantry Division met the Russians at the Elbe River. After a dismal winter that seemed to drag on eternally, April had flown past, which is what happens when an army is in the midst of a rout. The Germans were smashed, finished, kaput. Everyone on the American side wanted a piece of the fight. In March, the Ninth received its first black foot soldiers, men who accepted demotions in rank in order to get to the front. The African-American soldiers were so gung-ho, many of them went AWOL—not to get away from the fighting, but to get *closer* to it. One all-black squad neutralized a German tank that had blocked the Go-Devils' relentless advance.

On May 1, 1945; word came that Hitler was dead. The next day, Berlin fell to the Americans and the Russians.

Five days later, on May 7, 1945, Eisenhower ordered the end of all offensive operations. One minute after the church bells struck midnight on May 8, the war in Europe ended.

. . .

I do not know how Saford celebrated. Knowing Saford as I do now, maybe it's better that I don't. He didn't have long to soak it all in, because within three weeks of war's end, he was headed home. Some men were being sent to the Pacific, to help fight the Japanese. Not Saford. Drafted before Pearl Harbor, having killed even before the first guns fired upon the North Africa beaches, having fought across Sicily and Europe right into Germany, he had more than fulfilled his duty to Uncle Sam.

He left Europe on June 6, 1945—the one-year anniversary of D-Day—and arrived in the States on June 15. So many men were sent home, a week passed before his discharge was processed at Fort Meade, Maryland. From there he hopped a train to Roanoke, where he had some important business to take care of.

He had to pick up his car at the garage.

His old Buick had been mothballed since he had left Roanoke in 1941.

The car was in pretty sad shape when he saw it—all four tires had dry-rotted and needed replacing. But when Saford asked about the price of tires, he got answered with a question.

"You a doctor or a mail carrier?" the mechanic asked. "Only doctors and mail carriers can buy tires."

Rubber was still being rationed. Saford was incensed.

"Man, I've been gone for four years fighting for this country and you mean to tell me I can't get tires for my car?"

Only if he was a doctor or a mail carrier.

Saford called a mechanic he knew on Church Avenue, who fixed him up with four used tires. Two of them blew before he got out of town. He patched them and headed down the narrow road through Franklin County toward The Hollow.

He never called Dot. Never drove past her house. I never knew what happened between him and Dot after his return. Some members of the family say that he got a Dear John letter while he was overseas. Others say he came home wanting to be a free man after so many years spent in the country's service. Whatever the reason, that part of his life was over, as far as he was concerned. He tore on down the road on his four gimpy tires, a soldier boy finally headed home from the war—a war that was still not over for many American fighting boys, including Saford Hall's younger twin.

. . .

Clayton greeted 1945 in New Guinea, where he was recovering from the wounds he had received on Leyte. He loved the hospital, because it swarmed with army nurses who treated scores of wounded men from battle-torn islands across the South Pacific. Olive-drabbed women rolled up their sleeves and cleaned Clayton's wounds, changed his bandages, brought hot chow, and soothed his spirit. They were the first kind faces he had seen in months. For the rest of his life, he would speak fondly of them—I still remember his sermons about the "angels of mercy."

Soon, he was well enough to leave his hospital bed. Trouble was, no ships were headed back to Leyte anytime soon, so he was assigned to another outfit. Fighting had mostly died down in New Guinea, but pockets of Japanese resistance remained. Clayton thought he might get away with a few routine patrols, then hitch a ride back to the Philippines, where the Dead-eyes were cooling their heels and enjoying the sunshine after defeating the

Japanese. While his buddies in F Company passed the time between their shooting practice and meals by watching outdoor movies and swimming in the sea, Clayton strapped on his new helmet and headed into the jungles of New Guinea. Time to get back in the war.

His destination: the island of Biak. The Japanese had been run off this tiny island of coral and jungle months earlier, but an occasional sniper or straggler had to be cut down. The patrols, like every other jungle out-ing, were hot, sweaty, and miserable. The enemies were ubiquitous and fanatical—and those were just the mosquitoes. Clayton also got his first glimpse of native islanders, brown-skinned, grass-skirt-wearing men and women who emerged from hiding now that the shooting had stopped. He worried that they were headhunters.

The good news was that Clayton went on only two patrols on Biak. The bad news was why. During his second patrol, Clayton was hammered by a blinding headache. At first, he wondered if the pain had something to do with his head wounds. Sweat poured down his forehead and stung his eyes. He was dizzy and his pace slowed. A sergeant saw him dragging behind and stopped the patrol. He asked Clayton what the problem was.

By now, Clayton's teeth chattered, as if the strongest Arctic wind had blown away the jungle heat. He told the sergeant he would be all right. His head just hurt. The sergeant took one look at him and called for a medic.

"You've got malaria fever," the sergeant said. Clayton was loaded into a Jeep and driven back to camp. Within a few hours, he was back in the same hospital he had left just days earlier. At least he got to see the nurses again.

He was given quinine and other medicines to knock out the fever. He recovered well enough in a few days to get back in his boots and return to Leyte. The Deadeyes needed him.

. . .

The country boy from The Hollow rejoined F Company in the Philippines, where the Deadeyes waited to hear where they would be sent next. He was happy to see the familiar faces, and they were glad to welcome him back, even the funny-talking city boys. Clayton had grudgingly come to like the guys, even though he was a good five or six years older than the eighteen- and nineteen-year-old replacements who were filling the ranks of the battle-depleted company. He never bothered to learn most of the new guys' names. He called them "Young feller," just as he had called all the younger dudes since camp.

He even liked Fox, the hulking galoot from Illinois who picked on little guys and was always itching to fight. He was all right, Clayton decided, especially in battle. Near the end of the Leyte campaign, Clayton and Fox had been on a patrol that ran into a Japanese sniper. The shooter hid in a spider hole and occasionally popped out of the ground like a prairie dog to fire upon the patrol. Fox told Clayton to cover him as he sneaked around the sniper's position. When the sniper popped out again, Fox dragged the guy out of the hole by his rifle barrel. Then he beat the guy to death.

The Deadeyes were going to Japan. They all knew it and dreaded it.

Their mission sent them to the Ryukyu Islands, literally the "Southwest Islands." On March 6, 1945, the Ninety-sixth Infantry Division was told that its objective was to capture the largest of the Ryukyus, an island just 350 miles from the Japanese home island of Kyushu. An island called Okinawa.

The invasion would be called Operation Iceberg—a perfectly ironic military name for a mission that would bring all hell's fury.

. . .

F Company and the rest of the Deadeyes conducted training exercises through March, which consisted mostly of dress-rehearsal landings that introduced the new recruits to the fun and excitement of amphibious invasions. On March 27, 1945, F Company set sail aboard the troop transport USS *La Porte*. By now, every combat vet and green rookie had heard of Okinawa. On board the transports, soldiers were told that the Okinawa climate would be mild—much more comfortable than the jungles—that the people were of Chinese and Japanese lineage, and that the island had been independent before Japan annexed all of the Ryukyus in 1879 following negotiations with the Chinese that were arbitrated by—of all people—President Ulysses S. Grant.

Enemy strength on Okinawa was estimated to be more than 60,000. The Americans countered with 180,000 army troops and marines, plus the navy.

The night of March 31, 1945, the navy's biggest guns pounded the island. Destroying opposing forces on or near the beach was more important than the element of surprise. "Here we are, you bastards," the guns announced. Men attended chapel services on board the ships, and they read their army-distributed New Testaments. They were confident they would lick the Japanese. Hell, the Allies had run the Japs off every island they'd held. Why would Okinawa be any different? Sure, it's part of the enemy homeland, but still.

The Deadeyes were ready to finish this war. Things were going well in Europe. Maybe they'd get some reinforcements. Men came up with sayings like "Home alive in Forty-Five," "Back from the sticks in Forty-Six," and "Home or Heaven in Forty-Seven." Did the first saying have a remote chance of coming true?

For many—thousands, really—it did not.

A little bottle of liquor and a little rusty gun
Makes all of these young boys just think that they're grown

—"IF TROUBLE DON'T KILL ME, I'LL LIVE A LONG TIME,"
AS PERFORMED BY THE HALL TWINS

D-Day was taken. The term had been commonly used by the military to mark the scheduled start of any operation, but following the events of June 6, 1944, the name "D-Day" would forevermore be associated with Operation Overlord. The Okinawa invaders would have to choose another name for Operation Iceberg. So the commanders opted for L-Day, which, in the time-honored military tradition for completely misstating the situation, stood for Love-Day. The Japanese got it right, however. After three months of fighting, shelling, shooting, burning, killing, and dying that would lay an entire island and most of its inhabitants to waste, the Japanese had another name for the Battle of Okinawa: *"Tetsu no Ame."* The Typhoon of Steel.

The typhoon made landfall beneath a cloudless blue sky on April 1, 1945. The largest military task force ever assembled arrived aboard 1,300 ships that carried hundreds of thousands of men, a force that included six combat divisions and announced its presence with guns blazing, planes flying, and bombs dropping. F Company and the rest of the 382nd Regiment were held in reserve and would land several hours after the initial invasion. Clayton awoke to the voices of their division and battalion commanders, General James Bradley and Colonel Macey L. Dill, blasting over the ship's loudspeakers, wishing them good luck and God's blessings. The soldiers gulped down a breakfast of steak and reconstituted eggs, then went up on deck to watch the bombardment. Word came quickly that the 381st and 383rd had landed against "light resistance." It was time. Clayton and the rest of the 382nd disembarked shortly after 11 a.m. and headed for the skinny island that was sixty miles long and barely fifteen miles across at its widest. Until now, American forces in the Pacific had been called "liberators" for chasing the Japanese out of such places as Guadalcanal, New Guinea, and the Philippines. This day, they called themselves "conquerors," for they were hitting the Japanese on their home turf. It was Easter Sunday, a holy day for celebrating life, hope, and peace—which must have seemed like the worst April Fool's Day joke ever pulled.

The landing craft churned to the beach without harassment from bullets or shells. The amphibious vehicles crossed over a reef and an ancient defensive seawall and spilled their bellies full of soldiers onto the sand. Since it was Easter, the army had provided the F Company men with a lovely holiday meal of more rancid turkey packed in white thermal cans. The men strapped the cans to their backs, along with their rifles, grenades, knives, pistols, and other weapons of really massive destruction. When they hit the beach, however, they were told to drop the cans. The white cans against olive drab made perfect bull's-eyes for any sniper. The army might have had this invasion business down pat, but it couldn't do holiday meals for squat.

By 11:45 a.m., Clayton and the rest of F Company had landed at Brown Beach No. 2. The weather was lovely. The temperature was in the sixties, and a cool coastal breeze swept the bomb-cratered beach. One soldier called it "the most American weather we've seen." Within a few hours, the company had moved inland about 1,700 yards without detecting hide nor hair of the enemy.

"I've already lived longer than I thought I would," a young private exclaimed.

· · ·

In The Hollow, the peach trees would have burst into fluorescent pink blossoms, followed closely by snowdrifts of apple blooms. Had it been just two years since Clayton had last seen his mother and his old home place? Had it been four years since he and Saford sang together on the radio? A lifetime had passed since then. In Japan, the cherry trees were in bloom. The next time fruit trees bloomed in both countries, the war would be over, a fact inconceivable to the men who had just landed on an island where nearly every tree had been—or would be—blasted into sawdust and wood chips.

. . .

All the Deadeye regiments had landed near the middle of the long island and were now headed south. The marines fought to the north. Late on the operation's fourth day, F Company met its first real resistance. The Japanese felled trees across the road to Kamiyama. Two accompanying tanks had been knocked out by mines. Battalion commander Colonel Cyril D. Sterner moved his men and tanks across an open field and sealed caves and pillboxes, killing nearly 150 enemy soldiers.

Clayton and several soldiers stopped in front of a tank to await orders from F Company commander Captain James R. Barron. The captain had become a father figure to the "Fighting Foxes" of F Company. Barron had proven himself a terrific officer, a no-nonsense, GI-all-the-way guy who didn't play favorites among his men. He was a soldiers' officer. The men gathered around him as he looked through his binoculars. They waited eagerly for his instructions.

As Barron fiddled with his binoculars, a sniper's bullet struck him in the forehead. He died instantly. Clayton saw the whole thing. A couple of the guys saw the sniper in an open field and chased and riddled him with M1 fire. F Company had walked smack-dab into the Japanese front line and lost the only company commander it had known since Oregon. The real battle of Okinawa had begun.

. . .

The Japanese strategy was obvious—they were going to fight a defensive battle from the abundant high ground and inflict devastation on the Americans. The commanders of the mighty Japanese Thirty-second Army knew that they probably could not save Okinawa from the Americans, but they were going to make damn sure the Americans paid a high price for taking it. So high, in fact, that they would think twice before attempting a full-scale invasion of Japan. The Japanese soldiers were ordered to prefer death to surrender, to fight until the last man had either been killed or had killed himself.

Rifle platoons manned the front line. For years, the army had filled the rifle platoons of its infantry divisions with the less educated and the less wealthy—that is, guys like Clayton. The smart boys were sent to officer training school or the Army Air Corps or logistical teams. As F Company eyed the rocky, deadly hills before it, its ranks included guys from the wrong side of the tracks, farm boys, and one bastard from The Hollow. They would endure the brunt of the shelling and, if they survived and didn't crack up, they would meet the enemy head-on. They were the frontline grunts who, as a brigadier general once explained, had nothing to look forward to but "death, mutilation, or psychiatric breakdown." My Papa Clayton was one of those guys. The disposable ones.

Enemy machine gunners raked entire platoons of Americans from their high positions. F Company was pinned down at the bottom of a ridgeline they called Porter Hill. Supporting tanks were slowed by mines. The shelling continued.

The only way to advance was with help from the navy's big guns. However, the navy was engaged in a fight to the death with kamikazes and the Japanese navy. If the Americans lost the battle at sea, the men on the island would lose their support and be stranded. Finally, they received enough tank and artillery support to move on the hill and capture it. One hill down, but how many more to go?

The rock and shale were almost impervious to entrenching tools. Wasn't there a decent place to dig a foxhole in the Pacific? If it wasn't swamps in the Philippines, it was rocks in Okinawa. Clayton dug a hole close to the other guys, who burrowed in as deep as they could, then watched for enemy infiltrators. Clayton looked to his left and saw a Jap crawling toward Private Lloyd Jones's foxhole. He turned and fired quickly, right above Jones's head, and killed the enemy. Before Jones knew what the hell had happened, he saw the dead Jap rolling down the hill.

"Jesus!" he hollered. "You saved my life!"

Clayton didn't say a word. Jones sputtered words in adrenaline-fueled bursts.

"You killed him! You just saved my life! I'm gonna remember you in my prayers tonight, good buddy!"

"Thank you," Clayton finally said. "I'm gonna need it."

. . .

Forward, and now upward, the men of F Company moved, but when the Japanese weren't shelling the hell out of them, they were pitching grenades into their foxholes. Then came a roar from the heavens like nothing they had ever heard.

They were shells, enormous shells larger than anything that had ever been launched against them. The first one shook the ground with the violence of an earthquake when it hit and left a crater that would have swallowed a pair of tanks. Men wondered if those navy bastards were shelling them with their big guns by mistake. No, the barrage was coming from the hills directly in front.

They were 320 mm mortars, mammoth projectiles five feet long and more than a foot wide. These flying "boxcars" were terrifying, but the men soon learned that the shells buried themselves too deeply into the ground to cause much peripheral damage—a direct hit was its only effective strike. They also traveled relatively slowly through the air, allowing a man a chance to flee their impact (unless they were fired at night). Still, the concussion threw rocks and dirt clods and rattled the bones of every man and beast. Lizards as long as your arm flopped into foxholes to escape the earth-shaking pounding. Men wigged out and fled their holes, running and screaming that they couldn't take it anymore. Those who stayed prayed there wasn't a boxcar up there with their names on it. The collective psyche of F Company was near the breaking point. Just when things looked bleakest, it started to rain. Shrouded in ponchos and drowning in the merciless fire that flowed from a rocky peak, the men stared into the abyss. Then they learned President Roosevelt was dead.

Clayton was hunkered down in a muddy foxhole when word got to him. All the men were shocked at the news. Most had maintained their faith in Roosevelt's leadership; some were doubters, but few were as enthusiastic about Truman. Clayton thought that Truman was a dud. But what did it matter who was president? They were the ones in the foxholes. They were about to do the hard work again.

. . .

Clayton's C rations came with four cigarettes, which he smoked in succession to calm his nerves. On April 19, 1945, F Company and the rest of the battalion abandoned their foxholes beneath protective mortar fire: "The Big Push" was on. The Japanese had to be knocked off those hilltops if the operation was to succeed. Clayton was on the killing sides of those hills that day. Whether he killed a man with his bare hands or with a bayonet in the bloody foxholes near Tanabaru I cannot say. But I can tell you what he told me years later:

> *One side of the bayonet cuts, under the bottom. It's got a point out here. We had that point so sharp on our bayonets you could drag your finger across and it would cut your finger. We was gonna be sure that when we hit a Jap with a bayonet it went in him. What I didn't realize was how much trouble it was to get it out. When you'd stick one with a bayonet and go on in him, you know, you can drag that scutter. When you go to try and pull that bayonet out, you can drag him. You can drag that Jap with it. It creates a suction. We learned quick as we hit 'em with a bayonet, we hit 'em with a foot kick, too. Kick 'em off.*

Listening to Papa Clayton, whom I knew as a country preacher / hillbilly singer / cornpone comedian extraordinaire, give advice on how to properly extract a bayonet from another human being gave me a healthy dose of uncomfortable, "wish-I-didn't-know-*that*" reality. It was sort of like finding out that your wife is actually a man. Did I really know this guy? (I'm talking about my grandpa.) It's easy to lull yourself into believing that your grandpappy wasn't the type of guy to kill a person, that all the killing was done by the other guys, and your pawpaw merely ran bravely across the fields of fire and liberated oppressed people and marched in victory parades and lived happily ever after, when the truth is that he knew how to kick a man off a bayonet. There's only one way you know something like that.

◦ ◦ ◦

F Company took its hills after close fighting that included killing with those bloody bayonets. For their work, the men were taken off the front line and rewarded with ten days of sports and music. The division band traded M1s for clarinets and trumpets and played fourteen shows. Soldiers played baseball and volleyball during the day and relaxed at night with a movie—if you can call watching a movie that is interrupted by nine air-raid sirens relaxing.

The newsreels were entertaining, although not quite the same way. The men got a real kick out of the film clips from Europe, which showed soldiers dancing with fräuleins, staying at lovely chateaus, and skiing. Clayton and his buddies could only cuss under their breath. He looked for Saford in those newsreels.

To top it all off, when the announcement came on May 8, 1945, that war in Europe had ended, the men of F Company were strapping on their packs and heading back to the front.

"Good," the men said. "Now maybe they'll send some of those bastards over here and help us. They need to see what real fighting is like."

And that's how F Company celebrated V-E Day. Instead of riding victory parade floats, the Deadeyes trudged grimly down roads of ankle-deep mud toward the sound of artillery, passing the bloated, maggot-ridden corpses of Japanese soldiers along the way.

. . .

It seems cruel—if not downright sadistic—to spoil a guy with a week's worth of hot chow, ball games, love letters, movies, band concerts, and showers, then turn around and truck him right back into a combat zone. Talk about a shock to the system. Then again, maybe that's the only way to get him to fight. Give him a taste of what he's been missing. Let him remember the way of life he's trying to preserve. Remind him of his loved ones, the ones who miss him terribly and desperately long for him to come home in one piece. And let him know in very specific terms that the only way he will ever get back to the life he once knew is if he chases those lousy, stinking, goddamned Japs off those rocks and helps win this war.

F Company was one of the outfits charged with cracking the Naha-Shuri Line, a seemingly impenetrable bastion of Japanese defenses fortified by hidden caves and heavy artillery. The men reached the top of Dick Hill but were stopped by grenade-tossing Japanese on the reverse slope. They dug in for the night and responded grenade for grenade. Clayton covered his foxhole with his poncho and staked all four corners to the ground. The cover served two purposes: the poncho kept him dry, and grenades bounced off it.

As the battle of Okinawa completed its second month, American casualties of a different sort were piling up: the "nonbattle casualty." Infantrymen suffering from "combat fatigue" (or battle fatigue, shell shock, neuropsychiatric fatigue, or any other term the military used before posttraumatic stress disorder came into vogue) numbered 7,762 on Okinawa, according to the army's later studies. Strong men crumbled beneath battlefield stress. One F Company soldier cracked from the strain and ran from his foxhole toward the Japanese line, screaming and firing a machine gun before he was shot dead. Another man ran crying in the opposite direction, back to camp.

The number of combat fatigue cases was significantly higher on Okinawa than anywhere else in the Pacific, and there was a reason for that: all the goddamned shelling.

The Japanese had saved it all up for Okinawa. On other islands, they had fended off invaders with 105 mm mortars, which caused little physical or psychological damage. Here, though, the shells were two and three times larger, and there seemed to be a bottomless supply. Heavy artillery exploded constantly around the Deadeyes. Men lay in foxholes like living corpses in graves and took everything the Japanese threw at them, suffering the kinds of wounds that would hurt worse in years to come, the psychological kind for which the army doesn't hand out medals.

Another day, another hill to take. Hen Hill should have driven them all insane. F Company was repeatedly driven back by rifle fire, grenades, and mortars. A steady rain fell that night and didn't stop. No one moved a muscle for three days, until Clayton's platoon attempted to take Hen. They didn't make it. Clayton got almost to the top of the hill, so close to the top he could have dug a tunnel to the other side and shook hands with the enemy, but he was greeted with bullets and grenades. The men scampered back down and dug holes in the mud where they would remain for five more days, while grenades fell with the rain.

By now, F Company was a patchwork of war-torn veterans and green replacements. One of the new guys was a Tennessee kid named Raymond Jenkins, who ended up sharing some foxhole time with Clayton. Jenkins was young, eager, and understandably nervous. The grizzled veteran didn't have much to say—old guys didn't cozy up to the replacements. Their instructions to the green guys were simple: Keep your mouth shut and your eyes open, and, above all, don't foul up and get me killed.

But Jenkins was OK. He was a country boy who loved hillbilly music, and he reminded Clayton of other boys from the hills. Clayton still talked to Boone and Humphries, his buddies since Oregon, even though they were dug in with other guys. During those miserable days wallowing in the mud at the bottom of Hen Hill, the men talked about what they were going to do once this war was over. Boone had a grand plan. He was going to be a radiator repair man back home in North Carolina. Humphries wanted to get back to his wife, the girl he had married on furlough after his first choice had married somebody else.

Clayton, well, his prospects didn't look so hot. His banjo-playing gig was in jeopardy, considering that his boss had been killed in a car wreck. Maybe he and Saford could form a group of their own, just like in the old days, when they were country boys primed for the big time. They could lead their own group, make records, get rich, and have any girl they wanted. He could hear the crowds, the applause....

Well, enough of that. The rain let up. The order had come for Clayton's platoon to take the hill. Armed with rifles, grenades, and satchel charges, the platoon moved up the muddy slope. The men were near the top when enemy snipers opened up. The other platoons picked off the snipers as Clayton's group continued its advance. Grenades from the other side halted them momentarily, and more bullets zipped above their heads, but they pressed on to the top. Just before reaching the peak, the platoon lobbed several grenades toward the enemy positions. Unlike the Japanese tosses, the American grenades found their marks and forced the Japanese to leave exposed trenches and seek refuge in their caves and pillboxes. Battle-hardened and tested during too many combat actions to remember, Clayton went over the top.

A slithering line of men crashed over the hill like an ocean wave, washing down the other side and hitting the enemy with grenades and satchel charges. Fighting broke out across the entire ridgeline, as elements of different companies hurled themselves at the enemy. Now would have been the perfect time for the Japanese to surrender. The Deadeyes had heard rumors of enemy surrender—it sounded like it happened all the time in Europe, where entire companies of Germans threw up their hands and were afforded the comforts of American custody. Hot chow, showers, warm clothes, maybe even an all-expenses-paid trip to the States where they would serve their imprisonment picking apples in Virginia orchards. All of this awaited the Japanese, if only they'd just surrender.

Instead, they retreated to their caves and pillboxes and made a final stand. They would inflict as much carnage on the invading Americans as possible. When they could kill no more enemies, they would kill themselves—and anyone around them—by holding grenades to their chests, a "poor man's hara-kiri," the Americans called it. The military rulers of imperial Japan

188-IF TROUBLE DON'T KILL ME

had taught their soldiers that death was preferable to surrender. The Japanese army did not even bother to set up medical stations for their wounded. Those not well enough to fight would commit suicide. The Americans, they said, were dogs, barbarians who executed prisoners, murdered innocent civilians, and raped women. Even the citizens of Okinawa had been instructed to kill themselves and their families rather than become the slaves of the savage Americans.

The Americans obliged their enemies' desire to die on the battlefield. They killed the Japanese that had not made it back to the caves. They sealed others inside pillbox tombs with explosives. The ones who escaped and fled down the hill were cut down like rye stalks. If the Japanese expected savagery, the Americans would not disappoint. One man from G Company, Clarence Craft of Santa Ana, California, single-handedly killed thirty Japanese and was awarded the Medal of Honor.

And when the killing was over, the Americans did what all brave, honorable, decent soldiers had done throughout the Pacific war: They scavenged the carcasses for souvenirs. Men raced one another to be first to reach piles of dead Japanese, where they took flags and hand-stitched scarves from the waists of the dead. They disarmed corpses of their weapons, their firearms, their sabers. They relieved them of jewelry, the precious family heirlooms that had been given to war-going sons for luck. The scavenging became fuel for the imperial government's propaganda machine, which desperately needed to churn out new recruits for the futile Japanese cause. All over Japan, women, children, and old men learned to handle ancient weapons such as pikes and spears, and some even learned how to detonate explosives. They would be ready for those American dogs.

Clayton was not above looting the dead. He came away with a Japanese sword, a few medals, and some other trinkets that he kept in his duffel bag back at base camp. Lifting a few novelties off dead men who had tried to kill him seemed a minor sin compared with the butchery he had witnessed and carried out.

One day while on patrol, Clayton smelled a rank odor of decaying flesh. He looked around and saw no dead Japs—a rarity on an island where bloated corpses were more plentiful than fieldstones. (There was a story about a poor American greenhorn who had slipped and slid face-first down a muddy hill, and when he stopped at the bottom he discovered his pockets had scooped up pounds of maggots.) But the odor Clayton smelled emanated from the guy in front of him. When Clayton asked him what stunk so bad, the fellow took off his pack and pulled out his collection of gold-capped Japanese teeth, flesh and bone still attached, that he had carved out of the mouths of dead men.

. . .

As the Deadeyes prepared to deliver the mortal blow to the Japanese, the division had been fighting with little rest for more than two months. The men were the embodiment of misery—wet, wounded, tense, and constantly under siege. Their once ruddy visages had melted into classic dogfaces—unshaven, baggy-eyed, deep-lined, and weary. But it wasn't over yet. One more ridgeline loomed. They were beginning to learn that there were twice as many enemy troops as had been estimated when the battle began.

Two steep escarpments bookended a mass of hills near Okinawa's narrow southern tip. F Company would attack a peak called Yuza-Dake, a two-hundred-foot slope of coral that crouched like a boxer on the western flank of hills. To the east was the taller Yaeju-Dake escarpment, which would be left for the Seventh Infantry Division. The two peaks and connecting hills formed a natural saddle-shaped wall for the Japanese defenses, which numbered more than thirty-thousand. This was the final line that had to be cracked. Once it was rubbed out, nothing would hold the Americans back.

The first men to the top were fired upon by snipers. The rest of the company made it to the top without a scratch. The plateau was narrow, green, and adorned with a few trees. The company moved west to leave room for the rest of the battalion to complete its ascent. The men had only gone about fifty yards when all hell broke loose again.

. . .

Clayton never had many buddies in the army, which was probably a good thing, considering how many of those buddies died.

Surely, he had more friends in the service than he remembered as an old, ailing man. With just a month to live, though, he mentioned only three: Humphries, Jones, and Boone. They were all killed on Okinawa.

Humphries got it first. The slow-talking Ozark ridge runner was killed in a hail of bullets that met the company as it moved on the escarpment. Boone, Clayton's trusted buddy from North Carolina who remembered the Roy Hall band on WBIG and who wanted to be a radiator mechanic, was killed later on patrol. Jones died either from a sniper's bullet or artillery. Clayton could not remember, nearly six decades later. He just knew they were all dead.

F Company was under new leadership during this mission. Cledith Bourdeau had Captain Barron's old job as company commander. Bourdeau, a dark-headed, handsome Californian with a dazzling smile, had come over from first Battalion. Clayton's platoon had a new leader, as well, first Lieutenant Donald Seibert, a young replacement with no combat experience who had joined the company in the midst of the Okinawa battle. Clayton had his doubts about Seibert. Why wouldn't he? The platoon had cycled through nameless lieutenants who all seemed to crumble when the shooting started. Now, here comes a guy from the States who thinks he can lead a platoon of men who've been on the front line in two major battles.

Seibert, however, turned out to be a hell of a leader. He led the company to the top of the Yuza escarpment, where they were stopped behind an earthen berm by murderous sniper fire. Clayton saw a radio operator take a bullet between the eyes. It seemed that every foot of this hellhole would require a soldier's sacrifice.

Seibert hollered, "Let's move out!" Clayton and the others started to climb over the berm and were immediately soaked with fire: machine guns, rifles, small arms—the Japs hit them with everything, maybe even a rock or two. Seibert ordered the men back over the wall to safety.

Seibert refused to send his men back out into the field until they got support, which came in the form of a tank that made short work of the Japanese machine-gun nests, opening the door for the platoon to cross the berm and work across the open field.

The end was in sight; it had to be. The soldiers could look at a map, see they were nearing the tip of the island, and understand the Japanese were running out of places to hide. Trouble was, tens of thousands of enemy troops had fallen back to the south, making the last few miles of southern Okinawa the most dangerous place on earth. The Japanese command was largely intact, as well. They would not let their men surrender.

F Company took no prisoners, except for pitiful, straggling columns of Okinawan civilians desperate to flee the killing fields. Clayton had seen hundreds of civilian corpses strewn across the cratered, rocky land-scape. Most were women and children. Every available man had been dra-gooned into service by the Japanese. Hundreds of hapless people, mothers and children among them, had been caught in the murderous crossfire of the no-man's-land between the American and Japanese guns. Others were killed by Japanese soldiers when they would not abandon their hid-ing places inside the tombs or caves that the fighters sought to occupy. Still others died by their own hand. Following the orders from Japanese commanders and from the imperial government, entire families commit-ted suicide rather than be captured by the ruthless American soldiers. The real reason for such a wicked command was not to encourage honorable death, but rather to keep the population from giving critical information to the Americans. Many frightened families were given grenades to assist with the final act.

So they died. Clayton saw them as he worked his way to the sea. The sight of the mangled, decaying bodies of innocents was heartbreaking, even to a soldier who had long ago become inured to the shock of death, the smell of rotting flesh, and the immoralities of killing. He could not have known that he had not even seen the worst of it.

F Company tramped down the Yuza escarpment and plowed ahead toward the town of Aragachi. After a day of dodging bullets and blowing up caves, the Americans dug foxholes on the outskirts of a field. Just after nightfall, a few men heard rustling in the field. Another banzai charge? Hadn't the Japs abandoned that idiotic tactic? Flares burst above the land-scape but revealed nothing. After the flares burned out, the soldiers heard more rustling. Someone gave the order to fire, and a hail of bullets ripped across the field. After a few seconds of silence, a low moaning sound ema-nated from the area, followed by the most sickening sound the men had ever heard on a battlefield. Worse than the shouts of a banzai charge or the scream of a 320 mm shell.

They heard a baby crying.

No one knew what to do. Nothing in the field manual addressed the care of babies on a battlefield. Some men claimed it was a trick, a Jap ruse to lure them out of their foxholes and slaughter them. Others worried that the wails would drown out the sound of any approaching Japs. No one had a clue what to do. Then another sickening sound: a long machine-gun burst.

Then the most heartbreaking sound of all. Silence.

• • •

Papa Clayton was in a foxhole that night, probably close enough to have heard the baby's cries. This was a war story he never shared with any of us. I discovered it in another soldier's memoir. Papa Clayton would've been right there, hearing the cries, then the bullets, then nothing. I don't know how you get over something like that. He probably never did.

I can't get over it, either, and I wasn't even there. I can empathize with his reticence. Today, I will hug my daughter close and kiss her many times and tell her I love her. If my wife asks me what I wrote about today, I will not tell her, because I do not want to talk about it.

• • •

The Japanese would not give up. Their backs were against the ocean, they had lost tens of thousands of men, but still they resisted, harassing the Americans with small-arms fire. The Americans never slowed, plowing ahead to the outskirts of a small, bombed-out village where the Japanese were prepared to make a final stand. The village was called Aragachi, a name Clayton would remember until the day he died in his living room while waiting for that tomato sandwich.

The Deadeyes had shelled the hell out of Aragachi, setting ablaze the thatched roofs of wooden and rock huts. The village was infested with hundreds of enemy troops and an unknown number of civilians. By the time F Company arrived under clouds of phosphorus smoke on the evening of June 20, 1945, the village resembled ruins unearthed by an archaeological dig.

On June 21, the soldiers chaperoned mighty Sherman tanks into the rubble of the village. Infantrymen pointed out Japanese emplacements, and tanks responded with long streams of napalm-enhanced flame that incinerated the enemy. Japanese soldiers, some engulfed in flames, ran into the open only to be mowed down by M1-toting foot soldiers. Bullets flew from behind every rock and fallen house. F Company moved through the heart of the village, blasting and burning anything that moved. The men even employed an antiquated, yet effective, battlefield tactic by forming a long skirmish line of a dozen or more men, marching shoulder to shoulder through the center of the village. The formation resembled an old-fashioned Revolutionary War–era battle line, except these soldiers were armed with high-powered automatic weapons instead of muskets. The marching machine gunners swept their fire from side to side. Browning automatic rifle marksmen fired directly ahead. When these groups reloaded, the M1 riflemen, Clayton included, opened up. The company rolled ahead like a murderous bulldozer, forcing the Japanese forever backward.

Near the middle of the village, Clayton saw trouble on his left. A machine gun opened up on his squad and a tank. Clayton ran behind the tank and reached for the phone mounted on the back that allowed communication with the tank crew, but the phone had been blown off. He waved his arms frantically in hopes that the gunner would see him. He hollered, "Machine gun at nine o'clock!" Just then, he felt a whack against his right shin as if he'd been struck with a baseball bat. The tank spun quickly to the left and Clayton stumbled to the right and belly-flopped onto a pile of palm leaves and sticks that gave way like a floor caving in. He had fallen into a Japanese trench. Before he knew what had happened, a couple of Japanese heads rose from out of the leaves five feet in front of him... then a couple more... and a couple more.

And that's how it happens. One minute, you're alive, flailing in the cauldron of battle. Fighting, fighting, always fighting. A few more days, that's all you need, and you will have made it through. You will have survived this brutal war. You will live to see your home again. Your mother's worn and worried face, which you have not seen for so many years, will melt into sobs upon the return of her son, her brave son, gone all this time to fight for such a noble, divine cause. You will be celebrated as a hero for fighting this good fight, you will marry, and you will raise a family. If only you survive. But then it happens. Some son of a bitch from a wretched place called The Hollow falls right on top of you. Worse yet, he lands on his knees and elbows with his M1 pointing right at you, and you, armed with enough explosives to stop a tank, don't have so much as a pistol or a knife or any small weapon that could easily kill this man. So you do the only thing you can. You die.

Clayton opened up into the knot of Japs crouched in the trench. He emptied his eight-round clip and killed eight men in a matter of seconds.

The official citation for Clayton's Bronze Star award reported that Clayton was aided by at least two other men in killing the eight Japanese troops, whose intent most likely was to stop the tank. Other descriptions from that day mention the story of several soldiers killing a trenchful of Japanese. The citation reads:

*For heroic service in connection with military operations against the
enemy on Okinawa Island on 21 June 1945. While protecting a tank
which was supporting the attack of our troops upon the town of Aragachi, Sergeant (then Private First Class) Hall and two others killed
eight Japanese soldiers intent on neutralizing the tanks. The tank with
the three accompanying Infantrymen approached a ditch in which Sergeant Hall spied eight Japanese soldiers with demolition charges, hand
grenades and knee mortar shells, intended for the tank's destruction.
Sergeant Hall, with utter disregar [sic] for his personal safety, and
with full realization of the danger from this type of fire, ran to the
ditch, followed by the other two men, stood above and fired down into
the enemy engaging in a close up battle with them until the enemy were
all killed. His heroic service saved the tank and facilitated the accom-
plishment of the company's mission.*

Clayton always, *always*, contended that he fell into the trench. That
doesn't mean he got it completely right, but I believe him. I also accept the
army version that two other men were there. They just never fell into the
trench. Clayton did and he was the only man to climb out of that trench
alive, to eventually raise a family that would one day produce the likes of
me. Some days, I can't shake the notion that I should have made a whole
lot more of myself.

Right before tumbling into the ditch, Clayton had been shot in his lower
leg, but the wound required only a bandage. The day after Clayton's heroics, Okinawa was declared secure. The skirmishes, however, did not end.
The company began the mopping-up phase. A mop could never cleanse
the stench of death and devastation that had swallowed Aragachi, though.
On the day Clayton killed the eight enemy soldiers, the Ninety-sixth division's historian, Captain Donald Mulford entered the decimated village
and wrote the following:

*Aragachi was a living, stinking testimonial to the horror that war
brings to a civilian population. The men who of necessity had laid it
to waste were Americans, and though they hated the Japanese soldier,
they spared the natives whenever it would not endanger their own lives
to do so. But the natives here had been caught, partly by the force of*

circumstance and partly by fear of advancing Americans, a fear bred of constant propaganda by the Japanese Army.

Consequently they huddled in their holes, refusing to give up until burned or blasted out—some killing themselves and their children rather than face the horrors they had been led to expect. As morning came on the 21st, the town lay burned and broken under the hot sun with the sickly smell of death hanging like an unseen mist over the rubble. Old men, women, and children dressed in tattered black kimonos were herded to the rear by the dozens. One had to walk carefully, for the dead were everywhere.

Against the base of a stone wall was the naked body of an infant about a year old. No one seemed interested except the hundreds of flies that swarmed over it. There was little noise except for the occasional zing of a die-hard sniper's bullet and the distant chatter of machine guns.... For Aragachi, the war was over. The little town had paid the price for the empire lust of the Tokyo war lords.

And my Papa Clayton was there.

. . .

The army pushed southward like a massive press, squeezing thousands of innocents and many more frenzied enemy soldiers into a pocket of death, caught between the advancing forces and the sea. The estimated number of civilian dead has varied over the years, but most experts figure that at least 100,000 Okinawans perished, perhaps as many as 150,000. Even in the final days of the fighting, families continued to commit suicide rather than be captured by the bloody Americans.

For more than sixty years, the Japanese government has downplayed the role its former military commanders played in urging civilians to take their own lives. In 2007, the government began watering down its history textbooks for schoolchildren. This outraged Okinawans, including those who had lived through the battle and remembered well the military's gruesome instructions. They protested in crowds 100,000 strong, approximately one protestor for every civilian dead. They knew the truth.

. . .

I have read that Okinawa's Peace Memorial Park and museum is located atop breathtaking bluffs that offer panoramic views of the ocean and the neighboring cliffs. I've never seen it myself. I have long known that one of the ironies of terrible battles is that they are often fought in the most beautiful places—the rolling battlefields at Gettysburg, Pennyslvania, and Sharpsburg, Maryland, for example. Left to nature, the landscape heals itself; grass grows on hills where men died, and trees and bushes sprout from death trenches.

Those eight-hundred-foot cliffs are where many people—Japanese soldiers, Okinawan civilians, mothers, children—jumped to their deaths near the end of the battle. Even more died farther south. Their names are among the more than two hundred thousand inscribed on the Cornerstone of Peace, a series of black granite markers that form interlocking walls that crisscross the park. In photographs, the cornerstone reminds me of the Vietnam Veterans Memorial Wall in Washington, D.C., except with quadruple the number of names.

. . .

By battle's end, Clayton hated the Japanese with a passion. Then again, so did every other Deadeye. Clayton thought nothing of killing Japanese soldiers wherever he ran into them during the mopping-up phase. For the first time, large numbers of enemy troops were surrendering. A few handfuls at first, then scores, and finally hundreds and thousands of loincloth-wearing Japanese soldiers emerged from the sugarcane fields and rice paddies of southern Okinawa. Personally, Clayton didn't much care for taking prisoners.

Shortly after the Aragachi fight, he and another soldier kept watch over a small stream where a few Japanese had been observed—and killed—gathering water. Clayton saw a strange-looking woman he was sure was a Japanese solider in a woman's clothes. Clayton crept up behind and hollered. The person spun around quickly and pulled a pistol from his clothes. Clayton killed the cross-dressing Japanese soldier with one shot. Next, he probably frisked him for souvenirs.

Nearly nine months had passed since he had killed his first enemy soldier. He had been so scared then, stumbling upon a Jap in the jungles of the Philippines, that he almost vomited after killing the man. Remorse had long ago become a casualty of the war. Every day was like going to work. His job was to shoot Japs.

. . .

The bloody math is incomprehensible. The Allies (mostly Americans) killed more than 100,000 Japanese fighters. American losses have been recalculated several times over the years, with a total just over 14,000 generally accepted as a fair accounting of the dead and missing. More than half of those were soldiers, the rest marines and sailors. Tenth Army commander Lieutenant General Simon Bolivar Buckner, Jr., was killed, the highest-ranking U.S. officer to die from enemy fire during World War II. Brigadier General Claudius Easley was also killed on Okinawa. The top two Japanese commanders killed themselves.

Then there are the poor, innocent civilians. Okinawa was believed to have had a population of about 300,000 when 1945 dawned. By the end of the fighting, fewer than 200,000 were left alive. On a sliver of an island barely detectable on most schoolhouse globes, the combined number of American, Japanese, and Okinawan dead topped 250,000. F Company lost 40 men, twice the number that had died on Leyte.

Three hundred and thirty miles away, the main islands of Japan girded for invasion.

The battle of Okinawa has long been overshadowed by iconic World War II events such as the D-Day landings at Normandy and the images of the American flag raising on Iwo Jima. Yet, it was Okinawa—not Normandy, Iwo Jima, or Guadalcanal—that constituted the largest and deadliest land-and-sea operation of World War II. American casualties on Okinawa were double the number of Iwo Jima and Guadalcanal *combined*.

And *still* the killing was not finished.

. . .

The two young privates were green-as-grass rookies who arrived on Okinawa after the fighting was mostly over. One of them, just a kid who was probably pulling schoolgirl pigtails a couple months before, crowed about how badly he wanted to kill a Jap. The war might end before he ever got the chance, he whined.

Clayton tuned out the chattering as he walked along high ground just above flowering cane stalks waving in the sea breezes. Out toward the middle of the field, he noticed the stalks waving a little too much. Was a Jap in there? Civilians? He signaled to the two privates to move to the far end of the cane field. Clayton would enter the opposite end and chase whoever was hiding into a trap.

Clayton charged into the cane field, his face and arms slapped and scratched by the rough stalks, and chased whoever it was toward the two nervous privates. Clayton caught glimpses of the person through the rows of cane—a man in uniform, a Japanese solider. He plowed through the cane and ran the Jap over, dropping him with a rifle butt to the gut.

The enemy soldier writhed on the ground. He was as bedraggled and withered as the other few prisoners F Company had taken. He wore no hat or helmet, but his chest was unusually decorated with medals. On his hip, he carried a pistol, of which Clayton relieved him. Clayton hoped he had a saber, too, but he did not.

"You a colonel?" Clayton spit at the Jap.

The soldier attempted to rise, but Clayton caught him again with the rifle butt. He shouted at him to stay down. That's when Clayton noticed the fancy-looking wristwatch.

Clayton reached down and grabbed the Jap's wrist. The soldier wriggled his arm free, lunged his face toward Clayton's hand, and bit it. Hard.

Clayton hollered as he yanked his hand free. He came down with the rifle butt again, this time harder, squarely on top of the pitiful Jap's head. Clayton shouted at him to get up. He took the man's arm and lifted him to his feet. The Jap wobbled, barely able to stand. Clayton hated Japs, *hated* them.

"Boys," he said to the two rookies, who had stood by silently during the beat down. "Y'all want to shoot a Jap?"

The two guys were too stunned to answer at first.

"You mean, this close?" stammered the kid who had been all hot for killing Japs just a minute earlier.

"Yes, this close," Clayton said. "You'll never get an easier shot. You better shoot him now, or you might miss and he'll shoot you."

"I...I don't want to shoot a Jap like this," the soldier said.

"What difference does it make?" Clayton wanted to know. "You can shoot him from a hundred yards away or you can shoot him up close. I've killed a many of 'em, up close, far away. It don't make no difference where you do it."

"Well, you're a sergeant. If anybody shoots him, it should be you."

The other kid chimed in. "Why don't we just take him prisoner? Haul him back to headquarters and see if he's got any information?"

While Tweedledee and Tweedledum debated what to do, Clayton's gaze never left the Jap, which was fortunate for the three Americans, because he saw the enemy begin to reach inside his shirt for something.

Clayton reacted instantaneously. He brought the butt of the rife straight up with a smooth, sweeping arc, catching the Jap squarely between the eyes with a sickening smack of wood crushing bone. The enemy soldier fell immediately, dead from this final, mortal blow. Clayton reached into the dead man's shirt, which spilled a grenade onto the ground, the pin still fixed. The two greenhorns spoke nary a word.

"You see what I mean?" Clayton exploded. "You see what I mean? This is why you have to kill every Jap you see! Before he kills you first!"

Clayton kneeled down next to the dead enemy and reached for his shirt again. He ripped off a medal of oak leaves, removed the man's wristwatch, and shoved them into his pocket.

"Now you can take him to headquarters," he said to the rookies.

• • •

Ten days before Christmas, 1942, Clayton had awoken in a guest room of Roy Hall's house on Shadeland Avenue in Roanoke, where he had been living that fall. He had pulled on a white shirt with a Dr Pepper patch affixed to the left breast, slurped a cup of black coffee, put on his white cowboy hat, and rode with Roy to the WDBJ radio station, where they spent a packed morning with the band. They played a live program at 6:30, followed by a recording session in Studio B to make a week's worth of radio shows to be broadcast while the band members visited their families for Christmas.

During that morning session, Clayton had strapped on Roy's Martin guitar, the one with Roy's name spelled in mother-of-pearl along the fingerboard, and had sung "Old Shep," a hit song about a boy who cannot summon the courage to shoot his old, suffering dog.

> With hands that were trembling, I picked up my gun
> And aimed it at Shep's faithful head
> I just couldn't do it, I wanted to run
> I wish they would shoot me instead

Sixteen days later, Clayton traded his cowboy hat for a helmet, his guitar for a rifle.

Now, here he was, two and a half years later, standing on the last patch of green grass on a godforsaken island ten thousand miles from home, a place laid waste by bombs, flames, and bullets where a quarter of a million people had died, a few by his own hands. The cowboy who sentimentally sang about sparing the life of an old dog had become a trained, professional killer, and a good one, who had no problem cracking a guy's head open with a rifle butt. As he walked back to camp after that last patrol, he had to wonder if that cowboy kid would live again, or if he, too, was one of the casualties.

* * *

All the Deadeyes were pulled to the rear by July 1, 1945. Once on their new base, you'd have never known a war was still going on. The Deadeyes broke out the recreational boxes stuffed with bats, softballs, gloves, footballs, and volleyballs. If anything, the men were bored. They weren't in training, they weren't fighting, they were simply biding time. They suspected plans were being drawn up for an invasion of Japan (they were; Operation Olympic was scheduled for November), an invasion that would be spearheaded by a battle-tested division like the Deadeyes.

Finally, in late July, they were given their departure orders for Mindoro, a secure island in the Philippines. There, they would resume training and practice landings for the Japan invasion. They quickly packed for the move and then were told to speed it up because a typhoon warning had been issued.

That storm nearly got them. On July 29, 1945, the convoy of transports was struck by a massive typhoon. For nearly five days, Clayton's transport pitched and rolled so severely that the men huddled below decks, believing it would flip over. The soldiers suffered miserably, and many puked and messed their pants. Guys were as scared on that transport as they had been in combat.

Three days later, the winds died and the seas calmed. Men climbed to the decks, swallowed life-giving oxygen, and welcomed the sunshine. The storm clouds were behind them.

* * *

The news of the atomic bomb came over the ship's loudspeakers. Soldiers guzzled coffee and read mimeographed pages that updated war news and peace progress. On August 6, 1945, the first A-bomb was dropped on the industrial city of Hiroshima. The Japanese did not surrender. The second bomb was dropped on Nagasaki. Still, no surrender.

When the Deadeyes landed at Mindoro, the war wasn't over.

But on August 15, 1945, Japanese emperor Hirohito finally stood up to the hard-liners in the government and military. He announced Japan's surrender in a prerecorded radio address, which concluded, "It is according to the dictates of time and fate that we have resolved to pave the way for a grand peace for all the generations to come by enduring the unendurable and suffering what is unsufferable."

The guys who had been on Okinawa, not to mention the island's surviving civilians, also knew what it felt like to endure the unendurable.

After the Japanese surrender, the Deadeyes celebrated like a hundred Fourth of Julys. They fired guns, drank beer, sang songs, and danced with women from the Red Cross to the sounds and rhythms of the Ninety-sixth Infantry Division Band beneath a starry tropical sky.

World War II was over.

Nobody knows what I've been through
No one but God above

—"NO LETTER IN THE MAIL TODAY," A SONG RECORDED BY
BILL MONROE IN ATLANTA, 1940; THE SAME SESSION AT WHICH
CLAYTON AND SAFORD FIRST RECORDED WITH ROY HALL

A fighting army without a war is like a kid without school—only with more firepower. Men didn't know what to do with their sudden ration of free time. Military training was considered no longer relevant and was mostly canceled. Soldiers whiled away the hours playing sports, reading magazines, watching movies, and attending events at the enlisted men's club, "Fatigue Junction." Some took classes in math and science, as they prepared to return to a working world where knowing how to clean and reassemble an M1 rifle isn't a job requirement.

Clayton did what he always did with his free time in the army. He found a guitar and played in a band, one that specialized in hillbilly tunes and cowboy songs. Music really did seem to tame the savage beasts of Leyte and Okinawa.

Clayton's little band played shows in a bombed-out church on Mindoro. The crowd sat on old wooden pews and whooped and hollered like they were at an old-timey medicine show. They demanded that Clayton sing a song, like the ones he used to sing back at Camp White. But what songs did he remember?

He strapped on an old guitar, stepped up to the lone microphone, and flipped through the songbook in his head for a familiar tune. He complained that he'd lost the calluses on his chord fingers. He strummed a lonesome C chord over and over, natural as breathing. The words came back like the memory of a mother's face.

Clayton sang "Old Shep," the sentimental song about a boy and his dog. He crooned about good old days spent wandering over meadows and swimming in the old fishin' hole, where Old Shep miraculously saved his owner from drowning one day. He sang the line about being unable to put the old dog out of his misery and how he wished somebody would shoot him instead. By the end, Old Shep had gone on to where the good doggies go, frolicking in the fields of heaven.

When he was done, I like to think that the rowdy men grew quiet as they listened with ears still ringing from the reverberations of 320 mm mortars and machine guns. Maybe they recalled their own boyhood days, or remembered a favorite old dog or fishin' hole. Maybe, even after all the inhuman acts they had seen and committed, one day they could forget it all and never have to talk about things like that again. They would be OK. They would be human beings again.

 • • •

The army developed a point system called the Advanced Service Rating Score to determine who went home first. Soldiers earned points for service time, time overseas, campaigns, medals, and for having young children. Men who earned seventy points got a first-class ticket home. Clayton had sixty-seven.

Clayton occupied his time performing menial tasks, playing music, and hanging out with his new buddy: CoCo, a macaque monkey bequeathed to him by one of the seventy-pointers. CoCo's main job was requisitioning smokes and gum from unsuspecting soldiers and returning them to Clayton, who smoked and chewed up the loot. Otherwise, Clayton was bored, dying to get home. Chow was bad—the men joked that the bitter, nauseating, malaria-fighting Atabrine pills were the best part of meals. Brothels flourished, even though prostitution had been officially banned by MacArthur, who may as well have been ordering the tides to roll backward.

Finally, the army called Clayton's number. On December 15, 1945, he strode up the gangplank of a ship headed for California and sailed east. *East. Home.*

 • • •

204-IF TROUBLE DON'T KILL ME

Clayton's transport ship sailed slowly. He arrived in the Port of San Diego on January 3, 1946, almost three years to the day he had ridden the train to Camp Lee to be inducted. His duffel bag of Japanese souvenirs—sabers, guns, the watch he took from the Japanese soldier—was lost on the trip, but he didn't stick around to see if it would arrive. He boarded a train bound for North Carolina.

Clayton Hall became a civilian again on January 15, 1946, at Fort Bragg, where Saford had begun his own military hitch four and half years earlier. A clerk typed up his official Enlisted Record and Report of Separation / Honorable Discharge. Clayton provided a right thumbprint and signed his discharge, then personnel officer Captain J. B. Collier signed it, and that was that. He was issued his lapel button (which bore an eagle emblem that many an army man referred to as a "ruptured duck"), given a $100 installment of his $300 mustering-out pay, and handed a bus ticket to Mount Airy. He was on his way back home the next day.

The cold, damp weather was a shock to a man who had spent a good chunk of the past year and a half in the tropics. The temperature struggled to get out of the thirties, and the bus ride was shrouded in fog, rain, and a few snowflakes. When the bus traveled northward on U.S. 52 from Winston-Salem, the terrain started to roll and rise. He had traveled this route dozens of times before the war, when he played on WSJS and later when he and Saford had joined Roy Hall. Going home had never felt like this, though. The Virginia mountains were cloaked with fog, but he knew they were there—at least he hoped they still were.

The bus pulled into Mount Airy by midafternoon and dropped off Clayton near Main Street. He packed up his few belongings and walked to a barbershop, where his brother Sam cut hair. Clad in his wool army jacket and well-tanned from the Pacific sun, Clayton stood out among the winter-pale shoppers and businessmen on Mount Airy's gray street. Sam didn't even recognize his baby brother when he walked into the busy barbershop.

"Soldier boy, eh?" Sam said as he worked on a customer. "Have a seat and I'll be right with you."

Clayton sat down, knowing Sam didn't recognize him. "That's all right, I'll just wait my turn," he bellowed. "No sense in a fella giving special privileges to his brother." Sam nearly clipped off a customer's ear. He fumbled around, trying to get the scissors and comb out of his hands, finally just dropping them in the customer's lap.

All the men in the shop shook Clayton's hand, slapped him on the back, and welcomed him home. Saford had just been in the shop a couple hours earlier, Sam said. He might even still be in town. He offered Clayton a ride, and they set off down Main Street to look for Saford.

Saford had been home for nearly six months, and all these years later it's impossible to say what he had been up to in The Hollow or how he was greeted when he returned from war. Did he receive a hero's welcome? A parade down Main Street in Mount Airy? Perhaps he got only a pat on the back from the middle-aged guys too old to fight. Maybe the country people of The Hollow never even knew he was at war. They just assumed he was off playing music somewhere. It's all a mystery. All we know is that he didn't stick around Roanoke, he didn't talk about his wife, and he was living off his mustering-out pay from the army.

Sam drove slowly down the crowded street as Clayton scanned the sidewalks and café windows for any sign of Saford. The streets buzzed with postwar activity. Soldiers were coming home, getting jobs, and buying cars and business suits. Clayton would never find Saford in this crowd.

Then, there he was.

Saford strutted out of a soda fountain flanked by two girls. He was talking a mile a minute, spinning who knew what kind of tale. He wore only a light coat over his white shirt and necktie. He looked good. He looked the same.

Clayton climbed out the passenger side window, which faced the wrong side of the street, and sat on top of the door so he could look over the car's roof. He hollered across the busy street at Saford and asked if he needed a ride.

Who's hollering at me? Saford couldn't believe his eyes. He headed for the street, before he realized he had forgotten to bid the girls farewell. Cars blared their horns as he darted into traffic and ran down Sam's car, which had not stopped and was pulling away from Saford. Sam offered to cut a U-turn in the middle of the street, but Clayton ordered him to keep driving. Make him chase us.

Saford cut across to the sidewalk and caught up to Sam's car just as it stopped at a traffic light. Clayton leaped out and met his twin with a handshake and embrace. The symphony of car horns was the closest thing to a homecoming parade that they ever got. The Hall twins were together again.

· · ·

Here's how I picture Clayton's arrival at Mamo's house:

The twins chattered the whole way as Saford drove his Buick north on Wards Gap Road. I am guessing they did not talk about the war itself, except in the indirect language of "Boy, am I sure glad to see you again!" There had been times when they doubted that they ever would.

Saford pulled up to the little house below the mountain where he and Mamo lived. Pale gray smoke, hanging motionless in the rain like cobwebs, hovered above the chimney. Mamo was inside, weaving an egg basket from oak splits, humming "Get Along Home, Cindy" or some other old mountain song. She heard the car pull up, wondered who it could be, and peeked out the window. That's when she saw her baby boy.

"Clayton!"

Clayton climbed out of the passenger side and met his mother in the doorway.

"Hey, hey, Mama!"

Once she got over the surprise, I don't figure that Mamo wept or shouted or melted into an emotional, convulsing heap. That would have been against her nature. Instead, she would have wanted to know if Clayton was hungry. "Have you eat yet?"

She fed him beans and cornbread, the first down-home cooking Clayton had in nearly three years. Word spread to the kinfolks, and before too long, sisters, brothers, nieces, nephews, friends, and neighbors descended upon Mamo's little cabin to welcome Clayton home. Mamo cooked up fresh sausage from a hog she had helped butcher in the fall, and she fried half-moon apple pies in the iron skillet.

"Boy, you didn't make this big a fuss when I come home," Saford said, half-jokingly, half-jealously.

"You hush up," Mamo said. "I did so."

The family ate and fellowshipped. Somebody brought out a guitar, Saford tuned it and played it, and the twins sang harmonies that soared like birds escaped from cages. Yes, sirree boy, the Hall twins were really back together.

Which means, at some point, they would've scrapped with each other. Eventually, they talked about the war. Saford assured Clayton that no enemy compared to the Germans. Those guys were a war machine, buddy,

I'm telling you. They were the most disciplined, fearless, deadliest fighters the world had ever seen, and I helped whip 'em.

What the devil are you talking about? Clayton demanded to know. At least a German surrendered when he was licked. A Jap fought to the death like a dog. The only way to whip him was to kill him. You ain't fought a war till you've fought a Jap.

Like any good sibling rivalry, the argument escalated until somebody—probably Saford—bopped the other guy in the nose. Then the other dude—in this case, Clayton—retaliated. They punched and wrestled each other like boys on a schoolyard until Mamo stepped in and warned them that if they continued to act up this way neither one of them would get a fried apple pie. They obliged her, ate their pies, and sang until way past midnight, after everyone had left or gone to bed, leaving the twins to make music, just like when they were little boys, wondering what the future held.

That's how I picture it, anyway.

. . .

Most guys came home from the war intent on improving their lot in life. Many opened their first savings accounts with their mustering-out pay. Some went to college or trade school on the GI Bill to earn an education and learn skills that would lead to good-paying jobs.

Clayton and Saford took their $300 from the army and hollered, "We're rich! We'll never have to work again!" They just wanted to play music and have fun. They were the first beatniks, and they didn't even know it.

They wasted all of their mustering-out pay—and most of 1946, in the process—just by hanging out. They were like teenagers again, playing music in front parlors and at family reunions. They started going to church—not unlike most of their battlefield buddies who came home and thanked God for every day they were alive—joining nearby Mount Bethel Moravian Church. Clayton studied the Bible more diligently than Saford did, arriving early for Sunday school and even attending weeknight services and revivals. Both sang in the choir and even took up brass instruments to play in the church band. Those boys could play anything.

One Sunday morning in the Mount Bethel choir loft the ghosts of war returned to haunt Clayton for the first time. He had felt a little weak that morning but had decided to attend church anyway. During the service, he began to sweat profusely. He was burning up beneath his choir robe. A minute later, he was freezing. His head pounded. He asked Saford to help him up from the pew and escort him outdoors. Saford asked what was wrong with him.

"Malaria fever," Clayton said. He had relapsed.

Saford got Clayton back to Mamo's house, where she treated him with hot biscuits, honey, and tea. Clayton kept asking for water as he slipped in and out of consciousness for three days. Finally, his fever broke, and he recovered his strength quickly. At least this time, no one was ordering him to drag his sickly frame out of bed and back to the battlefield.

By the time the weather turned cool in late 1946, the twins had squandered their mustering-out pay without anything to show for it. No school, no jobs, no career track—nothing. Even after everything they had been through, they were still no better off than when they were seventeen, mostly uneducated and lacking prospects. The furniture factories of Bassett began to beckon again.

Meanwhile, their old pal Tommy Magness, who had not gone off to war, seemed to be doing just fine. No one knows for sure why Tommy wasn't called upon to serve. People have told me he had health problems, a weak heart, perhaps. Clayton told me that Tommy didn't fare well on the army's psychological tests and was farmed out. He had a wife and daughter, too, but so did a lot of other guys who sailed into the great void and never returned. Whatever the reasons, Tommy Magness fiddled while war raged. Shortly before Roy's fatal wreck, Tommy had gone to Louisville to play on the *Early Morning Frolic Show* on WHAS. While there, he got an offer to join a band led by another fellow named Roy—Roy Acuff.

Roy Acuff was the biggest star in country music, which still wasn't called country music. He was the headliner of the Grand Ole Opry, which had moved from Nashville's old War Memorial Auditorium to Nashville's even older and larger Ryman Auditorium in 1943. Thousands of fans bought his records and packed his traveling tent shows. He made movies for Republic Pictures. Tommy appeared in Roy's flicks *Sing, Neighbor, Sing* and *Night Train to Memphis*.

Tommy quit Acuff in 1946 to put together his own band. That's what he told Clayton and Saford when he drove down to The Hollow and invited them to join his group, Tommy Magness and the Orange Blossom Boys. He had a deal with WDBJ to start a new radio program, and he wanted the twins to fill out the group's lineup.

Good fortune had found them again. They got a second chance at their big break.

ROANOKE

Tommy Magness and the Orange Blossom Boys, 1947

In 1947, the twins joined the band "The Orange Blossom Boys" with Tommy Magness . . . [who] did two radio shows each day on radio station WDBJ.

—MOM, AGAIN, FROM THE GENEALOGY BOOK

Clayton and Saford were thrilled to get back to Roanoke. The street-cars still rumbled down Campbell Avenue, the Academy of Music still hosted concerts, and WDBJ still broadcast from its Kirk Avenue studios. To top it off, they were back on the radio, playing music. It was as if the twins had just awakened, Rip Van Winkle–like, from a five-year bad dream to find themselves back where they had always been, as if they'd never left . . . as if the war had never happened.

But as comforting as the familiar surroundings were, things weren't exactly the same. Roy Hall was dead, for one thing. Clayton and Saford had to mesh with new bandmates, which included a young hot-shot slide guitar player named Slim Idaho, and Warren Poindexter, a fine Roanoke singer and guitarist whom the twins barely knew. They knew Warren's wife, how-ever. Near the end of the war, Warren had married a young, pretty war widow in Roanoke—Reba, Clayton's old girlfriend. If Clayton felt awk-ward about the situation, he never said so. Besides, he'd have a new girl-friend soon.

Tommy had never led a band. Sure, he was the most famous musician to ever play in Roanoke, because not many Magic City musicians could brag about starring in movies with Roy Acuff, but he was a first-string fiddler who had played second fiddle to his bandleaders. Put him in a band headed by Bill Monroe, Roy Acuff, or Roy Hall, and he was a fiddlin' madman. How good would he be running his own show?

Pretty danged good, early reports indicated. The Orange Blossom Boys were fantastic. Tommy's fiddling was the musical centerpiece, but he was nearly upstaged by the incredible Slim Idaho, who made that electric, three-neck, pedal steel guitar wail. The twins were familiar with hillbilly and Western tunes, but this band could swing like any fiddle band from Texas or jazz combo from New York. Their sound was quite contemporary for country music, circa 1947. The ever-versatile twins sang together and comprised the rhythm section—Saford on guitar, Clayton on stand-up bass. Tommy's fiddling was fancier and faster than ever. The Orange Blossom Boys, who, naturally, employed "Orange Blossom Special" as their theme song, were like no band Roanoke had ever heard. On March 3, 1947, they made their debut over good old WDBJ, with the familiar voice of "Cousin Irving" Sharp at the microphone.

The program began with Slim Idaho making a train whistle sound from his slide guitar. The rest of the band kicked in, and Tommy fiddled the second part of "Orange Blossom Special" (the superfast part). Cousin Irving introduced the show and ordered up a hot fiddle number from Tommy, whose playing was outrageously good. His repertoire had expanded considerably over the last four years. He played such complex songs as "Alabama Jubilee" and even sang the verses while Slim wrung wailing high notes from his steel guitar. Tommy dusted off old favorites "Katy Hill" and "Black Mountain Rag," tunes he had known since he was a boy. On "Black Mountain Rag," he double-timed the final verse and it was all the band could do to keep up. Clayton slapped the bass ferociously. Saford and Warren chopped time on guitar. This band was *tight*.

The Orange Blossom Boys played every morning on WDBJ, raising the musical bar each time. Requests came in for "Arkansas Traveler," "Devil's Dream," and plenty of other numbers they didn't even know. Tommy would call Clayton up to the microphone and announce "Clayton, I believe it's time for me and you to do one ... and I don't believe I've done this one before!"

Clayton would laugh and say, "It don't make no difference," and the two of them would sing and play "Columbus Stockade Blues" as good as if they'd sung it a hundred times. The Orange Blossom Boys were good. Fan mail and requests for show dates poured into WDBJ.

It was just like the good old days, perhaps even better. Maybe the last five years *had* just been a bad dream.

. . .

Several years ago, I traveled a winding road over Windy Gap Mountain to visit Dorothy Wilbourne Spencer at her brick ranch house in Franklin County, Virginia, a home cuddled by gardens, flowers, and large shade trees. I asked her a question that had stumped me for quite a while: What on earth were you thinking when you married Saford Hall a second time?

Her answer was the only one that could have shocked me.

"We were never divorced," she told me.

That went against the family legend.

Maybe Saford told Clayton that he was divorced, or perhaps Clayton just assumed that was the case since Saford didn't seem to be in any hurry to shuffle back to Roanoke. Maybe Clayton knew his brother was still married. Whatever the truth, when Saford returned to Roanoke, he and Dot got back together and picked up where they had left off, except that she was now in her twenties, and she demanded that Saford behave better and treat her better than he had done before the war.

Clayton had no girlfriend, but Tommy and his wife, Tootsie—whom he'd finally married after divorcing his first wife, Ruth—aimed to fix that. Just a few weeks after Clayton returned to Roanoke, Tommy and Tootsie set up a double date among themselves, Clayton, and one of Tootsie's nieces, a pretty young girl from southeast Roanoke who lived high on a hill behind Mill Mountain. They fixed him up with Reba's baby sister, Elinor.

Elinor! The bratty kid who had been such a nuisance to Clayton when he dated Reba. She had tagged along and annoyed him on dates for two years. Elinor! Yes, he had written her a few times from the army, but that was only because she had written him first, and responding was the courteous thing to do. How old was she now, anyway? Fifteen or sixteen?

Old enough, it turned out.

Elinor met them at the door of the rambling old house on Gladstone Avenue where Clayton had spent many happy hours courting Reba. She wore a white skirt and a white top with a wide aqua and pink stripe that swooped down the front. Her wavy brown hair fell in waves across her forehead, and her curls in back dangled to her shoulders. She had wide blue eyes, a cute button nose, and ruby lips. She looked all grown up, at least to Clayton. He was smitten.

. . .

The foursome went to a movie downtown and stopped for a bite to eat afterward. They ate hamburgers, then Tommy drove everyone back to Elinor's house, where they . . . oh, fiddlesticks. Let's just cut to the chase. Elinor and Clayton got married three months later.

The thing to know about my family is that we don't waste any time when it comes to romance. We marry young and start popping out babies. My grandmother was sixteen when she married a twenty-eight-year-old combat veteran on June 14, 1947. She was seventeen when she gave birth to a daughter, my mother. My mom was seventeen when she married and when she had me. I, however, broke with family tradition in a major way and actually waited until my midtwenties to marry, and I didn't become a dad until I was forty. Mamo, of course, never married, but that didn't stop her from having those babies.

Clayton and Elinor were married at a parsonage in southeast Roanoke. Elinor's older brother Marvin was Clayton's best man; Marvin's young wife, Ada, was Elinor's maid of honor. According to the newspaper announcement, the bride wore a white, tailored gabardine suit with matching accessories, and a corsage of white roses and stephanotis. She carried a white "prayer book," according to the paper, covered with a dangling stream of flowers, and she wore a strand of pearls. The newspaper doesn't say that the groom wore a snappy suit with suspenders.

Clayton, ever the big spender and hopeless romantic, spirited Elinor away on an unforgettable honeymoon in that famous young lovers' getaway known as The Hollow, where they spent the week with Mamo and one of Clayton's nieces. That was the first time Elinor met Mamo, and the teenage city girl had no idea what to make of the old woman in long dresses whose hair was always piled into a bun. The Hollow seemed so foreign and strange to Elinor, Clayton might as well have whisked her away to the Philippines.

. . .

Elinor Glynn Holland Hall was—still is—a silly little girl crystallized in amber, the baby of her family. Her rambling, oft-repeated, somewhat absentminded, stream-of-consciousness, free-association style of conversing and storytelling has been as endearing to her relatives and friends as it has been occasionally irritating. Grandma doesn't have a filter. If a thought or story pops into her head, it comes out her mouth, usually in great detail, often repeatedly. Her memory, even in her golden years, is remarkable. She remembered every stitch and stripe of the white skirt she wore the night of her first date with Clayton, the same way many years later she would remember every medication Clayton was supposed to take and when he was supposed to take it.

So I can only imagine the stories Clayton heard that first night he took Elinor to the movies. She surely filled Clayton in on everything he had missed the past five years.

She must have told him that Reba had lived with her new husband, Donald Roman, in Kentucky until he was called overseas. She and her baby son, Donnie, then moved back to Roanoke, where in July 1944 the family got the news that Donald had been shot down over France. Every day after she got the news, she asked Elinor to go to the mailbox and bring back a letter that said it hadn't happened, that it was all a big mistake and that Donald was alive. Elinor did as she was told, but no letter ever came. Soon, Reba married Warren Poindexter and had a baby girl.

Elinor's biggest news, of course, was about how her daddy had died of an enlarged heart in 1945. He had come home from work one evening feeling ill and had asked Elinor to help him upstairs. He made it to the bathroom and vomited blood. After that, the doctor put him on a diet of prunes and black coffee, but he died anyway a year later, which meant her mama had to go to work at a mill in town. Not long before he got sick, her daddy had discovered a lovely cemetery while hunting near his old home place in Franklin County, and he had come home to tell Mama about it. When that eastern sky splits, he told her, that's where I want to meet the Lord. The place was so beautiful and the view of the mountains so spectacular that he bought plots not only for himself and his wife, but also for all four children plus their future spouses. He's buried there now, Elinor surely told Clayton, in that place called Mountain View. Isn't that a beautiful name? Wouldn't you love to be buried forever in a place called Mountain View?

I can hear her now—because, believe me, I've heard all those stories before.

The newlyweds' honeymoon in the country lasted only a few days.

They returned to Roanoke quickly so Clayton could get back to playing music.

. . .

Clayton and Elinor moved in with Elinor's mother on Gladstone Avenue—and that's when things began to change.

Slim Idaho left the band first, taking his innovative steel guitar with him to the Old Dominion Barn Dance on Richmond's WRVA. Within a year he was dead, killed in a motorcycle accident at age twenty-three, leaving a legacy as a pedal steel pioneer that lives on until this day.

Tommy hired Wayne Fleming, the twins' old buddy from Bassett, to play steel guitar. Wayne had played on the Grand Ole Opry before making records with Ernest Tubb.

The band handled the changes well, at first. Clayton and Saford reverted back to their silly ways and cornpone routines so quickly, you'd never know that two years earlier they were sitting in foxholes, praying not to die. One night while driving to a show date over the winding Catawba Mountain Road outside of Roanoke, the Orange Blossom Boys saw the aftermath of a terrible wreck that involved a truck from the Valleydale meatpacking plant. The twins, bless 'em, saw joke potential. During the show, Clayton stepped up to the microphone and told the crowd that he had just seen the awfullest wreck on the way to the show. A meat truck had been sideswiped by another car.

"Was anybody hurt?" Saford wanted to know.

"No," Clayton said, "but it sure tore the liver out of that truck!"

Bah-dum-bum.

Of course, Clayton and Saford's fun times never lasted long. In addition to the fiddle numbers and comedy routines, the Orange Blossom Boys were soon famous for their bandleader's heavy drinking. The twins had always known that Tommy liked the bottle, but he had kept his drinking under control when he worked for Roy Hall. The few times Tommy went on a bender and was late for a show, Roy would not wait on him. He left Tommy behind a couple of times and told him in specific terms that if he'd rather get drunk than play music, Roy would just hand the fiddle over to Saford. Tommy shaped up right quick.

But now, Tommy was the leader and didn't have to answer to anybody. Tommy and Tootsie had a little girl, Joan. Even though he had a family and career to consider, nothing wedged itself between him and the bottle. He began missing show dates, even though his name was at the top of the marquee. The ones he made it to, he was often drunk. One night before a show at the American Theater, witnesses saw Tommy in a back alley, swigging liquor from a bottle, chasing it with grape Nehi, and puking the mess back up. He kept up the routine until his liquor stayed down. He was in a bad way. While playing a dance at the City Market Building, a half-full liquor bottle fell out of his coat pocket and rolled across the stage right in front of his fans. He disappointed all who knew him.

. . .

The music the Orange Blossom Boys played was still sensational, however. Roy Hall's band had set the gold standard in Roanoke, but even his music sounded old-fashioned compared to Tommy Magness's hot band. Tommy was the Chuck Yeager of fiddle playing—he played so fast, he broke the sound barrier. The way he played "Orange Blossom Special" in 1947, replete with various train sounds, plucked strings, and fanciful shuffles, made his original 1938 version sound like a field recording of a blind ninety-year-old fiddler in the Ozarks. He was supremely talented. When Tommy called for a fiddle tune, say, for example, "Cotton-Eyed Joe," the rest of the band took a deep breath and knew they were in for a track meet. Wayne Fleming splashed copious electrified slide-guitar notes all over the map, Saford chopped a jazzy, swinging guitar rhythm, and Clayton walked up and down the fingerboard of the bass. When the band needed a vocal number, Saford was called on to sing "Foggy River," a bouncy pop-country number that had been a huge hit for Rex Allen. Saford got more requests for that song than any other, and the lyrics probably suited him better than any other song:

> Your love is colder than a foggy river
> Flowing over a heart of stone
> You left me stranded on this foggy river
> Drifting helpless and alone

The Orange Blossom Boys even made one—count 'em, one—78 record in September 1947. Recording for Roanoke's Blue Ridge Records at the Ponce de Leon Hotel on Campbell Avenue, the band lit through two songs: "Powhatan Arrow," an original number written and sung by Tommy, was sort of a melodic rewrite of "Natural Bridge Blues" and was inspired by Norfolk & Western's powerful new Class J passenger train of the same name; and the standard "I'm Sitting on Top of the World," sung by the Hall twins.

The Orange Blossom Boys were good, perhaps even *better* than Roy Hall and His Blue Ridge Entertainers. They were better than any band working in Roanoke, or, for that matter, anywhere in Virginia and North Carolina.

That's why it was such a shame when it all ended so suddenly.

· · ·

Tommy had been in Roanoke for more than a year and felt like it was time to move on. He heard about a radio station in Shreveport, Louisiana, that was booking hillbilly bands, so he sent them a copy of "Powhatan Arrow" / "I'm Sitting on Top of the World," along with a few radio transcriptions, to see if the management would hire them. The station was KWKH, a fifty-thousand-watt giant that was the most popular country music station in the country.

Around Thanksgiving, Tommy received word that KWKH wanted the Orange Blossom Boys. The band would be moving to Louisiana. Ready for a change, Clayton and Saford switched their musicians' union cards from the Roanoke chapter to a Louisiana local chapter. Dot and Elinor were not as enthusiastic about the move. Both were born-and-bred Roanoke girls reluctant to leave their families. The Orange Blossom Boys still had shows to play and radio programs to broadcast, but they made no secret that they were leaving soon.

The band had one major show date remaining on the calendar before the end of the year—a multiband affair at the majestic Roanoke Theater on Jefferson Street. They played their final morning radio program and said farewell to all their fans and all the folks who had written the radio station to make requests. They talked about the show that night at the Roanoke Theater and encouraged listeners to tell their friends and neighbors to come on down.

Somebody must have forgotten to tell Tommy. Five minutes before the curtain went up on the Orange Blossom Boys' final performance in Roanoke, the man whose name was at the top of the bill was nowhere to be found.

The boys in the band weren't sure what to do at first. The theater manager informed them that this was the second time a headline per-former had been a no-show *that day*. The Roanoke Theater had canceled an afternoon program because the scheduled performer never showed. (Forevermore, Clayton and Saford claimed that the first dude who stiffed the Roanoke Theater that afternoon was Hank Williams, who would have been twenty-four in 1947 and whose first records came out earlier that year. Clayton told me that ol' Hank had passed out drunk at the Ponce de Leon Hotel and never made the gig. When the legend becomes fact, as they say ...) The theater manager wasn't about to scrap another show, especially when the house was already full.

"Y'all get out there," he ordered the band. "Y'all don't need Tommy. You do the show!"

Saford led the band on stage, served as band spokesman, called the tunes, and got the show on the road. Really, the Tommy-less Orange Blos-som Boys had no trouble playing a show. Clayton and Saford could've car-ried a four-hour show by themselves. But this was ridiculous. Tommy had let the Orange Blossom Boys down many times over the last nine months with his drinking and his absenteeism, but this took the prize. Why were they uprooting their families, moving south, and sacrificing everything they had worked for, when Tommy could easily throw it all away in Shreveport and leave them stranded? When Clayton and Saford took the stage without their bandleader that night, they asked themselves those questions.

As the show rolled along, the band heard a scuffle backstage. Tommy had burst through the back door, drunk as a mule, wearing a heavy coat with cans of beer stuffed in every pocket—side, front, inside, anywhere he could hide a can. He opened his case and dropped his fiddle on the floor, where it reverberated with a *wang, bang, pi-tang* sound of pegs popping loose and strings unraveling. He picked it up and dragged the wrong side of his bow across the deadened strings. Just before Tommy made it to the stage, the theater manager corralled him in a bear hug and hauled him to a dressing room, barricading him inside. Tommy pounded on the door furi-ously, cussing and hollering, as his band played on without him.

The Orange Blossom Boys kept their composure and played the rest of the show without interruption. They thanked the audience for being so supportive and said they looked forward to a time when they could play for all their Roanoke fans again—which they realized would not come any time soon. The Orange Blossom Boys were done. They all knew it, Clay-ton, Saford, Wayne, and Warren. Everybody, that is, except Tommy.

When they sprang Tommy from his dressing-room holding cell, Tommy roared that he was glad he was leaving this Podunk town.

"Boys, we'll be on our way to Louisiana tomorrow!" he shouted.

Clayton corrected him.

"I'll tell you two who ain't a-going with you," he said. "Not with you like this."

They all quit. Tommy was undeterred. He headed down to Louisiana anyway. Clayton told people that Tommy recruited Jay Hugh Hall to go with him, but when they got down there, they were turned down by the KWKH management.

Tommy moved to Nashville and found work with Roy Acuff again. Within months, he was back in the movies, appearing with Acuff in *Smoky Mountain Melody*. That boy always landed on his feet.

As for Clayton and Saford, they had always landed on their feet, too. They had quit school as teenagers and went to work in a furniture factory, only to have Roy Hall rescue them from Bassett and hand them a music career. They had fought in some of the fiercest battles of World War II, but each managed to come home in one piece. They had squandered their savings and their opportunities after the war, but Tommy Magness came a-calling and made them stars again. Every time they fell, someone showed up with a net.

But not this time.

The twins worked briefly with their old pal Woody Mashburn in the Wanderers of the Wasteland, crooning such Western songs as "Happy, Roving Cowboy," "Cool Water," "Tumbling Tumbleweeds," and the mournful "He's Gone Up the Trail," which sounded like a eulogy for the twins' career:

> He's gone, he's gone up the trail
> His old guitar is still
> He's gone to meet that heavenly band
> That's led by Buffalo Bill

• • •

That group folded, too, and Clayton went to work at Johnson-Caper Furniture Company in southeast Roanoke. He and Elinor still lived at her mother's house, where Clayton read the Bible every evening. On November 30,

1948, Elinor gave birth to a baby girl, Sharon Renee. Mamo came all the way from The Hollow to see her new grandbaby. The next day, Saford and Dot stopped by the old Roanoke Memorial Hospital. Saford was ebullient over the sight of his twin brother's baby girl. He called her "Wee-waw." He called her that for the next fifty years, except for the times he called her "Nay-kid," which I assume played off the name Renee, an embarrassing nickname, to be sure, because it sounded like he was saying "na-ked," as in jaybird.

Whether it was because of his new responsibilities as a father, or because the Magic City had lost its enchantment, or because he simply wanted to get out from under his mother-in-law's roof, Clayton felt compelled to move. He longed for a little cabin in the woods, and he set out to find a country homestead where his young family could live far from the noisy streets and hot pavement of the city.

After he found just such a place, he regaled Elinor with fantastical tales of a land where the peaches and apples grew so large that you only needed two to fill a bushel box. The trees were all tall and green, the mountain streams clean and cold, and the people as friendly as any you could hope to meet. He wanted to live out his life in the only place he felt truly at home: The Hollow.

THE
HOLLOW

Clayton and Renee, circa 1953

In 1949, the band broke up, and Clayton, Elinor and Renee moved to Ararat. Later, the next year, they bought a cabin in the Mount Bethel community of Carroll County.

—MOM, FROM THE CARROLL COUNTY GENEALOGICAL BOOK, 1994

Only the old-timers still called it The Hollow. People below the mountain got their mail through the Ararat post office, which was ten miles away along roads that curled like blacksnakes.

Clayton, Elinor, and the baby rented a little cabin on Wards Gap Road for a couple of months before Clayton put a down payment on a tiny house and ten acres of land on the Carroll side of the Carroll County–Patrick County line. In January 1950, the young family moved into their four-room home made of black-painted logs chinked together with concrete, a cabin without heat or running water. An outhouse stood in the side yard. The front yard was dominated by a large white oak tree that would rain acorns down on a revolving fleet of broken-down rattletraps Clayton would own over the years. A long chicken coop sat at the bottom of a hill behind the house, just above a stream. Water for drinking, cooking, and washing was drawn from a well. The spartan accommodations provided quite a culture shock to Elinor, a young woman from the city who was used to the urban luxuries of bus lines, streetcars, ice cream shops, and indoor toilets.

She was a trouper, though, an independent gal willing to give this new lifestyle a try, especially since Clayton seemed much happier in the country. It wasn't easy, especially the whole business of doing your business in an outhouse, not to mention the threat of being chased by hogs. Clayton's brothers Sam and Mack lived on adjoining properties, and they kept hogs and grew peaches and apples. Sometimes the hogs escaped and wandered up to the house. One afternoon while Clayton was away, Elinor was in the side yard when she spotted one of the hogs coming her way. Scared silly, she made a break for the outhouse, where she locked the door and holed up for the rest of the afternoon. Each time she opened the door a crack to see if the two-hundred-pound porker was still there, the beast waddled up and rooted around outside. Elinor stayed put until Mamo arrived and found her daughter-in-law barricaded in the johnny house. Mamo nearly died laughing when Elinor told her that she feared the hog would eat her.

Clayton took a job with a construction company that kept him away from home for a week at a time. He painted buildings at the gunpowder plant in Radford, an hour away. He stayed at that job for nearly two years, living away from home four nights a week. Elinor kept the home fires burning with help from Mamo, who stayed at the house and looked after Renee while Elinor worked at a hosiery mill in Mount Airy. Elinor was independent, she knew how to drive a car and she taught some of the local girls how to drive, even if it went against their husbands' wishes. Clayton came home on the weekends, and he and Saford and all their brothers and cousins who were musicians played music in Clayton's living room every Saturday night—usually *all* night.

Clayton eventually quit the Radford job and found work at National Furniture in Mount Airy, where he could come home from work every night.

．．．

Saford came home, too. He and Dot split up for the last time in 1950, and he left Roanoke for good.

Their marriage didn't end for any single reason, but there wasn't a single reason for them to stay together, either. Dot was no longer the teenage girl whose domineering mother had convinced her that the handsome singer would make her a happy woman. She had long outgrown any schoolgirl infatuation she might have felt for Saford, and he had never done anything to make her happy. Saford showed no desire to improve, except for a short stint when he worked toward getting his high school diploma. He quit after only a few months, but he didn't tell Dot. She found out from Saford's buddies that he had actually been hanging out downtown when he should have been in class.

The end wasn't that hard. Saford simply came in one day and informed Dot that he was moving back home, to his real home. She wasn't invited. She wouldn't have gone, anyway. In a way, the breakup of her marriage felt like little more than the ending of a high school romance, which is what it sort of was for her, considering how young she was when she married Saford.

After the divorce, Dot married her old boyfriend from high school, the boy she had dated before Saford, the only boy she had ever really loved. They had two sons and Dot lived a long, happy life, playing piano in church and teaching piano to Roanoke children. After the boys had grown, she and her husband moved into the country, where even as she was dying from cancer she worked an hour or two every day in her flower beds, pulling weeds, cutting dead blooms, and never looking back to that time when she had been a child bride married to a high-strung musician and soldier boy from some place called The Hollow.

· · ·

Clayton taught Sunday school at Mount Bethel Moravian and sang in the choir. His ability to speak with confidence in front of large crowds earned him the responsibility of filling in for the preacher when he had to be away. Clayton quickly became a pillar of the church and of the little community that surrounded it.

The good Moravians would have been surprised to know that their favorite son was coming unglued.

Elinor saw signs of Clayton's temper early on. She knew he was the jealous type, so she didn't show him the newspaper clipping Reba had sent her about one of Elinor's old boyfriends. The young man had become an actor and was about to appear in a movie. But Elinor let it slip one day that Reba had sent her the news clipping and Clayton blew his stack. He tore through drawers in an old rolltop desk and tossed papers and letters all around the room.

"Where is it?" he demanded to know. "I want to wipe my ass with it!"

This was not the Clayton that Elinor had known when she was a little girl, the kindhearted country boy who would sit on the sofa with her sister and just talk for hours, the boy who read the Bible and discussed the book of Revelation with her mother. Fortunately, that Clayton was still around most of the time. But occasionally his anger boiled over and changed him, the way a full moon turns a man into a werewolf.

The person who really brought out the beast in Clayton was—who else?—Saford. Saford had his own temper issues, among his other problems. One day while the two of them played music on a cousin's porch, Saford grew irritated with Clayton's playing and smacked Clayton upside of the head. Clayton dropped Saford with one punch to the nose, and then he went home.

Mamo told Elinor she never could understand why her babies fought like they did. "I reckon every once in a while they have to see which one is the better man."

They even fought in front of Clayton's daughter, who was just a child. Little Renee watched her daddy and uncle rolling in the dirt, beating each other senseless, and she laughed. She thought that they were playing cowboys like in the Westerns.

• • •

Clayton and Saford made their peace the way they always had, by playing music.

Ralph Epperson, the twins' old pal from Blue Ridge School, who as a boy had been enamored with the technological revolution that was radio, had built the first commercial radio station in the area. The station went on the air in 1948 with a pledge to feature local talent and community news. Located at 740 AM, the station's call letters were WPAQ, not because it was an acronym for some slogan (like "We Piddle Along Quietly," for example) or the initials of a person's name, but because Ralph had been told that the letter Q really stood out in call letters and would make his station easy to remember.

Their professional days were behind them, but Clayton and Saford played on WPAQ frequently in the 1950s with a variety of bands. They taught a group of local pickers the old Roy Hall hit "Can You Forgive?" and recorded it live in the studio. They even formed a hot country band called the Swingbillies that made records for Ralph Epperson to play on the air.

By the mid-1950s, the music the twins had been playing their entire lives finally had a name: "bluegrass" music, named for Bill Monroe's band the Blue Grass Boys, a unit that had debuted in 1940 with Tommy Magness on the fiddle. Monroe's brand of up-tempo, acoustic-powered mandolin-and-banjo-led music had earned him the distinction as the "father of bluegrass," a title he held until his death forty years later.

The Hall twins were never called the "brothers of bluegrass," but they remained popular in their home community.

. . .

Tensions rose again. This time, though, it was over a woman: Saford's new wife, Clovie, whom he'd met at the furniture factory where they'd both worked. She wasn't bad looking—she had auburn hair and wore glasses—but she came with baggage. She had a cute little boy named Larry, even though she had never been married before. The thing that unnerved Clayton, was Clovie's deafness. Clayton could not understand why Saford would be smitten with a deaf woman. (If he had stopped to think about it, though, a deaf woman might be the only type who could stand to live with Saford for very long.)

Clovie went out of her way to communicate verbally, which meant she talked loudly and was often incomprehensible. She knew a little sign language—but nobody else in the family did, so what was the point?—and she often threw her hands about wildly as if gestures would help her be understood. Clovie's gyrations annoyed Clayton, who, even though he was a bona fide world traveler, was still burdened with backwoods aversions to people who were different.

"You don't love her," he told Saford. "You can't love her. I'll never understand you."

"I love her just as much as you love Elinor," Saford shot back.

Clayton managed to keep his prejudices to himself, mostly, especially around Clovie. He was too decent of a man to be mean to anybody. Besides, when Saford married Clovie and moved into a little house just a couple hundred yards from Clayton and Elinor, it didn't take long for Clovie to become a loving, accepted member of the family. She had a good heart, and she loved all of her new nieces and nephews. She liked Clayton and Elinor immensely and showered Renee with gifts of clothes, dolls, and coloring books. Her little boy, Larry, was adopted by all the cousins as if he was blood kin. Maybe Saford's new family would fit in after all.

The next thirty years truly were "The Hollow Years."

—NOT SOMETHING MY MOM WROTE

The genealogy-book version of Clayton and Saford's lives con-
veniently skips over this period. Not that it wasn't chock-full of wonderful
moments—the brothers settled into quiet lives raising their only children
(Clayton, a daughter; Saford, an adopted son), working at another furniture factory, worshipping in a historic Moravian church, making many new
friends, traveling to the beach when money wasn't tight and a car was road-
worthy, and playing music every chance they got. If either one of them
was here today, they might claim those years were among the happiest of
their lives. But they're not here and they would be lying.

I won't kill as many trees telling you about the next thirty years as I
did on the first thirty. In the process, I will give short shrift to my mother,
grandmother, brothers, and other people who were deeply close to Clayton
and Saford in the first few decades after the war. I apologize to them, but
they can write their own books. Besides, most of my family would agree
that the exciting part of the twins' shared story was the early days. Those
are the stories they regaled us with over and over again in my grandparents' cozy living room: the one about the time they walked to the White
Plains fiddlers convention in the storm with blue dye running down their
legs; the one about Roy Hall coming to Bassett looking for the Hall twins;
the one about Clayton buying his first car with money he had saved in a
sugar sack.

Not as much time was spent on the stories about how much they enjoyed applying stain and varnish to chests of drawers at National Furniture Factory in Mount Airy, North Carolina. Nor did they wax nostalgic about the fights they waged as old men, against their myriad health problems, marital duress, money issues, and each other.

But those thirty years are an important part of the story. That's when all the pent-up bitterness and stresses began to push against the surface, like lava awakening inside a dormant volcano. And when it erupted, the force blew the brothers apart.

· · ·

Mount Bethel Moravian Church was packed from pulpit to front door every Easter. Families who hadn't been to church since the Christmas candlelight service sprouted in pews like lilies in the field, men dressed in their best suits, ladies topped by flowery hats. Easter was the one time at Mount Bethel when even the preacher, Paul Snyder, didn't recognize every face. Elinor, who had met just about all the neighbors up and down Wards Gap Road, wondered who all these people were in her pew.

After the service, a snappily dressed woman walked up to Elinor and Renee, and she commented on how pretty Renee looked in her dress.

"I can't tell who she looks like," the woman said to Elinor, meaning that she couldn't decide if Renee resembled her daddy or her mommy. Renee thought the woman was silly. I look like Renee, she thought.

Pearl Tilley, a regular member of Mount Bethel, heard the lady's comment. Pearl strode by and said, "Ha! I know who she looks like!"

That didn't sit well with Elinor. What did she mean by "I know who she looks like?" Elinor demanded an explanation.

Pearl explained that she thought Renee resembled the Smiths, Pearl's own cousins. What makes you say that? Elinor asked. And that's when Pearl Tilley told my grandmother the story of Dan and Fitzhugh Smith and their relationship to the famous Hall twins of The Hollow.

· · ·

Dan Smith was Pearl Tilley's uncle, her mother's brother. Dan and Irene Smith had a large family of several boys and girls, all of them bright, hardworking children. Their daughters became teachers. The oldest son, Fitzhugh, had moved away to West Virginia to find work and rarely returned home.

Pearl told Elinor, "Now, you're going to hear that Fitzhugh Smith was Clayton and Saford's daddy. But my mother knew the truth. Uncle Dan was their daddy."

As Pearl explained it to Elinor, Irene Smith had fallen ill during the late summer of 1918. The flu epidemic had decimated Patrick County, especially children and the aged, but it's unclear what afflicted Irene. Mamo had been called to help nurse Irene back to health, to cook and to clean, and to care for the little Smiths, which included Fitzhugh, who wasn't so little. Mamo stayed at the Smith house for several weeks, just as she had done for other women over the years who had needed her domestic help. She and Irene were friends, and she even called Irene by her nickname, "Renie Gal."

But just as it had happened at some of the other places, Mamo departed the Smith house with a baby in her belly—except that this time, it was two babies.

Pearl told Elinor that the Smith family laid the blame on Fitzhugh, who would have been a teenager at the time. Fitzhugh moved away soon after, and the Smiths were spared any disgrace.

Elinor had never asked Clayton about his father, and Clayton had never volunteered any information. She never knew about the mean boys of The Hollow who bullied Clayton and Saford with taunts of "Dan and Fitzhugh...Dan and Fitzhugh." But now Elinor knew the truth.

Pearl Tilley wanted Clayton and Saford in the Smith fold. The Smiths were good people, and Dan and Irene's children, who would have been Clayton and Saford's half siblings, occasionally reached out to the twins, who thoroughly and unequivocally let it be known that they wanted to be left alone.

Pearl once called Elinor at home to tell her that the Smiths were holding a family reunion and that Clayton and Renee should come so that Renee could meet her cousins. Elinor asked, "What about me? Can I come?" Pearl replied, "Aw, you ain't no Smith."

Pearl tried one other time to reach out to the prideful Halls. She told Elinor that Renee was the spitting image of Dan's daughter Grace, who had been a schoolteacher. She thought it would be wonderful if Renee would come visit her aunt. She even sent a photograph just so Renee could see the resemblance for herself.

Renee wouldn't even look at it.

"I don't want to see what I'll look like when I get old," she said.

Mamo admitted to nothing. She never had to, because the family had adopted a don't ask, don't tell policy regarding her personal life. Most of Mamo's children eventually came to know who their fathers were, but none ever had any kind of personal relationship with the men.

. . .

Mamo's grandchildren—and there were many of them growing up along Wards Gap Road, nearly twenty in all—adored her. Who wouldn't love a woman who let you flip a fried pie in a pan, or played the card game Rook with you all night? My mother claimed she learned her numbers off of Rook cards. If Renee beat Mamo at a hand, Mamo would throw down her cards disgustedly and complain that the children's chatter had distracted her or that someone hadn't dealt the cards right. It was easy to see where Clayton and Saford had inherited their competitive natures.

Mamo loved her grandchildren right back, especially Renee, whom she believed was a living, breathing good luck charm. After Renee won a giant doll in a punch-board game at Lummy Chappell's store, Mamo spent every penny she had on Renee's punch-board habit (possibly laying the foundation for my mother's lottery-ticket addiction). Over the years, Renee won a cornucopia of cakes and gift baskets, fulfilling Mamo's belief that she was one special child.

Almost every Sunday afternoon in the summertime, Mamo invited her children and grandchildren to Clayton and Elinor's house for a day of food, family, and music. She would make huge pots of dumplings, pans of biscuits, and washtubs of lemonade. The boys—Clayton, Saford, Sam, their brothers, their cousins, and their nephews—busted out the fiddles and banjos and played until dark.

Mamo was still a fine singer herself, still preferring those old mountain ballads she sang as a younger woman working in the fields or making baskets. In the 1950s, a man came with a big reel-to-reel tape recorder and asked her to sing her favorite songs so he could save them for posterity. She hemmed and hawed at first, claiming nobody would want to listen to them old songs, not when she heard the kind of music her granddaughter Renee listened to—Elvis Presley, and all that rock and roll.

But she sang. She crooned the old mountain ballads about poor Ellen Smith, how was she found, shot through the heart lying cold on the ground; about handsome Molly, Barbara Allen, and a girl named Cindy, about whom she sang, "Get along home, Cindy, I'll marry you someday." The man made his tapes, and she never heard from him again.

Into her eighties, Mamo continued to doctor the aged and the infirm. When Renee fell gravely sick with rheumatic fever and missed several months of school, Mamo treated her granddaughter with pans of hot biscuits, honey, and foot rubs. At night, Mamo cried that poor little Renee (who wasn't that little anymore) would not make it in this world very long. She worried that she was too delicate. That might have been the only prediction that Mamo ever got wrong. Renee got well and returned to school, where she was an exceptional student.

Many evenings, Mamo made chicken and dumplings for herself, only to remember somebody else in the community who was hungry. She would pack the pot into one of her handmade baskets, wrap a few fried apple pies in a dish towel, and walk down Wards Gap Road to feed another hungry person.

Nearly everybody in The Hollow loved Mamo. They would miss her when she was gone.

. . .

Sometime in the early 1960s, Saford grew ill. Always skinny, he had shriveled below 120 pounds in his early thirties and was stricken with a continuous cough. A chest X-ray revealed a dire diagnosis: tuberculosis.

Saford's lungs had been scarred considerably from years of smoking cigarettes—he preferred Salems and Camels to Clayton's Winstons. He had also been subjected to poison-gas training before the war, not to mention the noxious fumes of furniture factories. He was a sick man.

He spent several months at Catawba Sanatorium in the rolling green hills northwest of Roanoke County, where he was treated with antibiotics and clean mountain air. By the time he returned home to Clovie and Larry, he was fully recovered, although he never again resembled the picture of good health. He continued to smoke, and he looked as thin and frail as a cancer patient. He and Clayton both continued to work in the furniture factories of Mount Airy, bringing home meager paychecks with which to pay off their grocery bills at the country stores. This was their lot in life now: work long hours, feed and clothe their families, play a little music on the side, repeat. Their chance for country music glory had long passed, and their battlefield adventures were just stories to entertain the family.

. . .

It must have been hard being Saford Hall's twin brother after the war. Saford loved regaling his copious nephews with war stories, telling them about meeting Patton, storming the beaches of North Africa, and chasing the Germans back to the Rhineland. He taught the boys how to shoot pistols by taking them down to a creek and setting up cans and bottles for target practice. He barked orders like the platoon sergeant he had been, instructing them how to hold, aim, and fire the weapons.

Clayton couldn't compete. He tried, repeating the stories of getting shot in the Philippines and the time he fell into the tank trap on Okinawa. But most of his stories didn't come easily—it's hard to explain to a gaggle of war-hungry boys what it's like to just sit in one place and have the shit shelled out of you day after day. Those stories weren't as exciting as Saford's incredible tales of escaping from Germans and slitting the throats of enemies.

It didn't help that, years earlier, right after the war, Saford had received a package that contained a cross-shaped medal and some papers.

"Looky here!" he exclaimed. "It's got Charles de Gaulle's name on it!"

Saford had been awarded the Croix de Guerre avec Etoile de Bronze— literally, a War Cross with Bronze Star, a prestigious commendation given by the French as thanks for helping with that liberation business.

Even with his Purple Heart, Bronze Star, and a breast full of combat ribbons, Clayton didn't stand a chance against Saford's braggadocio. So Clayton's stories got a little bigger with each retelling. Saford had been a platoon sergeant in charge of fifteen men (a fact verified in his service record). Soon, Clayton was, too, even though he had only been a squad leader, at best. Saford claimed that he had met Patton. Clayton claimed that he had killed eight Japs by himself. In the end, Clayton opted out of the war-story arms race. If Saford needed to believe he had been the better soldier, so be it. Clayton wanted desperately to leave the miseries of war behind, not relive them every day with his overly competitive twin brother who had Charles de Gaulle on his side.

. . .

The 1960s gave Clayton the chance for a clean break from refighting the Big One. He turned his attention away from war stories and got interested in county politics. The Halls were old-school, turn-of-the-(last-)century Democrats, who were fairly conservative when it came to social issues and religion but were liberal in their ideas that the government should help the poor and ask sacrifices of the rich. This was an odd position for Clayton to take, considering that, except for one or two visits to the VA Hospital in Salem, near Roanoke, for free medical care, he had never availed himself of the many government programs created to assist GIs returning from the war. He never went to school or learned a trade on the GI Bill. He never went back for a GED. Since his discharge in 1946, he had made his living with his own two hands, whether they were slapping a bass fiddle or slapping stain on furniture.

That didn't mean he felt government had no role in helping make people's lives better. Times certainly were not as hard as they had been during his poverty-stricken childhood in the 1920s, when a boy might eat one meal a day and be happy to have it, but even in the 1960s many neighbors, friends, and family were shamefully poor. Even in his own county, Clayton saw the economic disparity between country people and townsfolk, especially when it came to the sorry state of the schools below the mountain, where children were still taught by the warmth of coal-burning stoves. So this combat veteran, factory worker, family man, and Sunday school teacher took his stab at politics and ran for the board of supervisors—and lost. He never ran for office again.

Instead, he found a more important way to serve his community: He became a preacher.

He was not a trained minister; few mountain preachers could even spell "seminary," much less graduate from one. But he had a profound interest in the Bible, and he taught Sunday school at Mount Bethel Moravian Church, where he listened intently to the sermons of the Reverend Paul Snyder, a gentle pastor who favored a thoughtful, softer approach behind the pulpit over the hell-and-damnation hollering of many mountain preachers. Clayton soaked up anything he could about preaching, the Bible, and the Moravian sacraments.

Mostly, though, he wanted to preach the Gospel because of a promise he had made to the Lord during the war. Clayton told Elinor, "I promised that if the Lord let me come home alive, I would serve him the rest of my life."

Clayton was keenly interested in the book of Revelation, whose prophecies of fiery destruction and violence didn't seem so fantastic, considering

Clayton's own wartime experiences. But where others saw the apocalypse coming in the revelation to John, Clayton found hope that all bad times shall pass, that better things lay ahead, and that this mean old world we all live in would come to know peace.

Sometime around 1964, Reverend Snyder asked Clayton if he would take over Crooked Oak Moravian, a little church on an old gravel road called Bear Trail with a small congregation that had never prospered. Crooked Oak had been started by Clayton's own uncle, the Reverend Alfred Dawson, the husband of Mamo's sister Emma. Alfred preached his first sermon behind an actual crooked oak, which he used as a pulpit and where he laid his Bible. The namesake tree was felled to build the frame church, which was attended by a handful of congregants who had cycled through a series of young pastors they could not afford to pay. Reverend Snyder made his request to Clayton by slipping a note under his front door. Clayton accepted the offer and soon was preparing to become a preacher.

. . .

More changes were coming fast. Renee grew from a tomboyish imp who played with her boy cousins into a teenage beauty queen. Her light-brown hair had darkened considerably, and her wide brown eyes made her look like a Persian princess. She became a cheerleader and played clarinet in the band at Hillsville High School, a good thirty-minute bus ride over the mountain. She loved the Beatles and Sam Cooke, and she was a good dancer. She was quite popular, especially with boys, who called on her and wanted to date her. Clayton warned her, only half-jokingly, that he would shoot the tires out on the vehicle of any boy coming to see her.

"You'd better have a lot of bullets," Renee shot back.

She settled on one boy in particular—the fellow who had my name first. Ralph Berrier was two years older than Renee, a superb athlete who excelled at baseball. They met at the only place any hillbilly parents of mine could possibly meet—at the bowling alley in Mount Airy, North Carolina. Elinor, Renee, and Clovie had gone to town to do laundry on a Saturday night, and Renee convinced them to roll a game at the bowling alley. As the three ladies walked in, Ralph and a buddy were walking out. Recognizing the popular, athletic boy from the halls of Hillsville High School, Renee chirped, "You want to bowl a game?" Turns out that Ralph had never had a real date, and his buddy had dragged him to town to "find some women."

Ralph grew up in an apple orchard about ten miles from Renee's family, all the way across U.S. 52, which dissected the primarily "below-the-mountain" community of Cana. The sweethearts dated through Ralph's senior year, during which Renee was a sophomore and was voted the school's "Snow Queen." They stayed together even after Ralph was drafted at age eighteen—not by the military for service in Vietnam, but by baseball's Houston Astros. He reported to Florida for spring training and played for the Astros rookie-league club in Bradenton. He had been the best player in Carroll County, a slugging, left-handed power hitter who crushed base-balls over the old field house in right field. But in pro ball, everybody was the best player from somewhere, and young Ralph struggled. He was also homesick. A poor country boy from a family of apple pickers, he dreamed at night of mountain trails he had walked and woods he had hunted, and he wrote letters home to his mother wondering if anyone had taken over his job of mowing the cemetery at Flower Gap Primitive Baptist Church.

Renee made a road trip with Ralph's parents to visit him that summer in Florida, but mostly they kept their romance alive through letters. The next winter, as Ralph prepared for his second season in the minor leagues, he and Renee got married on December 22, 1965, the fiftieth wedding anniversary of Ralph's grandparents, Fred and Ella Leonard. He was eighteen, Renee had just turned seventeen and was a junior in high school. Like I said, we marry 'em off young in my clan.

Which brings up an embarrassing childhood story. When I was in the fourth grade at Lambsburg Elementary School, I somehow wound up making a speech about my family in front of the entire combined fourth- and fifth-grade class. I was blessed with the gift of gab at a young age, so I don't recall if the teacher actually requested that I speak to the class or if I just started spouting off because I thought everyone needed to know my family's secrets. Anyway, while enthralling my classmates with the impor-tant dates in my family's history, I somehow mentioned that my parents married on December 22, 1965, and that I was born on June 7, 1966.

And that's the precise moment when the cold, hard truth hit me.

The rest of the class needed the same amount of time to do the math as I did—about two seconds—and when the calculations were finished, the entire room roared with shocked laughter.

"You were born *six months* after your parents *got married?*" somebody hollered.

The audience whooped like a pack of hyenas. Even ten-year-olds know that it takes nine months' worth of simmerin' to make a healthy baby—and no one, then or since, had ever suggested that I might have been born three months premature.

"Oh my *God!*" I thought to myself. "My mom was *pregnant when she got married!*"

I was humiliated. I immediately sat down and never mentioned my family in public again. Until now, of course.

My mom had her own childhood foot-in-mouth moment, although not as embarrassing as my own. When she was a little girl, one of her playmates remarked how she couldn't wait until she was all grown-up so she could get married and have babies.

Little Renee didn't understand that at all.

"I'm not going to get married," she said. "My grandmother never got married, and she had ten babies."

Elinor heard her say that. She calmly pulled Renee aside and suggested that she not repeat that out loud.

. . .

Elinor cared for her new grandbaby while Renee attended summer school in order to graduate early. How many people can say they attended their mama's high school graduation? I can. I was there in the Hillsville High School auditorium when my mother became the first member of her immediate family to receive her high school diploma.

Ralph played three seasons in the minors before hanging up his spikes after the 1967 campaign. Renee and Ralph lived in a tiny three-room house Ralph's parents had built for them right in the middle of the family apple orchard. The house had running water but no indoor bathroom. The young couple was not used to using an outhouse. They had grown up poor, but not *that* poor. They had stepped back in time forty years to live like their parents had.

Clayton and Elinor stayed busy with work, church, and friends. They even traveled on weekends with other families to Claytor Lake, about an hour away, where they sunned themselves on the public beach and ate picnic lunches. Finally, Clayton found the slow, peaceful existence he had long sought.

Saford, not surprisingly, struggled with domestic life. He and Clovie argued frequently, often over money. Saford accused Clovie of buying too many appliances for the house. She bought a refrigerator and a washing machine, all on credit. Saford was up to his black-framed glasses in debt, and he let Clovie know he wasn't happy about it.

Clovie got her licks in by accusing Saford of womanizing, which he angrily denied. He swore up and down that he wasn't running around on her, claiming that this time he was telling the truth, a claim he continued to make right up until the moment the woman he was running around with showed up with a passel of kids.

She appeared at a show that Clayton and Saford were playing in Mount Airy. The twins had joined a red-hot group of local bluegrassers to perform at local festivals and fiddlers conventions. They even called themselves, of all things, the Blue Ridge Entertainers. During one of the Entertainers' gigs, a rumpled-looking lady wearing thick glasses and support hose arrived with several children. Somebody elbowed Elinor and told her, "That's the woman Saford's running around with." Elinor couldn't believe it. She was shocked that Saford would run around with another woman...so *frumpy* looking. Oh, she totally believed Saford was capable of cheating on Clovie. One time at a Christmas party, she had watched him dance with every woman in the house after he got into the punch bowl. He hugged them, squeezed them, and spun them like they were his dates. She figured he had a wandering eye. She just couldn't figure out what it was he saw in Miss Frumpy. She never knew. Thankfully, Miss Frumpy's kids were not his, but that provided little comfort. Saford and Clovie were on the rocks.

. . .

They thought it was emphysema at first. The wheezing, the coughing, the shortness of breath. Could it be tuberculosis? Weight was coming off. Strength was declining.

Mamo was dying.

Mamo the indestructible. Mamo the loving mother and grandmother. Mamo the fearless. Mamo the pie fryer, the basket maker, the healer. Mamo the legend. Mamo the great-grandmother I never knew. Mamo was dying.

She had been distressed with dizzy spells and breathing problems. As she grew ever weaker, she couldn't walk to the car without nearly passing out from exhaustion. Her boys took her to Catawba, the same hospital where Saford had recovered from tuberculosis. But Mamo's little lungs, which had breathed life into all those old mountain ballads, were riddled with scar tissue. They were giving out. As she lay in a hospital bed along-side other poor souls hooked up to oxygen tanks, Mamo told Clayton she was ready to go.

Clayton, however, was not ready to let her go. For one thing, the newly minted preacher man wasn't sure if his mama had ever been saved. Mamo went to church, especially when she was older and could go with her grand-children, but Clayton never recalled her saying anything about being bap-tized. He had to make sure his mama had been saved, otherwise he would never see her in heaven.

"Mama," Clayton said, "have you taken Christ as your Lord and Savior?"

"Yes, I know Jesus," she assured him.

"That ain't what I mean," he said. "Have you ever been saved?"

"What are you talking about?"

"I'm asking, have you given your soul to Christ and been saved?"

Mamo, weak though she was, got a little perturbed at Clayton's insinuations.

"What's this about being 'saved'? I said I know Jesus. I've lived a good life. Ain't that all that matters?"

Clayton grew impatient. "No, Mama. That ain't enough. Jesus has got to wash away all your sins...."

"What sins?" she interrupted. "I don't like that kind of talk."

"We've all sinned," Clayton said. "I don't mean nothing by it. It's just that you've got to ask Jesus to wash all your sins away. You've got to trust in the power of the blood."

"Well, I don't know...."

"I just want to make sure you're saved."

"I don't understand this talk about being 'saved.' I've lived a good life. I've loved everybody. I've treated people good. I ain't ever asked for noth-ing. Ain't that the most important thing? I've lived a good life?"

"No, Mama. It's not."

"Well, then," she said. "I don't know what to think about that."

Clayton prayed for his mother. He prayed that God would shine his love on her and forgive her all her many sins, that He would wash her sins away and leave her soul as white as the snow.

Judie Elizabeth Hall died June 4, 1968, one day after her eighty-ninth birthday. They buried her in the Montgomery Cemetery alongside her mother and her father, a man who had once boasted that he didn't want to spend eternity lying next to them leather-eyed Montgomerys. Clayton led the congregation in prayer, and he once again asked that God would bless his mother, and while He was at it, perhaps He could just forgive everyone in attendance of their innumerable sins.

Mamo was gone. Her grandchildren would miss the nights playing Rook and the Sunday afternoon parties. Most of her great-grandchildren would never know her. And her babies, those rascally twins, would no longer have anyone to step in and pull them apart when they fought. They would certainly miss that.

. . .

Clayton and Saford still had their happy moments. They played games of canasta, badminton, and golf together. Especially golf. Clayton's son-in-law, Ralph, introduced the game to the twins. They never excelled, but they weren't bad. My dad still talks about the day Clayton and Saford played eight consecutive rounds on the nine-hole White Pines Country Club all in one day, seventy-two holes in all. They walked every round, conspicuous by their quick little bowlegged steps.

They still played music with the newfangled Blue Ridge Entertainers, even appearing on local television a few times. I remember that when I was quite young a large crowd gathered at our house—by then we had upgraded from the three-room house to a four-room farmhouse that my great-grandfather had built—where we watched Clayton and Saford play some show on a low-powered North Carolina TV station.

That was near the end of the good times, though. Saford was unhappy with his life, and he projected that unhappiness onto others, including his twin. They saved their fights for the factory. They argued and occasionally came to blows over work. Clayton's expertise in color and stains had elevated him to the rank of quality control foreman at National Furniture Company in Mount Airy. He had an office where he filled out paperwork, smoked Winstons, and drank black coffee. He had the power to hire, fire, and discipline workers, which would drive the last wedge between him and Saford.

Saford constantly challenged Clayton's authority, even though the two didn't work in the same department. When Clayton hired Clovie to work in the finishing room, Saford went nuts, believing that Clayton had hired her just so she could spy on Saford while he was at work. Clayton said he hired her because she needed a job.

Months later, Saford pulled a one-eighty. Instead of coddling Clovie, he accused Clayton of being too hard on her at work, of treating her differently because she was deaf or because he wanted to show Saford who the boss was. Clayton called Saford crazy. He didn't treat Clovie any differently than he treated any other employee. When she did a good job, he told her so. When she needed to do something over, he told her that, too.

Saford's insecurities had made everyone close to him miserable—Clovie, Larry, and Clayton. He yelled at Clovie—who couldn't hear him—that she was going to bankrupt him. Clovie yelled, too—although Saford couldn't always understand her—and made manic gestures with her hands, which he also couldn't decipher. Clovie got her point across, though. She still accused Saford of running around with other women. Saford denied it. Teenage Larry took to staying out late just to avoid the arguments.

Clayton and Saford's last fight was a doozy. It happened at the factory. Clayton couldn't remember what it was about. He might have admonished Clovie for some work that needed redoing, and the next thing he knew, Saford stormed into his office, cussing a spittle-flying blue streak. At some point, Saford took a swing.

Then it was on. Arms and legs flailed as the two of them rolled out of Clayton's office. They toppled over each other like fighting dogs, one guy getting the advantage over the other, then losing it. Twenty-five years of simmering anger, bitterness, and blame that had slowly built up like steam in a boiler finally exploded in a blast of rage and fists. They fought right there on the factory floor, punching and scratching in front of an assembly line of coworkers who had probably seen it coming. Years later, men who worked at the factory would come up to my grandmother and apologize to her for not having tried to separate the twin brawlers out of fear of getting their own noses broken or losing a tooth. If only Mamo had been there to step in between them.

Finally, Clayton gained the advantage. He wrapped up Saford from behind in a steel-lock bear hug, lifted him off the ground, and toted him toward an open window. He would have thrown him out, too, had Saford not been able to spread his feet apart at the last second and brace himself against the frame like a cat that refuses to be stuffed into a carrier.

"He's crazy!" Saford hollered. "He's a crazy man!"

Clayton did not disagree.

"I am crazy!" he said, finally giving up and dropping Saford to the concrete floor in a heap. "You've *made* me crazy!"

That's when Saford left. Not just the factory, but Virginia. He moved away and found a job in Thomasville, North Carolina, applying finish to plastic mirror frames. He left so quickly, he didn't even take Clovie and Larry with him. He aimed to leave all his pain and sadness behind and start over. But things only got worse.

The first time Papa Clayton and I performed together onstage was during a countywide 4-H Club talent show in the spring of 1976. I had won the local competition at Lambsburg Elementary School with my impeccable a cappella version of "I Believe in Music," which had been a smash for the great Mac Davis. Actually, it was one of my mother's favorites. The lyrics scream "1970s" louder than a parade of tie-dyed Deadheads:

> *So clap your hands and stomp your feet and shake your tambourine,*
> *And lift your voices to the sky; tell me what you see*

Everybody!

> *I believe in music*
> *Oh-oh-oh, I believe in love*

Now, a Mac Davis song was great if all you cared about was dominating the Lambsburg market. But to compete in the county competition against the town kids from Hillsville and the burgeoning suburbs of Galax, I needed the heavy artillery. I needed Elvis.

And I needed Papa Clayton. I learned the words to "Love Me Tender" from a songbook of a hundred Elvis songs. Papa Clayton had no trouble

with the chords. Mom made me a little satin suit dotted with rhinestones—
this was clearly my Las Vegas period—and Papa Clayton and I took the stage
inside the posh environs of the Carroll County High School auditorium.

I won a red ribbon. That doesn't mean I finished in second place; a
bunch of people received blue ribbons and the rest of us got the red. I was
a second-class talent.

* * *

Ricky was his favorite grandson. Oh, I am sure Papa Clayton would deny
that he could ever choose one of his three grandsons over the others—I am
the oldest, Ricky is three years younger than me, Billy eleven—but Ricky
had to be the favorite. He was a live wire. He was rambunctious, loud,
hyper, and had a bad temper—which must have reminded Papa of two
other boys he once knew. Ricky was the only one of us he ever spanked
with a rolled-up magazine, but that just meant the two of them had a bond
neither Billy nor I could share.

Ricky could never sit still for more than thirty seconds, so Papa Clayton
took him outside, handed him a golf club and a plastic practice ball, and the
two of them duffed their way around the front yard for hours, hitting balls
toward "greens" of flower beds, oak trees, and car tires. He taught Ricky
how to play chess, which Ricky mastered as quickly as any five-year-old
ever had. One time, little Ricky even checkmated Uncle Asey, who quickly
claimed that, no, this was actually a *stalemate,* thus a tie, as he swiftly moved
the pieces to start a new game.

Papa Clayton also taught Ricky how to tie a necktie—where was I during all of these lessons? Watching *Planet of the Apes?*—in the double-knotted
Windsor knot fashion he had learned in the army. To this day, I can still tie
only a square knot.

But the greatest thing Papa Clayton ever taught Ricky to do was play
the guitar. Ricky must have been eight or nine, and I can still see the chord
positions Papa Clayton wrote in pencil on the pages of a small writing tab-
let. I might have tried a few chords myself, but I showed no real interest in
learning the guitar.

Ricky excelled on guitar and soon was playing with two of his classmates
at St. Paul Intermediate School. Ricky, Tony Jones, and Brad Hiatt formed
the famous Cana River Band, named for a body of water that did not exist.
They once played the Mount Airy fiddlers convention, unbeknownst to my

mother, who thought Ricky was just at a sleepover at Tony's house. The boy band received a huge crowd response, as you might expect of a kid act. Their selection was a vocal number by Ricky, a song called "Ugly Girl," whose chorus went:

Always marry an ugly girl, that's the only kind
She'll never ever leave you, 'cause she knows you won't mind

The biggest ovation, though, was reserved for the last verse:

Never make love to an ugly girl, she will never quit
She will think that it's the last she's ever gonna get

There's just something about an eleven-year-old boy singing a line like that that can drive an audience wild. Of course, had Ricky known that he would be asked to sing "Ugly Girl" at every cookout, birthday party, wedding, and family reunion for the next twenty-five years—the same way Papa Clayton kept requesting that he sing "The Little Drummer Boy" in church, even after Ricky towered over Papa by a good five inches—perhaps he would have chosen "Fox on the Run." His wife, who had to grit her teeth every time he sang about the advantages of marrying an ugly girl, would have preferred that, I am sure.

· · ·

We didn't see much of Saford when I was growing up. I have vivid memories of his visits to Papa and Grandma's house when I was small, and I certainly remember Clovie, always lively and boisterous, talking with her hands and telling me and my brothers how cute we were. Saford was forever laughing and telling stories. No signs of family tension were evident to a little kid—probably not to anyone else, either. The twins' separation served as a balm for the old wounds.

Saford and Clovie, however, were having a tough time, a fact I would not know until thirty years later. They did not leave Virginia together. Clovie moved to Thomasville several weeks or months after Saford had left. Family legend maintains that when she arrived, she went to the factory where Saford worked and asked to see her husband. She was informed that Saford was working in the shop . . . *with his wife.*

Clovie blew her stack. "I'm his wife!" she bellowed, as clearly as she could communicate. Saford apparently had set up housekeeping with the same woman he'd been running around with in Mount Airy. That little party finally ended with the landfall of Hurricane Clovie.

Saford, Clovie, and Larry lived in a rented house on Unity Street—an ironic address for this household. The family was hardly the picture of domestic tranquillity. All Saford had done was relocate his troubles from Virginia to North Carolina. The single bright spot in his life had not changed—music.

Shortly after he arrived in Thomasville, Saford formed a bluegrass band. He invited musicians to jam sessions every week on Unity Street. One night, a neighbor attended—a fortyish fellow with swept-back hair and sideburns—and lamented that he had never learned to play music like that. Saford told the fellow if he would get himself a cheap guitar, Saford could teach him to play it in thirty days.

So the guy did as Saford instructed and sure enough, a month later, Benjamin "Buster" Brown could strum through simple bluegrass patterns. Buster's wife, Madge, was so shocked by her husband's sudden musical prowess that she asked Saford if he could teach her how to play the big bass fiddle. Within a few months, Saford had even taught the Browns' sons to play guitar and banjo. Pretty soon, they had a family band.

They called themselves Buster Brown and the Thomasville Playboys, even though Saford was the most accomplished musician of the bunch and the guy who did all the talking. They played local dances and fiddlers conventions all over North Carolina. Saford's fiddling was better than ever. He had nearly fifty years of fiddle playing under his belt and knew as many tunes as there were birds in the trees. He played the fast numbers clean and briskly and could gear it down into beautiful slow tunes such as "Roxanna Waltz" and "Faded Love." He was a consummate showman.

Soon he had a protégé.

John Hofmann was a tall, strapping teenager with blond hair and an inquisitive, chatty personality. Saford met the boy during a Christmas square dance, when the young man walked up to him after a set and told Saford that he was the best fiddle player he had ever heard. Nothing endeared a person to Saford more quickly than flattery.

John asked about Saford's fiddle, an old Stainer model with a fearsome lion's head carved out of the headstock. The instrument looked older than it was, and was spotted with cigarette burns from the Salems Saford smoked as he played. John told Saford he was learning fiddle and asked Saford for his phone number so that he might call on him for a lesson. Saford told John that he didn't have a phone—that his wife was deaf and couldn't hear one ring—so he invited the teenager to his house for a lesson.

The next day, on a Sunday afternoon, John took his cheap fiddle to Saford's new house on Cox Avenue, which he rented from Buster Brown's father-in-law. Saford welcomed John inside, pulled up two chairs in the front room, and set a smoking stand with an ash tray between them. He asked John if he smoked, and the boy admitted that he did.

"Most good musicians do," Saford said, as he offered John a smoke and an ice-cold bottle of Dr Pepper.

He asked John to show him what he knew. John fiddled rough-hewn versions of "Boil Them Cabbage Down" and "Old Joe Clark," two fiddle standards if ever there were any. Saford complimented John on his playing—take it from me, Saford Hall encouraged and instilled confidence into every young fiddle player he ever met, whether he could play a lick or not—and he showed John how to play "Walking in My Sleep." John was amazed. This man could play a tune using all four strings!

"That's in G chord," Saford said.

The hour got late as John sat enraptured, listening to Saford play and tell stories. This man had made records. This man had played on the radio. This man made out like he had been famous at one time. See that Dr Pepper bottle you're drinking, Saford told him, that was my sponsor. That was all before the war, you see, which ruined everything.

John Hofmann returned, again and again. Saford showed him how to play "Sally Goodin" and "Dusty Miller." He taught him "Fisher's Hornpipe" and "Soldier's Joy." John drank in fiddle tunes like they were Dr Pepper, and he inhaled Saford's stories like cigarette smoke. This old dude was the real deal.

● ● ●

The only music Clayton played was in church. He sang in a gospel trio with two other church members, Brenda Ayers and Rebecca Hiatt, as part of the Crooked Oak Singers, an outfit that made a joyful noise at churches, revivals, homecomings, and all grade of worship service for several years in

252-IF TROUBLE DON'T KILL ME

the 1970s. Papa Clayton's signature song was an old gospel standard called "Thank You, Lord, for Your Blessings on Me," which neatly summed up his autumn years.

> *I've a roof up above me, I've a good place to sleep*
> *There's food on my table, and shoes on my feet*
> *You gave me your love, Lord, and a fine family*
> *Thank you, Lord, for your blessings on me*

One year, the church gave him a guitar as a present, but he never played it very much. It wasn't nearly as good as the 1940s Martins the Blue Ridge Entertainers favored. Besides, his duty now wasn't to play hillbilly music, it was to serve the Lord.

Clayton never became an ordained Moravian minister. Achieving that rank would have required attending a seminary. Crooked Oak Moravian Church, which struggled with membership throughout the 1970s and '80s, survived only because the main church's Southern Province deemed it a "mission," almost an outpost in the wilds of southern Virginia. That meant a poor, self-educated country preacher could lead the congregation. Clayton was eventually appointed an acolyte, a lay pastor who could administer the sacraments—which, in our church, meant serving tiny glasses of grape juice for communion.

The passage of years has diminished many specific memories of Crooked Oak, but a few survive. I can still see my baby brother Billy, a toddler of two, crawling up into the pulpit while Papa Clayton preached, spouting a baby-talk sermon of his own. I remember the way Papa Clayton signaled the end of a sermon: "As Mozelle comes to the piano," which was Mozelle Allen's cue to approach the piano bench and play the introduction to the benedictory hymn, "Just as I Am." I can still hear the benediction Papa Clayton prayed at the doorway at the end of every service: "May the grace of our Lord and Savior Jesus Christ be with and abide with you both now and evermore. Amen. Thank you for coming. God bless you." I can still smell the church's musty odor in summer, long before we installed air conditioning, and I can still hear the groans and creaks of the old wooden pews, which had been donated by another church. I remember the smell of beeswax candles from the Christmas candlelight service. But I don't remember much about Papa Clayton's sermons, except for this: He packed them with war references.

Sometimes they came in the form of a joke, like the Sunday morning he mentioned at the beginning of a sermon that the power had been out at his house, forcing him to "dry shave...like I used to do in the army!"

For his next birthday, the congregation gave him a rechargeable razor, so he wouldn't have to "dry shave" again.

Other times, the war references cropped up from nowhere, like sniper's bullets fired from the trees. Why did Papa Clayton preach about how he ordered men to lay down crossfire on enemy soldiers? Was he advising Joshua how best to attack Jericho? Did the Hebrews lay down a crossfire against the attacking Roman army?

He praised the "angels of mercy," the army nurses who took care of him after he was wounded and sick with malaria. Angels would seem like appropriate sermon fodder, but I don't remember what the context was.

I realize now that more was going on with Papa Clayton than just the spirit working his tongue. Yes, he practiced the mountain-style, free-association approach to sermons, where you never wrote out anything, you just started spouting off, but all those tales of crossfires and battles and army nurses seeped into his sermons not because he enjoyed talking about the war, but the opposite. He *couldn't* talk about it. The pulpit was an outlet for what was eating away at him. He had no one to confide in, not even his twin.

. . .

I discovered the metal lockbox while searching for an old letter Clayton had written from the army. Grandma kept it inside an old rolltop desk, stuffed with papers and letters saved over decades. I never found the letter I was looking for, but I uncovered something even more meaningful: numerous pieces of correspondence from various government agencies and political power brokers, which included the Veterans Administration, the Disabled American Veterans, accountants, and even U.S. congressmen, most written in the 1970s and early '80s, some older. They were answers to Papa Clayton's pleas for help, and they were not the answers he wanted.

The earliest letter was dated March 9, 1949, the day the VA informed him he would draw a monthly award of $13.80 for, according to the letter, "Malaria, neck wound and nervousness."

He suffered recurrences of malaria for more than ten years after he returned from the war. The first time Elinor saw him sick with fever scared her to death. They were still living in Roanoke, still in her mother's house, when Clayton passed out in a feverish pile. He didn't respond when she tried to wake him. He was unconscious for hours, and when he finally awoke, he instructed her that if she ever saw him like that she should pour water onto his tongue.

My mother remembered seeing him sick when she was a child. She remembered that he burned like a woodstove, and that she could feel the heat from his body across the small living room. He suffered his last malaria attack just shy of his fortieth birthday.

But the "nervousness" was chronic. He had difficulty sleeping. Pressures at work mounted. His $13,000-a-year job as quality control supervisor at the furniture factory made him responsible for every piece of furniture that left the premises. But as he sent back cracked tabletops and wobbly table legs for repair, Papa Clayton had no one to watch over him as he slowly fell apart.

He recognized that he was not a well man. He tried to call out for help, but his pride prevented him from announcing to the world that he was sick. As he approached his sixtieth birthday, he desperately wanted to retire from the furniture factory. He could not focus on his work. He suffered from anxiety and knew his mental condition was deteriorating, even as he tried to hide his impending meltdown from the rest of his family, friends, and coworkers. He wrote to the VA to see if he could get an increase in that tiny monthly payment he received for his old wounds, which would allow him to retire early. The VA responded:

> March 28, 1977
> Dear Mr. Hall:
>   After carefully reviewing the report of your 1-18-77 examination and all other evidence of record, it has been determined that your service connected nervous condition should be evaluated at 10% disabling rather than 0% disabling. However, this increased evaluation does not affect your previously assigned 10% combined evaluation. Your reward will remain unchanged.

He wrote to veterans' advocacy groups, including the American Legion and the Military Order of the Purple Heart, who asked him to fill out more forms and send them to other offices. He wrote to his congressman, who contacted the commonwealth's War Veterans Claims Division, who instructed Clayton that he file a "Notice of Disagreement" with the VA's decision, which would result in him receiving a "statement of the case," whereupon he would have sixty days to file his appeal. Should he have any more questions, he could contact them.

He had lots of questions, but he wasn't getting any answers. All he wanted was for the government to understand that he needed just a tiny bit of help, just a few dollars more per month so he could quit work and escape the pressures that were burning away his insides. He even underwent a psychiatric evaluation. He dutifully filled out the paperwork, made his appeal, and waited. Five months later, his congressman replied:

> April 26, 1978
> Dear Mr. Hall:
>   Enclosed is the copy of a decision we have received from the Board of Veterans Appeals on your claim.
>   This appears to be self-explanatory and we regret that it is not more encouraging.

Attached was a four-page summary of the board's findings. In January 1977, Clayton had undergone a psychiatric examination at the VA in Salem, Virginia. The appeals board summarized the particulars under the heading "Evidence":

> A psychiatric report noted that the appellant had complained of his nerves and an inability to sleep. He reported that he had to 'go to the bathroom' frequently. He was worried some about his problem in starting a stream. He was reported to be alert, in good contact, well oriented and agreeable and friendly. He was calm and appeared comfortable. He indicated some elements of depression; his memory was adequate. He represented a rather 'give up attitude,' developing multiple somatic complaints, and losing interest in his work. He was apprehensive and concerned that he would have to give up his job. A psychosis was not indicated. He denied [being a] danger to himself or others. A diagnosis of anxiety neurosis was made.

Now, put yourself in the appeals board's shoes. A fifty-eight-year-old man experiencing difficulty "starting a stream" was probably not grounds for 100 percent disability, otherwise every fifty-something man in America would be drawing disability. Unhappiness with work was probably not a red flag to the board, either. Call it a "Civilian Catch-22": any fellow who wants to quit his job can't be crazy. The psychiatrist's original notes remarked that Clayton appeared "calm," "friendly," and "agreeable." In other words, he was too proud to show how he really felt, too stoic to tell them his insides were tied together with spaghetti noodles. He shot himself in the combat boot with his calm demeanor and brave front. But that's all it was, a front.

The appeals board decided "Anxiety neurosis is productive of no more than moderate social and industrial impairment." It concluded "The scheduled criteria for a rating in excess of ten per cent (10%) for anxiety neurosis have not been met. . . . Entitlement to an increased rating for anxiety neurosis is not established. The benefit sought on appeal is denied."

It was an appropriate decision, given the evidence. But did the board really have all the evidence? Did the psychiatrist ever ask him what it was like to fight on Okinawa? Did the members of the appeals board ask what it felt like to crouch in a foxhole and watch a platoon of screaming Japanese soldiers charging you? Did anyone ask if watching his captain die from a bullet to the forehead shook him up a little? Clayton gave the right answers to all the wrong questions. He looked fine on the outside, which was all that mattered.

Besides, this was in the mid-1970s. The VA must have been processing thousands of claims and appeals from damaged World War II vets. What's one more? What's one man out of a million?

If Clayton was angered or frustrated by this decision, he kept it to himself. He continued to work, and in the summer of 1980 he was honored for twenty-five years of service at National Furniture. He still smoked Winston cigarettes, drank coffee by the potful, and ate good ol' fatty country cooking. He preached every Sunday at Crooked Oak Moravian Church and he sang gospel music with his friends. He seemed to be holding up well.

But what no one knew was that when he went to bed on the night of December 20, 1980, my strong, proud Papa Clayton was a broken man.

●　●　●

My mom, Grandma, and I went Christmas shopping in Winston-Salem the Saturday before Christmas, leaving Papa Clayton at home. He had just received his Christmas bonus from the furniture factory and was planning to do a little shopping of his own on Sunday, just before the candlelight service at Crooked Oak.

But Papa Clayton did not make it to church the next day. Early on the morning of Sunday, December 21, 1980, Grandma called Mom to tell her Papa Clayton was horribly sick. His malaria had recurred.

The recurrence seemed odd to Mom. He hadn't suffered a relapse in more than twenty years. But he woke up sick in the middle of the night and talking gobbledygook, babbling like a feverish madman. He vomited up thick, milky bile, which had not happened before.

Mom and Dad took my brothers and me to Papa and Grandma's that afternoon. My parents recognized immediately that this was more than just malaria. Papa's left arm and leg had gone numb. "They're gone," he kept saying. Dad called the rescue squad, which carried Papa Clayton to the hospital in Mount Airy—where he was examined and sent home.

The next day, Grandma took Papa to their family doctor, Eric Jarrell, who looked at Papa for two minutes and immediately sent him to the VA hospital in Salem. Papa Clayton stayed at the VA for the next thirty-three days and underwent surgery to remove an arterial blockage.

He had suffered a stroke.

. . .

I was fourteen when Papa Clayton had his stroke. I barely remember him when he was still strong and active, playing golf, pitching horseshoes, working every day. My memories of him were forged when I was in high school, when he was old and weak and moved slowly around with a cane.

He never worked again. He surrendered his position at Crooked Oak, although he attended semi-regularly when he was able. The paralysis in his left arm and leg was mild, more like constant numbness, but it was debilitating. Grandma stayed home to care for him. He drew $532 a month from Social Security and about $50 a month in veteran's benefits. They were damn near broke.

About a year after Clayton's stroke, Crooked Oak sponsored an auction to help pay his medical bills. The organizers held it on the grounds of Mount Bethel Elementary School on a clear spring day in 1982, following one of his many lengthy hospital stays at the VA. Even though the temperature was mild, Papa Clayton sat in a lounge chair, wearing a big, heavy coat. He looked extremely tired, old, and beaten.

But he continued to fight. He petitioned the VA for more benefits but was denied almost every time. The VA insisted that Papa Clayton's health problems were not service connected. His congressman intervened, but the VA held firm:

> Feb. 13, 1981
>
> Mr. Hall is service connected for a nervous condition, malaria, and residuals of a gunshot wound to the neck. He has submitted evidence claiming an increase in his service-connected disabilities, but the evidence did not show that he was treated for any of his service-connected conditions. Therefore, no change in the evaluations is in order.

His "nervous condition" worsened. His poor physical health depressed him. For the next five years, he spent months at a time in the VA hospital, where he was treated for "nerves and depression." In 1983, he submitted to the VA an income / net worth statement that revealed that he had mounting bills and only $2,100 to his name.

That was the same year I spent an incredibly boring week at Boys State. We "delegates" were supposed to be learning all about state government from a brigade of old American Legion dudes. After a long week of drudgery and army chants, I couldn't wait for my mother to rescue me and two high school buddies who had been imprisoned.

On the way home, we all joked about the old guys. I told my pals how the boys in my company...platoon, barracks, whatever they called it...how we laughed at the way one seriously old dude pronounced "MAC-Ar-thuh!" Those old bastards were a riot! We continued to yuck it up right up to the moment my mother drove us to the VA hospital to see my grandfather.

Papa Clayton spent a good chunk of the summer of 1983 hospitalized for his nerves. We met him outside, away from the depressing confines of the hospital, where carcasses of shattered men rolled around in wheelchairs, talking, sometimes shouting, to themselves. Broken combat veterans sat in the bleachers of the VA ball field where the local American Legion teams played—where I would play one day—and constantly razzed players on both sides. *"Get this guy! He cain't hit! This guy cain't pitch! Come on now! You ain't got nothing! Nothing!"*

Papa Clayton looked well—but tired. We told him we had just attended Boys State—making it sound much more interesting and dignified than it actually was, and leaving out the parts about making fun of the old soldiers who shepherded us through the inner workings of government. He was proud of us ol' Carroll County boys. He had spent his week in a VA work-shop, making leather belts for me and my brothers. He hand-stamped our names on the belts, complete with silly-looking footprint and horse-head stamps. He even made a leather billfold for me. The workshop was meant to be therapeutic, a way for him to focus on a task and take his mind off all his troubles. I am sure I never wore that belt. It looked sort of 1970s-ish, and this was the ultramodern era of 1983.

My mom snapped a few pictures, then drove me and my buddies home from our week of state-sponsored hell. Papa Clayton disappeared inside the hospital, melting into the phalanx of old, decrepit soldiers, who, like him, were simply fading away. My buddies and I never spoke of the old soldiers at Boys State again.

• • •

Saford fared no better. He might've appeared a tad healthier than Clayton, which wasn't saying much. Still, he didn't look good. He smoked two packs of Salems a day, and his frame had withered to the point that one close friend said he looked like a Holocaust victim.

By the early 1980s, his personal life was a shambles. Clovie continued to accuse him of womanizing, and even though she might have been wrong this time, Saford's track record did not allow for the benefit of the doubt. Their marriage was not long for this world.

Even Saford's music suffered. He was still the front man for Buster Brown and the Thomasville Playboys, who played square dances every weekend. But somewhere along the line he and Buster fell out.

John Hofmann, the young man who came to Saford's house to learn how to play the fiddle, became a close friend. During the first few years they knew each other, John and Saford fiddled nightly, swigging Dr Pepper, smoking cigarettes, and telling stories. John became a good fiddle player quickly. He accompanied Saford on several trips back to the hills of old Virginia, where they competed in every backwater fiddlers convention Saford knew how to get to. John even beat his mentor at one contest by playing one of Saford's favorite tunes, "Sally Goodin."

Within a few years, John was traveling to fiddlers conventions alone. He became a professional and by 1980 had landed a major gig as the fiddler for country singer Mickey Gilley right at the peak of the *Urban Cowboy*–mechanical bull era. At the pinnacle of John's career, he played with Gilley during the 1981 Grammy Awards telecast. Saford, proud of his best pupil, couldn't believe it when John sent him a Mickey Gilley tour jacket. Saford wore it everywhere, even when the weather was warm.

Saford made a few more close friends, most notably Bruce Moseley, a terrific guitarist who started playing shows with the Buster Brown band around 1984. Saford loved Bruce's style—he was a tight rhythm player who could pull off blistering flat-picked rockabilly solos. Bruce was a cool dude, his hair combed back in a pseudo-pompadour like a Baptist preacher, and he knew every corny joke in the book. Saford was inspired by his playing. It reminded him of the swinging hillbilly music of the Orange Blossom Boys.

Alas, nothing good lasts for a Hall boy. Bruce didn't stay with the Buster Brown band long. When he left, Saford thought about quitting, too.

Trouble was, quitting music would have left Saford with utterly nothing to look forward to each day. After nearly thirty years of marriage, he and Clovie were finished. She packed her bags and headed back to Virginia, leaving Saford with the house, from which he was about to be evicted. His landlord, Buster Brown's father-in-law, had died and the property was for sale. Saford was about to become homeless.

He was in bad shape, financially and physically. He carried barely 120 pounds on his five-foot-seven frame, and he tired so easily that he could no longer perform his job at Thomasville Furniture Industries, Inc. Luckily for him, his boss was a good friend who assigned Saford mostly supervisory tasks that did not tax him physically. Saford's lungs, damaged by years of smoking, tuberculosis, factory fumes, and exposure to poisonous gases during army training, seemed ready to give out. Like Mamo, and now Clayton, he was wasting away to nothing.

Saford Hall had squandered every relationship he'd ever had—with his wives, his stepson, and even his own twin brother. Now, on the verge of becoming a homeless man, Saford was sick, probably dying, with nobody to take care of him. He moved in with his stepson Larry's soon-to-be-ex-wife for a while in a broken down house trailer, which really got folks talking. What had become of the gallant World War II hero, the man who had won medals and helped conquer Germany? He was now in his sixties, chain-smoking his way to oblivion in squalor. Saford had truly bottomed out. When he was diagnosed with an arterial blockage that required surgery, his only hope for adequate treatment was the VA hospital in Salem.

When he got to the hospital, a familiar face was waiting for him.

. . .

Sometimes, it seemed as if they shared one life force. When Clayton and Saford were together, they were strong, healthy, and, with notable exceptions, mostly happy. When they drifted apart, they grew weak, atrophied, and sick, their very bodies seeming to vanish like morning mist right before our eyes. This shared life force, or soul, or whatever you want to call it, is probably part of the mythology of twins—along with the myths that they can finish each other's sentences; they're always polar opposites; one is a leader and the other a follower; one is an old instigator, the other a peacemaker; one plays fiddle, the other banjo; and so forth.

Clayton's health had been dreadful. His frayed nerves required yearly hospital stays at the VA. He was still partly debilitated from the stroke and had developed diabetes. He underwent colon surgery to remove a tumor, which was hard on the family, as we worried that he might have cancer and might not be strong enough to survive the operation. But he made it through, and as they wheeled him back to his room from the OR, he told Mom and Grandma, "I'm an old toughie."

Damn right he was.

He had to be, because less than a year after the colon surgery, he was back at the VA for yet another major operation. A blockage in his left coronary artery needed to be cleared.

That was the same week in 1986 his twin brother checked into the VA because he had a blockage in his *right* coronary artery. The twins were together again, to have their broken hearts mended.

Their procedures were scheduled for the same time, an arrangement the ICU nurses hated: "They're identical twins! What if we get confused and give them the wrong medicine?"

But the twins' surgeon, Dr. Jorge Rivera, instructed the nurses that the twins were to remain together. Making a mistake with their medications was not an issue. In fact, it was impossible. They suffered the same ailments and were on the same meds. He wanted them together for a bigger reason, which was now plain to Clayton and Saford.

"They are good medicine for each other," Dr. Rivera told the nurses.

Lying in their hospital beds, awaiting their twin surgeries, Clayton and Saford made their peace with each other. Whatever had come between them—anger, bitterness, jealousy—had been eradicated by the sicknesses that nearly killed them. The twins survived their ailments and their surgeries, which not only removed arterial blockages but seemed to clear out the remaining resentment that had clogged their relationship. They were too old, with too few years left, to lose another day of their lives apart from one another.

Following his surgery, Saford returned briefly to Thomasville, just long enough to pack up his few earthly possessions. His old buddy John Hofmann was back in town, too, having left the road for good. John and his new bride had decided they would add a room to their house for Saford. John loved Saford dearly. The thought of having him around full-time, playing fiddles and drinking Dr Pepper until the sun came up, lifted his spirits.

John drove to the trailer park where Saford lived to tell him his plans. He arrived in time to see Saford packing the last of his things into a friend's car. He was moving back to Virginia.

"You weren't even going to say good-bye?" John asked his mentor and friend.

Saford was too embarrassed to answer. They shook hands and Saford climbed into the car and headed up the road, back to Virginia, back to the mountains, back home. John returned to his own home, where that night, reflecting on the loss of his old friend, he bawled like a baby.

A couple of Saford's nephews put Saford in a trailer on a piece of Patrick County property owned by Johnny Vipperman, one of Saford's many music-playing cousins.

Within months, that dumpy little trailer became the scene of some of the hottest jam sessions to ever hit Patrick County. All of Saford's old pals came by to pick. Johnny Vipperman, who had played a week with Bill Monroe before being shipped off to the Korean War, and Clayton were regulars. The trailer was cramped and hot, a perfect terrarium for the rebirth of Clayton and Saford's final act.

They would start over, they decided. They would start a band.

They were sixty-eight years old.

For therapy, Saford and Clayton put together a new band called
"The Hall Twins and the Westerners."

—MOM, 1994, THE GENEALOGICAL BOOK

And this is how I *really* remember Clayton and Saford: standing on my parents' front porch, identically clad in blue-and-white checked shirts and matching tan cowboy hats, Saford sawing the fiddle, Clayton cradling a guitar. Alongside them was a band of similarly dressed, mostly gray-haired musicians. The twins looked rejuvenated, healthy and happy.

The date was June 7, 1992, my birthday, just two days after my wedding day. My parents threw Ruth and me a postwedding party headlined by the famous Hall Twins and the Westerners. A large crowd of family and friends sat on folding chairs in the front yard, listening to and enjoying the show. My extended family from Roanoke and Richmond had heard the Hall Twins many times. Ruth's family from Maryland, on the other hand, had not. The simple, country scene of old guys playing bluegrass and Western songs at a cookout was probably a bit unsettling to such sophisticated folks, whose own grandfathers surely did not do those sorts of things, but everyone maintained their composure.

Saford stepped up to a microphone, fiddle in hand. Clayton stood a few steps off to the side, stationed behind his own microphone. Saford did most of the talking, as always.

"Now, here's a little number Clayton and I had the privilege to record with Roy Hall and His Blue Ridge Entertainers in Atlanta, Georgia...oh, how long ago Clayton? Two or three weeks ago?"

"Yeah, man!"

"Anyway, here it 'tis, called 'Don't Let Your Sweet Love Die'!"

They harmonized on the chorus:

> Don't let your sweet love die like flowers in the fall
> Don't take away the smile and leave the tears
> My heart believes in you, please say you love me too
> Don't leave me here to face the lonely years

Their sweet love had not died. Those old songs and comedy routines fit Clayton and Saford as comfortably as their matching cowboy shirts. Saford had never stopped performing, so he still remembered the words that Clayton had forgotten. For his part, Clayton followed with the high tenor on the verses he could remember, playing a steady rhythm the whole time.

The Hall Twins and the Westerners played together for about ten years—ten phenomenal, miraculous, gift-from-God years. They performed nearly every weekend at playhouses, church picnics, pinto bean suppers, WPAQ's *Merry-Go-Round*—playing for people who remembered the old songs and missed them.

These are the good old boys I knew. The stories of their blue period were just that—stories I would piece together years later, when it would be hard for me to reconcile the young combat soldiers and brawling, angry middle-aged men they had been with the funny, lovable old-timers I knew and loved.

· · ·

My family often repeated the tale of how Uncle Saford had saved Papa Clayton's life by coming home and getting him back out playing music. And it's true—Clayton's health improved remarkably once he rejoined his other half. But some of the credit for Clayton's rebirth needs to be shared with my mother. In 1986, not long after Papa Clayton's last major surgery, Mom withdrew a wad of money from her bank account and sent Papa and Grandma on a vacation to a place Papa Clayton had always talked about: Hawaii.

He had never forgotten the beaches of Honolulu, where as a much younger man he had swum in the Pacific Ocean, watched the girls dance in their grass skirts, and reveled in the final summer before everything changed. In some ways, Hawaii was the last place where he was truly himself—before the Battle of Leyte, Tabontabon, screaming shells falling on his head, towering escarpments to scale on Okinawa, Japanese soldiers hiding in tank traps. That gilded summer of 1943 in Hawaii was his last taste of paradise before being initiated into hell.

Papa and Grandma spent more than a week in Honolulu. They went with a tour group of other old-timers, including several WWII vets who, like Clayton, had spent many happy hours on the island before they were shipped off to war. They took in a Hawaiian revue of music and dancing, dined at a luau, and were serenaded by Hawaiian actor and singer Al Harrington, who had been on *Hawaii Five-O*. They joined other combat veterans and their wives and visited the USS *Arizona* Memorial. Pearl Harbor looked much different than it had in 1943, when the bombed hulks of ships still jammed the harbor. Paradise had returned.

Clayton wore a flowery Hawaiian shirt every day. Mom had bought him a pack of shirts before he and Grandma embarked on their grand getaway, and Grandma bought him a few more at a used-clothing store after they arrived in Honolulu. Just before they returned, Clayton bought a grass-skirted hula doll as a goofy gift for one of his neighbors back home. But on the return flight, he confessed to Elinor. "I don't want to give my hula girl away!" So he kept it on top of the stereo cabinet in his living room, a grass-skirted memento not only of a perfect vacation but of a time and place long passed.

. . .

He came home reborn.

Which leads to this further debunking of the family myth: Clayton wasn't the only one whose life was saved by Saford's return. Clayton saved Saford, too.

Saford's rebirth was more spiritual than physical. I never knew the man whose personal life had disintegrated so terribly and so sadly in Thomasville. I never saw the guy who had been a poor husband and father. The Saford Hall I knew was happy, funny, and a complete cutup. He even drove a Yugo and was proud of it. That Saford was the front man for the Hall Twins and the Westerners.

The Westerners started out with just the twins, their cousin Johnny Vipperman, and a local banjo picker, Bill Smith. One night early in the band's history, the boys were playing a show at the Fairview Ruritan Club near Galax, when in from the cold walked Bruce Moseley, Saford's old guitar-picking buddy from Thomasville, the dude with the fancy fingers and goofy jokes. Bruce and his wife, Jean, had been traveling on the Blue Ridge Parkway when they heard a radio commercial for the Hall Twins' show.

"That's Saford!" he hollered when he heard the spot.

Bruce had been searching for Saford since he fled Thomasville, but nobody could tell him where the old fiddler lived. After they reconnected with Saford, the Moseleys hightailed it for Virginia every Friday afternoon after work. They spent every weekend in Saford's trailer, where folks came for the music and for Jean's fried chicken. The gatherings were almost on a par with Mamo's weekend parties at Clayton and Elinor's house.

Those jam sessions in Saford's cozy trailer birthed the Hall Twins and the Westerners. When it was really packed, the heat was almost unbearable, especially at night, when Saford turned off the air conditioner. There was no place to sit, so Saford played his fiddle while sitting on the commode of the bathroom at the end of the hall.

The "classic" Hall Twins and the Westerners lineup was Clayton, Saford, Bill Smith (banjo), Johnny Vipperman (guitar and vocals), Bruce Moseley (guitar), Jean Moseley (electric bass), and a washboard-playing fellow Saford knew from Thomasville, who claimed his name was Val Jello. In 1992, the Westerners recorded a collection of old Roy Hall songs and Western and gospel numbers that included "Red River Valley," "Peace in the Valley," and, of course, "Don't Let Your Sweet Love Die." They put it out on cassette tape, titled *Then and Now*, to sell at their gigs.

The Hall Twins and the Westerners performed on the Radford University campus during the annual Folk Arts Festival when I was a senior. Did I walk a half mile to see them? No. The show was on a Saturday morning and I was probably a tad groggy. This began a regrettable era for me— the era when I didn't attend nearly enough Hall Twins and the Westerners concerts.

I had my opportunities. They performed all over southwest Virginia in the early 1990s, which coincided with the beginnings of my journalism career and its concomitant sixty-hour workweek. The shows I missed were legendary: the Mount Airy Autumn Leaves Festival in 1989 (that's the show where Saford announced, "I'm seventy years old!" And Clayton replied, "I'm seventy, too!"); a concert at a local high school practically in my backyard in 1995 (Ruth went to that show with a friend; I took calls on the sports desk); numerous performances on the *Merry-Go-Round* in Mount Airy (I'm not sure I knew what the *Merry-Go-Round* was until it was almost too late); and, most regrettably, the twins' 150th birthday party in 1994.

Fortunately, I got to see a few shows, because the Hall Twins played so often. A lot of people remembered the boys' time with Roy Hall and His Blue Ridge Entertainers.

A Roy Hall revival had been rekindled in the late 1970s, when a small Virginia record label called County Records issued fourteen Roy Hall numbers on an LP titled *Roy Hall and His Blue Ridge Entertainers: Recorded 1938–41.* An article about the album appeared in *Bluegrass Unlimited,* an influential publication dedicated to bluegrass and old-time mountain music.

Clayton was interviewed for that article, headlined "Roy Hall & His Blue Ridge Entertainers: Almost Bluegrass." One of his most famous stories was boiled down to a single sentence: "Clayton Hall contends that in one unusually good week his share of the band's earnings provided him with a new automobile."

By the late 1980s, somebody else came looking for the Hall twins.

• • •

Kip Lornell was a young professor and music historian at Ferrum College in Franklin County, about forty-five minutes south of Roanoke. He worked for the Blue Ridge Institute, Ferrum's center for the study and preservation of southwest Virginia folk life and culture.

Lornell had taken a keen interest in the Roanoke Valley's folk-music history. He was surprised, however, to learn that much of Roanoke's country music had been influenced not so much by mountain string bands, but by bolo-wearing Western bands that played on the radio. Roy Hall's name came up frequently in his research, as did the names of Tommy Magness and the not-related-to-Roy Hall twins.

The Blue Ridge Institute made a name for itself in the 1970s and '80s by producing a landmark series of albums called *Virginia Traditions,* records themed around genres from Tidewater blues to southwest Virginia ballads. In 1988, Lornell spearheaded the institute's final LP, *Early Roanoke Country Radio,* an album that featured old radio transcriptions that dated back to WDBJ's earliest days in the 1920s. The pièce de résistance of the vinyl LP was side two, which was anchored by a pair of fifteen-minute radio programs—one by Roy Hall and His Blue Ridge Entertainers, one by Tommy Magness and the Orange Blossom Boys.

The Blue Ridge Institute had come into possession of seven Roy Hall programs and a few Tommy Magness shows that a former WDBJ employee had saved from destruction when the station moved from Kirk Avenue in the 1960s. Prior to the album's release, a Roy Hall radio program had not been heard publicly in two generations.

At the drop of a needle, the scratchy sound of 1942 crackled to life.

> *She'll be drinking Dr Pepper when she comes*
> *She'll be drinking Dr Pepper when she comes*
> *She'll be drinking Dr Pepper and we'll all go out and he'p her*
> *She'll be drinking Dr Pepper when she comes*

Then came the voice of "Cousin Irving" Sharp, as reassuring and comforting as St. Peter welcoming blessed souls at the pearly gates. "Well, hello there. We've been expecting you. It's Dr Pepper Time. Time for another quarter hour of your favorite old-timey songs presented by Roy Hall and the Blue Ridge Entertainers, brought to you by your friendly neighborhood Dr Pepper dealer."

Irving called for "Fisher's Hornpipe" from Tommy, who fiddled so fast, he transcended time and space and transported Roy Hall and His Blue Ridge Entertainers back to the future. As much as I'd like to tell you that the *Early Roanoke Country Radio* album zoomed to number one on the *Billboard* country charts, won a Grammy, and made national celebrities out of the Hall Twins and the Westerners, the truth is that its appeal was pretty much limited to Roanokers old enough to remember local country music radio of the 1940s.

But that was good enough. The local media jumped all over the surviving Roanoke musicians. The *Roanoke Times & World-News* published a story about the record. Roanoke public radio station WVTF invited Clayton and Saford to be interviewed by host Bill Vernon for his popular *In and Around Bluegrass* show. The twins were media darlings, spinning their timeworn stories and reciting their old comedy routines for their grandchildren's generation.

Nobody talked about the war or lamented what might have been. Nobody talked about unsteady nerves, depression, or sickness. Clayton and Saford only sang, told stories, laughed, and sang some more.

. . .

The Blue Ridge Institute made a documentary about Roanoke country radio, narrated by Franklin County native David Huddleston (yes, Coen Brothers fans, *The Big Lebowski*!). I never saw it when it aired, but I did make it down to Roanoke for the big reunion show at Smith Park on the Roanoke River during Roanoke's annual Festival in the Park. Clayton and Saford easily were the MVPs (most valuable pickers) of the afternoon, as they represented three classic Roanoke bands: the Blue Ridge Entertainers, the Orange Blossom Boys, and the Wanderers of the Wasteland.

The boys were in their element. Snow-haired men and middle-aged women in big glasses sat in lounge chairs beneath the old oaks and sycamores that shaded the stage. Clayton and Saford hadn't played a real show in Roanoke in . . . how long? Forty years? Probably not since the night Tommy Magness showed up drunk at the Roanoke Theater and the Orange Blossom Boys busted up. They picked up where they had left off, singing the same songs, yukking it up between numbers, doing the same comedy bits.

I sidled up to the stage and snapped pictures with my new 35 mm Minolta. What a cool story these old dudes have, I thought, a primordial outline beginning to evolve in my soft little brain. Somebody ought to write a book about them.

They sang their song they wrote for Mamo, "When Mother Prayed for Me":

When mother prayed for me
Down on her bended knee
A blinding tear rolled down her cheek
When mother prayed for me

She held me in her arms
Her eyes lifted heavenly
When she asked God above to shine down his love
When mother prayed for me

The crowd loved it. The twins' harmonies were pitch-perfect. They hardly seemed real, these two look-alikes singing old songs that dated back before the days of television and FM radio. But there they were, singing on a stage in Roanoke, almost fifty years after they had arrived in the Magic City by driving the wrong way down a one-way street. They had endured. The crowd cheered. Fans did not rush the stage and cause it to crash to the ground. They did not demand the twins play five shows. They just wanted one good one, and they got it.

• • •

The Hall Twins and the Westerners performed at house parties, VFW dances, Democratic fund-raisers—anywhere folks wanted to hear classic bluegrass and Western songs. They peddled their cassette tape *Then and Now* at show dates. They videotaped a thirty-minute program of music and stories that aired in 1993 on some fly-by-night cable channel called the Americana Network based out of Branson, Missouri. They taped it in my parents' living room, right about where we recorded Saford's war stories that day Ruth gave me the fiddle for my birthday.

Thanks to Papa Clayton's connections to the Moravian church, the Hall Twins and the Westerners were in constant demand on the gospel-singing circuit. Not a month passed when they weren't invited to play a revival or homecoming service.

They played just about every Moravian church from Winston-Salem to Carroll County. Along the way, they met a fellow traveler from the world of country music and the Moravian faith: George Hamilton IV, the old singer best known for his 1961 number one hit "Abilene."

> *Abilene, Abilene*
> *Prettiest town I ever seen*
> *Folks down there don't treat you mean*
> *In Abilene, my Abilene*

Hamilton loved the twins, and he invited them to accompany him at other Moravian churches around Winston-Salem, the epicenter of the church's southern branch. In 1993, he even took them to his old stomping grounds in Tennessee—a little place called the Grand Ole Opry.

Hamilton had been a member of the Opry since his heyday in the early 1960s. The Hall twins went with him to Nashville, where Hamilton played a show at the Ryman Auditorium, the "Mother Church of Country Music." Clayton and Saford made the six-hour trip, staying in a campground cabin along the way, just so they could visit the Ryman and watch their friend. During his set, Hamilton introduced Clayton and Saford and asked them to stand. Hamilton told the audience that these old boys had played the Grand Ole Opry back in its beginnings in the early 1940s. The crowd applauded respectfully, even though surely no one in the audience had ever heard of the Hall twins. That didn't matter to Clayton and Saford, who stood, waved, and grinned like they were famous.

They never took the stage on that trip, although they did meet country star Vince Gill. They also paid a visit to the Country Music Hall of Fame on fabled Music Row. They went looking for an old friend, whose name was enshrined among the immortals Roy Acuff, Bob Wills, and even Elvis Presley. Along the "Walkway of Fame," they read the familiar names of Bill Monroe, Johnny Cash, Loretta Lynn, Gene Autry, Chet Atkins, and Patsy Cline, until, at last, they found it, written on a slab of stone in the ground for all the world to see: Tommy Magness. Class of 1980.

Saford snapped a picture, and the twins headed home.

. . .

A few final words about Tommy Magness.

After the Orange Blossom Boys imploded in 1947, Tommy fell in with country music legend Roy Acuff again for a couple of years. No moss ever grew on Tommy's fiddle, and by 1950, he was back in Roanoke, right about the time the twins were leaving. Once again, he led a band. Once again, he broadcast over WDBJ. Once again, it all fell apart.

He called his band the Tennessee Buddies, and it featured two young hotshots—guitarist and singer Red Smiley and banjoist Don Reno. The Buddies were good, and Tommy taught them many of the old hits he had played with Roy Hall: "Don't Let Your Sweet Love Die," "I Wonder Where You Are Tonight," and "I Know You're Married but I Love You Still." The group held one recording session in Cincinnati for the Federal label in 1951, under the guidance of producer Syd Nathan, a music pioneer whose work with rural white and urban black musicians (including James Brown) laid the groundwork for rock 'n' roll and earned him induction into the Rock and Roll Hall of Fame in 1997.

Reno and Smiley eventually kicked out Tommy, who still battled the bottle, and formed their own band—the Tennessee Cut-Ups—and became bluegrass music legends. The duo of Don Reno and Red Smiley became household names in Roanoke, literally, because they played in most households every morning by way of WDBJ *television*. They were the daily musical act on *Top o' the Morning*, a news and entertainment program hosted, naturally, by "Cousin Irving" Sharp, who had moved seamlessly into the new visual medium. Reno and Smiley scored a slew of bluegrass hits. Many of them were penned by Reno himself, but others were the old Roy Hall songs they had learned from Tommy.

But Roy Hall was dead and with him part of Roanoke's musical past, and soon Tommy Magness would be, too. From that point forward, when people spoke of the history of bluegrass music in Roanoke, they didn't talk about Roy Hall, Tommy Magness, or the Hall twins, or their cute little programs on WDBJ radio sponsored by Dr Pepper. They spoke of Reno and Smiley, *Top o' the Morning*, and the show's sponsor, the Kroger grocery store chain.

Roanoke had changed. The Academy of Music, where the Blue Ridge Entertainers had played scores of Saturday Night Jamborees with the likes of the Sons of the Pioneers, the Carter Family, and Roy Rogers, deteriorated and was razed in 1952. The city even had a new nickname, which originated from a ridiculous plan by a local merchants group to erect a ninety-foot freestanding neon star atop Mill Mountain as a promotional gimmick before the 1949 Christmas shopping season. The shining star immediately caught on with the public and was allowed to stay permanently. The Magic City was eclipsed by a giant neon-powered star. To this day, Roanoke bills itself as the Star City.

Tommy moved back to Mineral Bluff, Georgia, land of his birth, where he married one of his old girlfriends, a small, middle-aged woman named Leah. His health declined, and he suffered a series of small strokes that caused numbness in his hands, making it difficult to play. Other than his immediate family, few people in northwest Georgia knew that Tommy Magness was a music legend. Sometime in the early morning hours of October 5, 1972, Tommy Magness suffered a heart attack and died in his sleep just before his fifty-sixth birthday. He would be little remembered for most of the next twenty-five years.

Then, in the late 1990s, Sony Music issued a series of CDs intended to chronicle the best of American twentieth-century recorded music. Through mergers and acquisitions, Sony absorbed many record labels, including Columbia, which through its subsidiaries had issued the greatest popular songs ever recorded. Sony greeted the new millennium with a series of compilations that featured the best of twentieth-century jazz, pop, folk, classical, show tunes, rap, and country—practically any genre that Columbia recorded.

The country CD was assigned to famed music historian and pop culture critic Billy Altman, a guy who wrote about rock for *Creem* and *Rolling Stone*, who has been a curator for the Rock and Roll Hall of Fame, and who writes for the Huffington Post. Altman is the classic musicologist snob, a dude who knows more about Chuck Berry's session musicians than any teenager knows about the latest *American Idol* champ. He knew his country music history, and he knew about a certain historic recording that had never been released to the public. He was sure the master still existed, though, buried deep in Columbia's vault.

After a few calls, Altman found it—an original acetate recorded in Columbia, South Carolina, in 1938 by a hillbilly singer from North Carolina and his young fiddling prodigy. Roy Hall and Tommy Magness's original version of "Orange Blossom Special" had survived for sixty years. Altman included it in Sony's *Country: The American Tradition* CD. Right between the Sons of the Pioneers and Gene Autry, you'll find Roy Hall and His Blue Ridge Entertainers, the band that did not include Saford and Clayton but which was much improved after they joined. In 1999, Sony compiled all the discs into a *Soundtrack for a Century* box set, which means that Roy Hall sits alongside the likes of George Jones, Thelonious Monk, Bob Dylan, and Aerosmith.

I bought the country music anthology just so I could play the original "Orange Blossom Special" for Papa Clayton. He had heard Tommy play the song a thousand times, but he had never heard the original recording. Papa listened to his long-dead buddies, as a nervous twenty-one-year-old fiddler shuffled stiffly through the tune. After hearing the historic recording, Clayton looked at me and said, "Boy, Tommy didn't do much with that one."

. . .

Saford died first. I watched him dying, wheezing, gasping for oxygen as he lay mostly lifeless in a hospital bed in Galax, Virginia, on a cold February night. I could not bear to stay until the end, so I hightailed it home and got the news the next morning that he was gone.

In late 1997, Saford got pneumonia, which ravaged his long-scarred lungs.

His health spiraled downhill for the next sixteen months, until he died of pulmonary fibrosis on February 11, 1999. He died from roughly the same causes that had taken Mamo thirty-one years earlier and would claim Clayton four years later. I was a pallbearer at the funeral, during which I saw something I never thought I'd see—Papa Clayton bawling uncontrollably as the family was led into the funeral home's chapel. The old toughie couldn't help it. As Clayton walked down the aisle toward the flag-draped coffin, Saford's voice sang sweetly from the public-address system, because my mother had chosen the Hall Twins and the Westerners' version of an old hymn called "Come on In" as the prelude. The twins harmonized on the chorus:

> *Come on in, the battle is over*
> *Come on in, your race is run*
> *Come on in, heaven is waiting*
> *A crown of life you now have won*

Saford was buried in the Montgomery Cemetery, close to Mamo, Granny, and Pappy Hall. When he died, he barely had a penny to his name. An insurance policy paid for some of the funeral expenses; friends and family picked up the rest. Another friend spearheaded a fund drive to buy Saford a headstone engraved with a fiddle. Even in death, Saford relied upon the kindness of others.

● ● ●

Incredibly, Clayton's health improved the first couple of years after his twin's death, but eventually, he, too, grew weaker and labored to breathe. He died on April 22, 2003. (Strange twins fact: If you take Saford's date of death—2/11—and double or "twin" it, you get 4/22.)

Clayton had decided years earlier that he did not want to be buried in the Montgomery Cemetery, which had badly deteriorated from neglect—a few tombstones had fallen over, the rutted gravel road that led to the graveyard was all but impassable due in part to a couple of fallen trees, and the only person who even bothered to mow was his *older* brother Asey, who by the time Clayton died was nearly ninety. Considering the graveyard's sad shape, Clayton had agreed to be buried in Elinor's family's cemetery in Franklin County, the place her father had discovered on a hunting trip so many years before.

The twins lie in eternal rest some fifty miles apart. Strangely, I have never been bothered by this. Some people think it's a shame that the twins are not together. Some family members have talked of actually exhuming Saford's body and moving it to the Franklin County cemetery. Perhaps that will happen someday. To me, though, it seems entirely appropriate that Clayton and Elinor will be together, while Saford wanders off on his own.

. . .

Their last gig was a classic. As they got older, the Hall Twins and the Westerners were regulars on WPAQ's *Merry-Go-Round,* the live radio broadcast that began in 1948. The Hall twins had been among WPAQ's first performers, and their swingin' brand of acoustic country music and bluegrass stood out in a region famous for old-time mountain music.

WPAQ had become an institution, a place where the rural and small-town folks of southwest Virginia and northeast North Carolina could tune in to hear their musical heritage doled out in generous heaps of fiddle and banjo tunes. The station gained such a reputation among bluegrass and old-time mountain music fans, performers, and scholars that Rounder Records issued a CD of WPAQ recordings called *WPAQ: The Voice of the Blue Ridge Mountains.* The CD's selections were all by the home folks, including one song that Clayton and Saford had helped record around 1950—an up-tempo version of the old Roy Hall tune "Can You Forgive?" retitled "Forgive Is Number One." Rounder was the biggest label that ever put out one of their recordings.

In June 1998, just before the release of that CD, WPAQ hosted a gathering of musicians and musicologists for a series of workshops to discuss the radio station's impact on the local culture. The workshops culminated in a big concert at the Andy Griffith Playhouse, an old school converted to a concert hall and named for Mount Airy's most famous native son. (Locals still lay claim to the fact that Mount Airy served as inspiration for the fictional small-town utopia of Mayberry. Years later, that inspiration reversed itself as Mount Airy morphed into a real-life Mayberry, home to the Mayberry Mall, Aunt Bea's restaurant, Floyd's Barbershop, and other Mayberry-themed enterprises that attract Andy-philes to town.) Naturally, local favorites the Hall Twins and the Westerners were on the concert bill along with the headline act, Wade and Julia Mainer. That's the same Wade Mainer of the old Mainer brothers band that inspired those twin bastards from The Hollow so many years earlier. Wade Mainer was ninety years old at the time and still performed on rare occasions. Mike Seeger, brother of Pete Seeger and a famous roots-music performer and music historian in his own right, was one of the masters of ceremonies. The Hall twins were thrilled to be included.

There was only one problem. Saford was dying. He was tethered to an oxygen tank twenty-four hours a day and was almost too weak to sing or play the fiddle. He had no business being onstage.

A few days before the show, Clayton visited his ailing twin at the little house on Wards Gap Road that old friends Bruce and Jean Moseley had bought for him. Saford was a thin doll of himself. He could speak only a sentence or two without coughing or wheezing, but he told Clayton he would play the show. They talked about the old days, even about their M1 rifles. Old soldiers never forget their rifle's serial number, Saford told Clayton, who agreed.

But try as he might, Clayton could not come up with his number.

Saford couldn't remember his, either. They both thought and thought, then each began to chuckle until Saford started coughing again. He hacked up gobs of phlegm from the depths of his scarred lungs as Clayton reached for a box of tissues.

"I'm a goner this time," Saford said.

Clayton started to protest, telling Saford he shouldn't think that way, but his older twin cut him off.

"My time is done," Saford said. His coughing subsided. "I know I ain't been the best person all the time. But I did the best I could. I've seen and done things that not a lot of country boys ever get to do. I know I ain't got much time left, but I know where I'm going when my time comes. I did my best to live a good life. That's all any of us can do, ain't it? Just live a good life? When it's all said and done, ain't that enough?"

Clayton gazed at his withered, dying other half. It was like watching himself fade to nothing.

"Yes," Clayton said. "It is."

* * *

The stage manager at the Andy Griffith Playhouse was skeptical—and nervous. This poor old guy can't possibly play fiddle while hooked up to an oxygen tank, can he? Will he even survive the walk to the stage?

Saford wasn't well. Even a few steps winded him, so he limited his move-ment as much as possible. He wasn't sure if he could play and sing. My family attended the show in hopes of lending moral support to the old boys, but I am sure we all had the same thought: that this time, in front of a packed house, Clayton and Saford might embarrass themselves. We also knew that this was probably their last show, although none of us said that. What a shame they had to go out like this.

We weren't the only ones who felt that way. Saford was scared, too. That's why he brought along a hired gun—his old friend and protégé from Thomasville, John Hofmann.

John had driven to Virginia to pick up Saford before the show, but when he arrived at his friend's house, Saford informed John that his fiddle-playing services were sorely needed. John politely refused at first, claiming he didn't even know all of Saford's songs, especially the Western numbers. Saford was determined that John would play.

"I've never asked you for nothing," Saford told him sternly, oxygen tubes hanging from his nostrils. "But I need you to do this one thing for me."

John could not refuse his old friend.

. . .

The twins talked to the Mainers backstage. They had met Wade Mainer years before, back when he brought his band to Roanoke during the peak of Roy Hall's career. Mainer was cordial; he remembered the twins from Roy's band, and he certainly remembered Roy's brother Jay Hugh, who had worked with him in the 1930s. They didn't make much small talk; besides, Saford could barely talk at all.

The show began when a local family group called the Slate Mountain Ramblers whipped the audience into a frenzy with a half hour of incredible old-time fiddle tunes. On came the Hall twins. Saford was adamant about leaving the oxygen tank backstage, although it would have helped save his breath for singing. He took his place behind the microphone. Clayton sat next to him and waited for Saford to call a tune. Already, Saford was too winded to sing. Huffing and puffing as if he had just run a half marathon, Saford pointed to John and asked him to play "Soldier's Joy," one of the first fiddle tunes Saford had learned as a boy in The Hollow. John obliged, and with Clayton playing rhythm guitar, they zipped through the tune.

Saford caught his breath long enough to sing harmony with Clayton on "Cool Water." This was not the greatest Hall Twins show of all time, but the boys were holding their own. Saford didn't have the energy for a comedy bit, which was just as well. "Orange Blossom Special" was not an option. How would they close out their brief set? Only Saford knew.

"For our last number, we'd like to do an old song that my brother and I had the privilege to record with Roy Hall and His Blue Ridge Entertainers in Atlanta, Georgia," Saford said. "It's called 'Don't Let Your Sweet Love Die' and it goes something like this."

He motioned to John, who fiddled his way through the intro. Clayton fell into the rhythm as if finishing a twin's sentence. Then, with voices of angels, they sang as one:

> *Don't let your sweet love die like flowers in the fall*
> *Don't take away the smile and leave the tears*
> *My heart believes in you, please say you love me too*
> *Don't leave me here to face the lonely years*

From somewhere miraculous, Saford found his voice:

> *I drifted all alone, no one to call my own*
> *Then you came like an angel from the sky*
> *You said we'd never part, don't leave and break my heart*
> *Be mine alone, don't let your sweet love die*

> *When flowers fade away, they'll bloom again someday*
> *Will you love me when the rosebuds open wide*
> *Or is your kiss to be only a memory*
> *I need you so, don't let your sweet love die*

Saford sang beautifully, as good as ever, summoning a voice that filled the hall. To this day, I do not know how he did it. Was it a voice from God? From his soul? Or just from his gut? His singing was free from the wheezes, rasps, and coughs that were killing him. Clayton's harmony and chugging rhythm were spot-on. John, the veteran pro that he was, had no trouble finding a melodic hook on which to hang a fiddle solo. The performance was a triumph.

How many times had these old bastards been counted out? How many times did they rise from the canvas to deliver the counterpunch? How much pain, loss, and suffering could two men possibly endure time after time, and yet still go out singing and smiling? They were undefeatable. They would not be embarrassed. War could not kill them, bitterness could not separate them, and sickness would never, ever keep them from the stage.

I was not there the first time Clayton and Saford played together on Granny Hall's porch, where they sang and danced for pennies tossed by weary travelers. I was not yet born to see the dye running down their arms and legs the night they stole the show at White Plains and won first prize. I was not there the day Roy Hall came to Bassett, or when the Blue Ridge Entertainers made records in Atlanta, or when the twins played at the Academy of Music. I was not even there for their 150th birthday party, or their many *Merry-Go-Round* shows. But you can be damn sure I was there the night they played their last gig.

Clayton and Saford repeated the last line of the chorus, the international bluegrass code for "OK, we're through now."

I need you so, don't let your sweet love die.
I need you so, don't let your sweet love die.

The audience rose as if electric shocks had been sent through their seats, exploding into cheers. Sure, the twins probably scored a few sympathy points, seeing how few expected poor, sick Saford to even survive the performance, much less sound as good as he did. But Clayton and Saford earned those cheers. They always could please a crowd.

Clayton and Saford stood up and took their final bows. The bastard sons of Judie Hall, the good-looking boys who made records with Roy Hall, the soldiers who won a World War, the old men who could still put on a good show, hugged their instruments to their chests and exited the stage, disappearing behind the curtain as the sound of applause and hollers rang in their ears.

The crowd wanted more.

Acknowledgments

I have a notebook from a long-forgotten college course about early European literature that must have been as interesting to me as listening to *The Canterbury Tales* read in its original Middle English. On the right side of one page, written next to actual class notes that included the words "Dante," "Virgil," and "Dark Foreboding," is an outline for a story. It's my grandpa's story. The date on the page is February 9, 1988.

That's how long this book has hung over my head. I often doubted that I'd ever get around to it. I didn't know enough about Clayton and Saford's story, about bluegrass music, about World War II. . . . I didn't know enough about anything, really. But I kept gathering thread, not actually starting until 1994, when Clayton and Saford told some of their war stories to mom's video camera, and I kept at it for the next fourteen years, even after the two of them died, until Crown Publishers accepted my book proposal in 2008—a mere twenty years after my primitive lit-class outline.

I will never be able to thank everybody who helped me make this book a reality. I mentioned a few names in the Sources section of those who provided wonderful vignettes and pearls, but so many others helped, too. To everyone who took time to talk to me, to tell me about their lives, to play music with me, or to assist me in any way, I am eternally grateful for your help. Please know that little pieces of you are in this book.

Peter McGuigan, my agent at Foundry Literary + Media, was the first person in the publishing industry who actually believed in this book. Without him and his assistant, Hannah Brown Gordon (now an agent herself), I would be handing out collated copies of this manuscript at family picnics, or giving them away at Christmas. Mary Choteborsky, my editor at Crown, performed an incredible job getting the book into shape and making this as much her project as mine. To her, her assistants, and everyone at Crown, especially Jennifer Reyes, Brett Valley, and publicist Courtney Greenhalgh, I am forever indebted to you all. Likewise, I thank my bosses at the *Roanoke Times* for allowing me two leaves from work that allowed me to complete this book.

My family has provided encouragement for years, long before I ever thought I had it in me to write a book. My wife, Ruth, has been a "book widow" for several years now, probably feeling like a single parent at times while she cared for our daughter, Lucy, as I slogged away in my cluttered upstairs office in our little house. Honey, I finished it because of you. I'll bet you wish you'd never given me that fiddle.

Although it is too late to thank them properly, the only reason there is a book at all is because Clayton and Saford Hall led such incredibly rich lives. You know that this story has to be true because no one could make it up. Whatever the book's failings are as a tribute to two great, flawed men, the effort to tell their story properly is heartfelt and sincere, even if I didn't finish it while they were still around to bask in the glory.

Sources

Most of the research done for this book resulted from hundreds of interviews conducted mainly between 1994 and 2008. The primary sources were
Clayton and Saford Hall; my mother, Renee Manning; my grandmother,
Elinor Hall; my great-uncle Asa Hall; and scores of other family, friends,
soldiers, and historians. I am indebted to people such as Rufus Hall, Ever-
ett Dawson, Mamie Helen Bateman, Ralph Epperson, Johnny Vipperman,
Clarence Marshall, Bruce and Jean Moseley, John Hofmann, Dorothy Spencer, my dad and brothers, and scores of other people who told me their
stories to help hang the flesh on the bones of this tale.

The Blue Ridge Institute at Ferrum College provided invaluable WDBJ
radio recordings from 1941 to 1942, as well as recorded interviews with
many long-gone radio pioneers, which included Clayton and Saford. I am
the happy beneficiary of the hard labors of institute director Roddy Moore
and former staffer Kip Lornell, whose work in the 1980s provided a wealth
of sources that I would have sorely lacked otherwise.

The main sources for "The War" section were interviews with men who
fought. I am grateful to Donald Huber, Jay Waxman, Raymond Jenkins,
Wayne Page, and Donald Seibert, among others.

The primary books, articles, and manuscripts used for World War II
research included:

Ambrose, Stephen E., *Citizen Soldiers: The U.S. Army from the
Normandy Beaches to the Bulge to the Surrender of Germany—June
7, 1944 to May 7, 1945*, New York: Touchstone Books, 1998.

Atkinson, Rick, *An Army at Dawn: The War in North Africa, 1942-1943*, New York: Holt Paperbacks, 2003.

Davidson, Orlando R., *The Deadeyes: The Story of the 96th Infantry Division*, Nashville: The Battery Press, Inc., 1981.

Dencker, Donald O., *Love Company: Infantry Combat Against the Japanese, World War II*, Manhattan, KS: Sunflower University Press, 2002.

Dwight D. Eisenhower's official report on Operation Torch found at www.american-divisions.com.

Histories and reports from the U.S. Army Center of Military History, http://www.history.army.mil/.

Johnson, Chalmers, "The Looting of Asia," London Review of Books, vol. 25, no. 22 (November 2003), pages 3–6.

King, Jr., Clyde Raymond, and George Sadallah, "The Fighting Foxes," a self-published history of the Ninety-Sixth Infantry Division, 382 Regiment, Company F.

Mittleman, Joseph B., *Eight Stars to Victory: A History of the Veteran Ninth U.S. Infantry Division*, Nashville: The Battery Press, Inc., 2003.

Personal papers of Lt. Col. (ret.) Donald Seibert.

Peterson, Lance Cpl. Bryan A., "Memorial Park Honors Lives Lost During Battle of Okinawa," http://www.okinawa.usmc.mil/.

Pyle, Ernie, *Here Is Your War: Story of G.I. Joe*, Lincoln, NE: University of Nebraska Press, 2004.

Reed, John S., "Okinawa: The Battle, the Bomb, and the Camera," *Prologue* 37, no.2 (summer 2005), pages 18–23.

Rottman, Gordon L.; Peter Dennis, illustrator, *World War II Combat Reconnaissance Tactics*, Oxford, UK: Osprey Publishing, 2007.

In addition to interviews with bluegrass musicians, several sources detailed the early days of bluegrass and Roanoke:

Dotson, Rand, *Roanoke, Virginia, 1882–1912: Magic City of the New South*, Knoxville, TN: University of Tennessee Press, 2007.

Rosenberg, Neil V., *Bluegrass: A History*, Champagne, IL: University of Illinois Press, 1993.

Wolfe, Charles K., *Classic Country: Legends of Country Music*, New York: Routledge, 2000.

Index

About the Author

RALPH BERRIER, JR., is a reporter at the *Roanoke Times,* for which he has written extensively about Virginia's musical heritage. His work has been honored by the Scripps Howard Foundation's National Journalism Awards, the American Association of Sunday and Feature Editors, and the Newspaper Association of America. He is also an avid bluegrass and old-time fiddle player who lives in Roanoke, Virginia, with his wife and daughter.